CW00971605

Eastwood on Eastwood

Eastwood on Eastwood

Michael Henry Wilson

CAHIERS DU
CINEMA

Contents

Page 2: 'To be able to work at something you enjoy doing is a great privilege.' Eastwood on the set of *True Crime* (1999).

Left: 'I wanted to make the movie so badly that I was willing to pay them!' Eastwood takes a break during the shoot of *Mystic River* (2003) in Boston.

Prologue:
The Maverick's Path

'Today, I do what I want to do and the way I want to do it. It took me some time to get there', Clint Eastwood remarked in February 2005, before receiving his second Oscar for *Million Dollar Baby*. What an amazing path he has blazed in three-quarters of a century, from adolescent wanderings to Hollywood triumphs! This individualist, who values authenticity above all, has kept his cards close to his chest. Shielded by the power of his celebrity, he has been one of the most secretive, and therefore most subtle 'smugglers' of the American cinema. He has eluded the trappings of stardom so well that he never stops surprising us. With him one has come to expect the unexpected. Working his way up step by step – from actor to producer, from director to composer – he has managed to remain a nonconformist who is not afraid of challenging or unsettling his audience. Particularly remarkable has been his progression from genre films to uniquely personal ones. This has elicited the admiration of his peers, led by Steven Spielberg and Martin Scorsese, as well as the respect of his elders and mentors, from Frank Capra to Alfred Hitchcock to William Wellman to Orson Welles.

At the onset, questions keep popping up, sparking paradoxes. How did a young actor raised in the system manage to achieve creative autonomy? How did he come to see directing as the extension of his acting craft? How did a star that could have rested on his laurels take advantage of his hard-won status to bring to life projects that couldn't have been launched otherwise? Who else would have dared to brush off commercial failures (*The Beguiled, Honkytonk Man, Changeling*), swim against the tide (*Breezy, White Hunter, Black Heart, A Perfect World*), or seize hard-edged subjects that terrified all the studios (*Mystic River, Million Dollar Baby*)? How did this professional become, almost unwittingly, an artist? Is it because he never believed in the marketing studies and audience polls that are now the norm in Hollywood? Because he trusted only his instincts? Or because he considered himself first and foremost a storyteller and embraced only stories that he personally wanted to see on the big screen?

Dream or Nightmare?

Eastwood's life and career are proof that the American dream can still, occasionally, become a reality: the skinny kid of the Great Depression would grow into a superstar; the freewheeling Oakland youth would be elected mayor of Carmel; the novice who champed at the bit under his Universal Studios contract would end up controlling every phase

When justice can only be poetic: Eastwood and the 'Bird Girl' of *Midnight in the Garden of Good and Evil* (1997), filmed in Savannah, Georgia.

of the filmmaking process to harvest a wealth of prestigious awards. But he is well aware that this elusive dream – which he called 'the craziest idea in history' at the time of *Bronco Billy* – is too often discredited, betrayed, if not perverted. As he explored its many facets, from the Civil War to the Pacific War, from bebop to country music, from urban criminality to the conquest of space, he paid special attention to the flaws, the excesses, the 'craziness'. Fable after fable, you see him being drawn to the marginalized, particularly those individuals who are at odds with the system – whether it be police or army, Washington or Hollywood – and who dare to expose its corruption.

Our maverick has always had a predilection for Americana, a genre now obsolete in Hollywood. Witness his provincial chronicles and ballads of the lost continent: the Oklahoma of *Honkytonk Man*, the Idaho of *Pale Rider*, the Texas of *A Perfect World*, the Iowa of *The Bridges of Madison County*, the Savannah of *Midnight in the Garden of Good and Evil*, the Detroit of *Gran Torino*... He may have been, with Robert Altman, one of the last explorers of the hinterland, straying from well-travelled roads to reveal previously unseen locations or forgotten communities. There is no complacency or nostalgia in his approach, though. The point of view he favors is that of the stranger passing through, of the vagabond who is eager to resume his travels. Don't expect the quaint wholesomeness of a Norman Rockwell, but rather the disturbing strangeness of an Edward Hopper. The gloom and doom of film noir have spread over the canvas. The weirdest perversities may emerge from underneath the surface, and violence threatens to burst through the veneer at any moment. God-fearing country folk can be as dangerous as the wild beasts that prowl city jungles. The most threatened species is always the outsider, constantly at risk of being hunted and maybe lynched. As the Francesca of *Madison* knows so well, one can be stifled even in the wide-open spaces. The American heartland is rarely a friendly place in which to live...

The Stranger dear to Eastwood only rides through it – just long enough to embody the fantasies of its inhabitants or to express the most secret neuroses of his environment. A nomad by definition, he is not destined to plant roots anywhere. His past, haunting him like a curse, won't allow it. Unpredictable, capable of the best and the worst, he is liable at any moment to swing towards one or the other extreme. If he is a predator, he may be the most vulnerable character in the story (*The Beguiled*). If he dispenses justice, he may be the most deadly (*High Plains Drifter*). Is he a liberator or an exterminator, an archangel or a demon? He can only be the catalyst, the one who probes hearts and minds, precipitates conflicts and prompts the others to accomplish their destiny. Even a gentle fellow like Bronco Billy is no stranger to ambiguity. Adored by kids because of his good heart, he may be the most candid character ever essayed by Eastwood, but has spent seven years in a penitentiary for a crime of passion. Furthermore, his spectacle is a facsimile: the legendary cowboy is really a New Jersey shoemaker who left his humble workshop to resurrect the old West under the big tent. His mantra is that of an actor: 'I am who I want to be.' This could be his creator talking about himself today.

Eastwood is quick to acknowledge that his travels opened his eyes. He was in Spain, filming an Italian western inspired by Akira Kurosawa's samurais, when he realized that America was not the only playing field. This was a beneficial estrangement. The unusual experience confirmed to him that there was more to the art of film than Hollywood movies. As soon as he returned to the United States he formed his own production company, Malpaso, to better resist interference from the major studios. Above all, he wanted to be responsible for his successes and failures. By running the show, he would be the only one held accountable. If his body of work never conformed to any aesthetic or ideological grid, it is probably because he became aware of the power of the medium while working abroad, far from Hollywood. He also learned from his accomplices, Don Siegel and Sergio Leone, themselves experienced 'smugglers', how to make codes and conventions work for him – notably by subverting the black and white morality of genre films. Later, he had no qualms in demystifying the Man with No Name or Dirty Harry, the two roles that had made him a cultural icon. He would even make a mockery of his image as a macho fighter by standing up for misfits, loners and dreamers, characters who fled from warped social values into imaginary worlds.

Unlike most of the directors that directed him over the years, Eastwood managed to preserve his independence. Early on, before stepping behind the camera, he felt the need to renew himself, to avoid being pigeonholed, even when the formula was as lucrative as the *Rawhide* series or the Leone westerns. Along the way, he may have upset some timid souls who preferred the clean-cut Rowdy Yates to contract killers. More than once he eschewed expectations by portraying unsavoury individuals, the kind that would draw first, shoot anyone in the back, spit on the bodies of their victims and assault women to have their way. The heart of these hunters was sometimes blacker than that of their prey. Eastwood didn't shy away from self-parody either. Take, for instance, the whacky free-for-all saga of Philo Beddoe, an unpredictable eccentric who prefers the company of an orangutan to his clique of country rednecks (*Every Which Way But Loose, Any Which Way You Can*). Even better, Eastwood had the audacity to grow old with his characters. Instead of cheating or hiding the effects of age, he used them to expand his choices and deepen his compositions. This meant ignoring the cult of youth and the obsession with box-office blockbusters that have dumbed down Hollywood movies since *Star Wars*.

Eastwood didn't wait for the last ride of William Munny, the farmer of *Unforgiven* who can hardly stand in the saddle, to take advantage of his wrinkles. As early as *Honkytonk Man*, he embodied a man prematurely aged by his excesses and a terminal case of tuberculosis. Red cannot make do without his young nephew. (Eastwood recruited his son Kyle for this crucial role.) At the end of his rope, he has to pass on the torch. It is the boy who will leave in search of the promised land, California, with his guitar and an Okie girl, after the elder has succumbed to his illness in a seedy motel room. Eastwood has always had a fondness for these anachronistic lost souls who can be at once comical and pathetic. In *Heartbreak Ridge*, Sergeant Highway is a grizzled alcoholic veteran, but he endears himself to his young Marines by never missing an opportunity to ridicule the technocrats of the new army, his *bête noire*. In *Space Cowboys*, the 'ripe stuff' is the 'right stuff': our four retirees may be senior citizens, but they have something to teach their younger colleagues. They certainly don't need computers

to manoeuvre the space shuttle for an impeccable landing. Though retired, Detective McCaleb, an old-school cop allergic to cell phones, is still fighting bureaucratic red tape in *Blood Work*. The older generation has a definite edge over the new one, and it is only appropriate since they are the last individualists – and possibly the last idealists – in a world of atrophy and uniformity.

Unlike the Eastwood heroes of yesteryear, these dinosaurs are not indestructible; they are not self-sufficient any more. But with age, they have gained a new heart. This happens literally in *Blood Work*, where Detective McCaleb receives a heart transplant from a young Mexican woman and devotes his last investigation to solving the crime of which she was a victim. One could apply this metaphor of rebirth to the filmmaker himself. As soon as he fashions a mythology, he is likely to turn it over or subvert it – at the risk of alienating fans of his earlier films. 'I need new variations or original themes', he maintains. 'Otherwise, it is not stimulating to me, it's not a challenge any more.' This is why he was able to invest himself in the High Plains Drifter's fury as much as in the Pale Rider's detachment; to project the blasphemous irony of film director Wilson (*White Hunter, Black Heart*) as well as the deep passion of photographer Kincaid (*The Bridges of Madison County*); to inhabit the America of Bronco Billy after that of Dirty Harry; or to paint the Iwo Jima of the vanquished, following the portrayal of their conquerors. From the growing body of his work emerges a strange human comedy, which may be richer for being politically incorrect now and then. Carnies and sax players cross paths with mercenaries and serial killers. Women are capable of the same violence as men, while displaying a much superior intelligence. It's an unvarnished America, slightly unhinged, part circus and part jungle – a continent where it is not always easy to sort out the righteous from the sinners, or to distinguish the dream from the nightmare.

The Prince of Chiaroscuro

There is a Walter Mitty in Clint Eastwood. His profession enchants him because he is able to lead multiple existences with impunity, while embodying for sheer pleasure all sorts of ambiguous, unpredictable individuals whose behavior can be at times highly reprehensible. As a matter of fact, he holds his 'double' at such a distance that he can question it from one film to the other, and sometimes within the same film: 'I know it's not me. There is what I am as a person and what I represent as an actor. And that image only exists in the mind or the eyes of the audience.' In other words, this persona should not be considered as an entity that is resurrected like a phoenix from film to film. Rather, to use one of his favorite words, it is like the jumping-off point for a series of 'variations'. It is no coincidence that the director of *Bird* often borrows from the vocabulary of jazzmen. Eastwood's youth was rocked by the 78 r.p.m. records of Blue Note; his first hero was Lester Young. Jazz was his school, the school of nonconformism: 'As soon as I hit a piano, I knew one shouldn't be afraid to be different.' The music scores of his films have perpetuated that passion, but the spontaneity of jazz inspired him on many other levels: in the choice of his subjects, the rapidity of his shoots, and even at the editing table where the rhythm of a scene may come to him, sometimes, '… like the rhythm of a piece comes to a soloist who improvises on a given theme'.

That jazz magic can be felt too when Eastwood composes with light and darkness: their interplay creates as many potential 'variations' as a musical theme. Whatever the genre he is working in – western or cop drama, blues or ballad – he will satisfy his taste for chiaroscuro. In bisecting the screen between light and shadow, he distils the discomfort of suspense and ambiguity. To him, directing means animating an ever-changing, uncertain space, where anything can happen. For the characters, navigating through the darkness can be a matter of life and death. This is true even in interiors, where the lighting is sometimes so sparse that protagonist and antagonist may be mistaken. We'll even find instances where they trade roles. Since *Play Misty for Me*, the chiaroscuro commands both the dramatics and the aesthetics of this filmmaker (as confirmed by the sophisticated pictorialism of 'Vanessa in the Garden', so unusual for a television episode). This is one reason why it is preferable to discover his films on the big screen, where the subtlety of his cinematography can be best appreciated. It would also be a mistake to lock his visual strategy into a systematic analysis, as it evolves from one project to another. Thus the tension created by the chiaroscuro doesn't always express the precariousness of life or the irony of fate: the love scenes of *Breezy* and of *The Bridges of Madison County* fade away in a half-light that is at once discreet and suggestive. Conversely, broad daylight can conceal as many dangers as the darkest night: in *The Gauntlet* the machine-gunning of the Greyhound bus by Phoenix police occurs at high noon, just as the execution of Kevin Costner takes place under a bright sun in *A Perfect World*. Both are perfect examples of films 'noirs' in color.

As a director, Eastwood has carefully avoided the pitfalls of conceptual rigidity. He is an 'impressionist' who wants to remain receptive to the spirit of places, to life's serendipities, and first and foremost to his instincts. He intends to capture the inspiration of the moment, in himself and among his collaborators. His predilection for the first take, often the purest, the most authentic, is legendary. A project will hold his attention only if he sees in it an opportunity to expand his register or experiment with a brand new field of ideas and emotions. Maturity has only reinforced his self-confidence. Far from repeating himself, as he did in mid-career when Warner Bros. was pushing him to resuscitate the threadbare *Dirty Harry* series, he is determined more than ever to innovate. Even his subjects are getting bolder, from pedophilia (*Mystic River*) to euthanasia (*Million Dollar Baby*), from the deconstruction of American patriotism (*Flags of Our Fathers*) to that of Japanese militarism (*Letters from Iwo Jima*). The 'little detours' of *Honkytonk Man* and *Bronco Billy* have become his royal road. 'I prefer to tackle new stories and new ideas instead of recycling those that have already been treated by others', he says, alluding to the current epidemic of sequels and remakes. It is no wonder that he is nostalgic for the time when studios felt a responsibility to develop original projects, and employed large stables of screenwriters for that purpose. In the mercantile world of current Hollywood cinema, his position has never appeared more eccentric. The heir of a bygone golden age, he is one of a kind in today's youth-obsessed industry. He is a living paradox: an icon who remains marginal and somewhat subversive.

If Leone and Siegel paved the way for him, Eastwood is arguably indebted to William Wellman as well. The old master directed him in his last picture, the partly autobiographical *Lafayette Escadrille*. Like the director of *Wild Boys of the Road*, Eastwood is inclined to debunk myths, stripping classical genres of their customary trappings in order to expose the failings of men and their institutions. He too has undertaken a counter-history of America, where rebels and have-nots occupy the foreground. For 'Wild Bill' Wellman, reckless adventurers, grizzled veterans and fallen women were the salt of the earth, but he never allowed them to shed tears on their road to sacrifice. He knew that the power of the unspoken is worth a thousand speeches. Underplaying emotions was his favorite strategy. Eastwood, from *Breezy* to *Million Dollar Baby*, has retained the lesson of Wellman's *The Ox-Bow Incident* and *The Story of G.I. Joe*: the purest, most honest lyricism is the one that stabs sentimentality and cuts to the bone. In *The Bridges of Madison County*, Kincaid turns his back to the camera as soon as tears come to his eyes. Emotional devastation calls for utmost sobriety; heartbreak demands radical minimalism. Wellman would have been on familiar ground in *Gran Torino*, where Walt Kowalski redeems his life by sacrificing it.

Long before it set its sights on the horrors of Iwo Jima, the cinema of Eastwood had ventured into the furthermost bounds of grief. Inspector Harry Callahan and Charlie Parker belong to the same breed as Ira Hayes. Wounded men whose searing pain cannot be assuaged, they lack the most basic instinct for self-preservation. If monsters obsess Harry to the point where he turns into one himself, Bird is the victim of his excessively sharp sense of hearing, of what you might call a heightened sensory overload. Sapped from the inside by an ulcer, constantly in a state of withdrawal, he is gradually overwhelmed by the cacophony of an increasingly hostile environment. So is Harry, the cop haunted by the cry of the victims he has been unable to save. When he wonders aloud about the dissonances of Stravinsky's *The Firebird*, Parker must be talking about himself: 'If one could hear all the sounds in the world, one would go crazy.' Both characters experience intolerable static in all their being, and they desperately attempt to exorcise it, one with his sax, the other with his Magnum 44. They pursue their self-destructive path with the same integrity, living each moment as if it were the last, burning all their bridges in one interminable sleepless night. To follow these hapless characters, Eastwood finds the right distance, the one that came naturally to Wellman. He is at once fascinated and sympathetic, but refuses to 'romanticize' them.

As he matured, Eastwood's empathy for the outsiders expanded and deepened until it embraced all victims. It appears that the lonely hero of the early years has grown in tandem with the filmmaker himself. First and foremost, he had to overcome his fierce individualism and decide to take sides with the oppressed. There is a world of difference between the cynicism of the Italian westerns and the fervor of *Pale Rider*; the bitter sarcasm of the *Dirty Harry* series and the subdued sadness of *True Crime*; the horseman of the apocalypse in *High Plains Drifter* and the angel of mercy in *Million Dollar Baby*. Nothing seemed to affect the impassive, laconic pistolero of Leone. This heart of steel was only allowed one kind gesture per adventure: you saw him shelter a pretty woman and her child named Jesus (*A Fistful of Dollars*); shoot down apples for an urchin (*For a Few Dollars More*); offer a few puffs of his cigar to a dying young soldier (*The Good, the Bad and the Ugly*). But nothing could divert him from his goal; no one had any hold over him. Such an inflexible character appeared destined to end as a robot in the *Westworld* amusement park, and one can understand why Eastwood was itching for new 'variations', new opportunities to spread his wings.

In his following pictures, gestures of compassion are at first dispensed sparingly. The sheriff of *Coogan's Bluff* jeers, 'Pity? What color is it?', but by the end he grants his prisoner the cigarette he had denied to the captive Indian in the prologue. The High Plains Drifter's only selfless act is a gift of blankets and candies to an old Indian and his two children. Josey Wales, who is just as driven an avenger, shows a little more humanity as he collects along the way a bunch of outcasts, including a couple of Indians who, like him, have lost everything. He even finds them a place of refuge, where he himself may not be ready to settle. Though Sergeant Highway behaves like a martinet in *Heartbreak Ridge*, he sometimes plays Santa Claus to his Marines, particularly those who come from underprivileged backgrounds. As for the character of Wilson in *White Hunter, Black Heart*, he sympathizes instinctively with the Africans during their soccer match against British colonials. This will leave him even more shattered when his hubris provokes the death of his trail guide, Kivu. We also see Bronco Billy stretch altruism to martyrdom when he lets a vicious sheriff humiliate him in order to snatch a young Vietnam deserter from jail, even though he strongly disapproves of the boy's insubordination.

The Widest Palette of Emotions

These sentiments clearly signal that, over the years, pathos has been rediscovered, even if it remains understated, filtered through the restraint dear to our best classical storytellers. Emotions, in all their range and colors, have actually been at the heart of Eastwood's poetics. Passion quickly ceased to be perceived as a weakness, let alone a psychosis (*Play Misty for Me*). *Breezy*, his third directorial effort, testified to a new awareness. This underrated gem painted with exquisite sensitivity the transformation of a fifty-year-old through his encounter with a teenager. Frank (William Holden) is a real estate developer who looks down upon the have-nots, a driven businessman who thinks he is immune to the flames of love. He is one of the living-dead, laboring under 'the black cloud' of cynicism and resentment. His world comes tumbling down when he falls for Breezy (Kay Lenz), a flower child who goes with the flow. This will-o'-the-wisp rescues him from his humdrum existence. (The enchantress is the antithesis of her fellow hippie Linny, the depraved junkie of *Coogan's Bluff*.) Frank also receives a gentle lesson in tolerance. He who compared drop-outs to 'the flotsam of low tide' begins his rebirth when Breezy leads him to the beach to experience the ocean's vital energy. For the first time, the flights of the heart prevail over masculine reticence. For his unlikely couple, Eastwood opens floodgates that would never be closed again.

One finds the same dynamic and quiet lyricism, modulated with even more subtlety, in *The Bridges of Madison County*. Genders are reversed: Francesca (Meryl Streep), the farmer, is the living-dead, and her liberator is the reporter-photographer Kincaid, who provides her with more magic in four days than she has known in twenty years of marriage. Through his emotional acting, Eastwood gives us the most vulnerable of romantic lovers. Aware that Francesca represents his last chance for happiness, Kincaid is more open than her and so devastated by their separation that he eventually dies of a broken heart. Passion is not possession any more. It is the spark of life itself, one that rekindles our desires and forces us to open our eyes. Eastwood's camera suggests this reawakening of the senses when it captures Francesca unbuttoning her dress to assess her naked body in the mirror or peeping longingly at Kincaid as he splashes himself at the pump. If you remove sexuality from the mix, you will observe the same alchemy in *Million Dollar Baby*. Frank has become Frankie, the trainer who buries himself in his job, and Breezy is transformed into Maggie (Hilary Swank), a displaced young dreamer barely making a living as a waitress. Of course this is a father–daughter couple, but Maggie's courage rubs off on Frankie, who taps into his own again after years of cautious hibernation. Maybe grace is at work in such improbable pairing. Their unexpected communion will elevate them far beyond the circumstances.

The impassivity and solipsism of the Man with No Name have been superseded. If the iconography of the Italian westerns reappears here and there, Eastwood is merely playing with it or defusing it in jest. Bronco Billy is shot against the light when he draws his guns and shouts, 'Stick 'em up!', but it is a game meant to impress his most impressionable audience: children. The gunslinger is only an impersonator. In *Honkytonk Man*, Red enjoys a bath in a watering hole, with a cigar in his mouth like the High Plains Drifter, but starts running for dear life as soon as a bull shows up. The cool dude is anything but a daredevil. In the Leone films, the fascination exerted by mercenaries and bounty hunters rested on their invincibility. But this superhuman quality soon became a source of humor and caricature. Like the Road Runner in Chuck Jones' cartoons, the Harry Callahan of *Sudden Impact* cannot show his face anywhere without triggering a volley of projectiles. He leaves a string of dead bodies in his wake. The reverse angle shot of his silhouette is both iconic and ironic as he appears to the surprised mafiosi, his head profiled against

the neon lights of a fairground, brandishing his eternal Magnum, as indestructible as the Terminator. Like the myth of the Man with No Name, the fable of Dirty Harry dissolves into parody. Witness the detective commandeering a bus full of pensioners to chase a harmless bank thief. Excess and insanity are the norm as in a grotesque nightmare. Humor and horror mix in a chaotic and rather uncomfortable marriage.

Eastwood has long favored optical conjuring tricks that give his persona a supernatural dimension: the hero appears or disappears like a ghost. This cinematic illusionism can be found in Leone, naturally, but also in Siegel's pictures, from *Coogan's Bluff* (Coogan emerging from nowhere to capture an Indian or to catch up with a suspect at the Cloisters) to *Escape from Alcatraz* (where Morris vanishes into thin air, leaving only a white chrysanthemum on the shore, the signature of his successful escape). Later, Eastwood re-orchestrated these effects in his own films, mainly when his character was making an entrance or settling accounts. The High Plains Drifter arises from the desert like a mirage and dissolves back into it in the same way. In the meantime, he metes out punishment with a disconcerting offhandedness, drawing his gun in a split second, lighting sticks of dynamite with his cigar, accumulating outrageous provocations – such as having the villagers repaint their town in hellish colors. In a striking vision, the Stranger is profiled against a wall of flames, as awesome a figure as William Hart when, in *Hell's Hinges*, he torched a western town to purify it. In *Josey Wales* the backlighting is integral to transforming the hero into a living legend. His features can barely be distinguished when they are framed by the threshold of the cantina where he is about to kill two degenerates, or later, when he stands on a sand dune to annihilate a gang of smugglers in one violent outburst. Maybe there is no saga without dazzle, no magic without chiaroscuro.

In *Pale Rider* the Preacher's biblical aura is suggested by the film's very title. Again, the dispenser of justice is conjured up as an apparition: his silhouette takes shape between heaven and earth, amid snows and clouds. He is the spirit of the Frontier. He springs up from the collective psyche so clearly that his entrance into town is framed from the point of view of witnesses, in subjective shots that feel like incantations or hallucinations. During the final duel he is given such attributes as ubiquity and omniscience. He even remains invisible, as elusive as immanent justice, when he disposes of Sheriff Stockburn's six deputies. We are suddenly faced with a reincarnation of the Man with No Name, whose invulnerability defied plausibility. This wizardry reappears in *Unforgiven*'s magnificent chiaroscuro, when William Munny returns to the saloon where he was tortured in order to seek revenge on Little Bill (Gene Hackman). It is a stunning backlash of his repressed past: far from being rehabilitated, Munny is still the killer who would shoot anything that moved or crawled: women, children, animals, unarmed men. After the execution he vanishes for ever, just as Frankie vanishes at the end of *Million Dollar Baby* when the black sun of melancholy has consumed his world.

Like *Josey Wales*, *Pale Rider* opens on a devastating raid perpetrated on innocents – in this case, peaceful prospectors. Yet this injustice will lead to resistance rather than vengeance, to a collective struggle rather than an individual vendetta. Coming down from the heavenly mountains, the Preacher galvanizes the oppressed by showing them how to lead a fight, before saddling up and fading into the scenery. (His compassion even turns into a gift of love when, like the otherworldly emissary of Pasolini's *Teorema*, he yields to his hostess' desire and grants her a night of passion.) If Josey Wales unwittingly became the champion of the disenfranchised, the Preacher embraces the cause of the miners voluntarily and his solidarity soon extends to the entire community. However, this providential man is not one of the innocents. He is a former desperado and therefore accustomed to expeditious, devastating methods. His previous existence is never quite defined, but easy to picture if we recall the mercenary of yesteryear. Risen from the depths of his past, the sheriff's arrival gives the Preacher a personal motivation that may overlap with that of the filmmaker: isn't the extermination of the long-coated killers akin to the death knell of the Man with No Name and his amoral ways?

What is truly unique to Eastwood in this tale is its ambivalence – the marriage of rectitude and darkness. The defrocked pastor is really an anti-hero whose day of reckoning is upon him. He has no gospel truth to dispense; he only reveals what was already latent; he even carries the mark of Cain under his collar. Nonetheless, he is endowed with a mysterious grace. Should we see him as the phoenix of the West, who delivers a rebirth to those who invoked him? Doesn't he ultimately embody the myth that Bronco Billy, another former convict, will strive to re-create with his carnival? In contemporary America, a Wild West show can only be an insane asylum – a melting pot for every kind of 'craziness'. Yet Billy, who gathers a fraternity of castaways, knows about solidarity. With him, everyone is entitled to a fresh start. The ranch he promises to his troupe could be the one Josey Wales was seeking in Indian territory. Admittedly, the legend of the West as Billy re-enacts it in the circus only fascinates children, but that doesn't prevent him from demanding that his fellow performers show an utter respect for timeworn rituals. Somehow, he too is a modern Pied Piper who rekindles buried desires, an inspirational figure who allows every actor 'to be what he wants to be'. His message is the one that runs consistently throughout Eastwood's body of work, from *Breezy* to *Million Dollar Baby*: dreams are our Fountain of Youth. They are the most precious, powerful reality that we can manifest here on earth.

The Enigmas of the Bird Girl

Eastwood has often stated that no one film has the power to change the world or even make it more equitable. This hasn't stopped him from expressing a point a view or rather a succession of points of view. Characteristically, he prefers to describe them as variations: 'There may not be one Clint Eastwood message, but there are probably a variety of messages, because I try to say something different with each film.' Although he eschews repetition and self-consciousness, one can't help noticing that the projects he is attracted to, as well as the films he was impacted by (from *The Ox-Bow Incident* to *Paths of Glory*), revolve most often around the law and institutions. In a country as young as the United States, these are still precarious constructions and they are continuously being challenged. Because it thwarts or shackles the individualism that built the nation, the legal machine remains a source of angst, if not controversy and heartbreak. In Eastwood's morality plays, justice is always in question, as it may shift at any moment and turn into its opposites: ambiguity and unfairness, imperfection and blindness. It is on such travesties that the dream trips and shatters. The protagonist of *Dirty Harry* is so disgusted by the city's establishment that he ends up tossing his badge into the San Francisco Bay.

In *Midnight…*, the garden of good and evil is a cemetery, where Eastwood frames at length an enigmatic statue, the 'Bird Girl'. The little fairy's eyes are not blindfolded, but she has an ineffable expression as she holds out two bowls resembling a pair of scales. Is it for the birds or the passers-by? Is she inviting us to weigh life's pros and cons? Or defying us to choose between right and wrong, light and dark? If truth is only 'in the eyes of the beholder', as suggested by a narrative designed like a *trompe-l'oeil*, it will forever remain elusive. Jim Williams (Kevin Spacey), the suspect whose eyes evoke 'the tinted windows of a sleek limousine', spins several versions of the fateful night of crime, until they become superimposed on one another like the palimpsest he has been restoring. Ultimately, he will die from a heart attack at the very spot where he probably gunned down his lover. After all, the

magic spells of voodoo may well be more reliable than the jurors of Savannah. There is just as much irony in *True Crime*, where three flashbacks on the same act of violence are required to determine the innocence of Beechum (Isaiah Washington), a black man presumed guilty because he is young and black. A final twist reveals that the real culprit is … another black man, yet even younger.

Hasn't such relativism always been at the heart of Eastwood's concerns? It is already evident in his first project as a producer, *Hang 'em High*, which draws a parallel between vigilantism and official justice. Violence is not a game any more, nor the euphoric spectacle it was in Leone's westerns, but an object of serious study. What is shaping up, under the skilled direction of Ted Post, an old accomplice from *Rawhide*, is the world of moral chiaroscuro. The film predates *Unforgiven* by more than twenty years: the West is already a nebulous minefield where an innocent can become guilty by mere association and be strung up on the spot without trial. Jed, the unsuspecting cowboy, is the first in a long series of traumatized heroes who stagger along, wounded in the soul, more dead than alive. With a noose around his neck, he barely escapes a lynching. Later, when he accepts the tin star, it is for the sole purpose of taking revenge on his attackers. It is his turn now to demand an eye for an eye. Inexorably, the hunter begins to mimic those he is tracking down. The tragic chain of events that will unfold in *Unforgiven* and *Mystic River* is already in place: an infamous act spreads through the social body like a cancer. Once hired by Judge Fenton (Pat Hingle), an inquisitor intent on hanging people 'to make an example', Jed discovers the inequity of repressive acts perpetrated in the name of law and order. From then on he is caught between two types of atrocities, those committed by lynching mobs and those decreed by the special court. The film's climax is the ritual of the public hanging, a circus as vile as the summary execution in *The Ox-Bow Incident*. Furthermore, the curious bond that forms between Jed and the victim of a rape (Inger Stevens) suggests a convergence of destinies that anticipates that of Josey Wales and his flock, or Harry and Jennifer in *Sudden Impact*.

Because the relation of the individual to the law is always problematic, it gives rise to new variations from one film to the next. The protagonist is caught in a cross-fire, torn between two extremes, doomed to wander between opposite winds, like Ethan Edwards in *The Searchers*: vengeance or justice, insurrection or repression, crime or punishment. In the westerns that followed Eastwood's return to Hollywood, even the mercenary is forced to take sides or to question the cause he is serving. Ethical frontiers get blurred in *Two Mules for Sister Sara*, where gold leads a Southern contract killer to fight with the Juaristas, while the hooker with a big heart turns out to be a revolutionary militant. In *Joe Kidd* the bounty hunter turns against the Yankee 'imperialists' who pay him to slaughter Mexican dissidents. *High Plains Drifter* goes further, ascribing to the Stranger the same methods as the rabble that tortured his brother. This implacable ghost has come back to punish an entire community, one that failed to render assistance to a person in danger. Not content with demanding an eye for an eye, he flushes out the ignominy of his fellow citizens by forcing on them his most absurd whims. Like Albert Camus' Caligula, he sets up a reign of terror, raises the arbitrary into a system, and undermines each of the town's institutions. Derision is his most effective dynamite. His behavior, seemingly aberrant, ends up unveiling everyone's complicity. He is perfectly consistent in only sparing the town's downtrodden: a dwarf and an Indian family.

The saga of the avenger is always ambiguous. Witness Josey Wales, another of the living-dead, who has lost his wife, his son and his farm in a massacre. Again, the trauma transforms the survivor into an executioner. His vengeance is boundless for he encounters as many scoundrels among the Confederates as among the Unionists. In the throes of despair, the renegade becomes an exile in his own land. He is more inclined to make peace with Indians than the US Cavalry: aren't Comanches and Cherokees, driven away from their territory, following the same 'trail of tears' as him? The William Munny of *Unforgiven* is swallowed up into the same kind of hell. Seemingly reborn as a farmer, the ex-killer can talk about nothing but 'sin' and 'expiation', yet takes up the gun again on the pretext of punishing a cowboy who has viciously abused a prostitute. The irony here is that one of the worst criminals appoints himself a righter of wrongs. Once more, the infernal cycle of violence is set in motion by an unforgivable iniquity. It will be the case again in contemporary America, whether in San Francisco, where revenge is the last resort of a rape victim (Sondra Locke in *Sudden Impact*), or in Boston, where a father blinded by grief carries it on against the wrong person (Sean Penn in *Mystic River*). These victims all place personal justice – a primal, visceral catharsis – above legal justice, that cold-blooded monster which indifferently crushes victims and culprits alike.

Ambiguity and Derision

The Man of the West is not the only one to be confronted by the perverse effects of law and order. Now this role falls mainly to the policeman, the second pillar of Hollywood's genre cinema. Eastwood strips him of his decent manners and his good conscience. The strict moralism of yesterday is obsolete; today's cop is no white knight, but a civil servant caught in the net of a system that is either dysfunctional or downright corrupt. *Coogan's Bluff*, which serves as a link between the westerns and the *Dirty Harry* series, contrasts the simplistic justice of a hard-headed cowboy and the pragmatic justice of his urban colleagues. Coogan ignores the most basic rules of procedure and ethics, starting with a suspect's rights. Naturally, this macho bully is out of his league in Manhattan. His professional transgressions ruffle the local bureaucrats, who know their turf intimately. As Lieutenant McElroy (Lee J. Cobb) puts it: 'This isn't the OK Corral. We have a system. It's not much, but it's better than nothing.' In *Dirty Harry*, on the other hand, the protagonist upholds exactly the opposite. He could abide by the system only if it were beyond reproach. Since it is not, the only judge he can rely on is himself; he fashions his own system. Harry could probably subscribe to a stark observation made by Vidocq, the first modern-day detective, as quoted by Jean-Pierre Melville in his film *Dirty Money*: 'The only feelings that his fellow men have ever inspired in a policeman are ambiguity and derision.'

Inspector Callahan provokes 'the powers that be' even more than the criminals. His superiors never stop reproaching him for his 'Wild West shows'. It is only on account of his efficiency that he is assigned the most dangerous cases. The dirty work is always for *dirty* Harry, and the character's pathos stems from his grim solitude. He cannot have a private life because he has created a vacuum around himself. With neither roots nor ties, the only thing left is an all-consuming obsession. The recurrent image of the series is that of Harry returning to his pad and waiting alone, in the growing darkness, for a sleepless night. He dispenses justice, but is not one of the righteous. Instead, he is the Don Quixote of urban crime, fighting, most of the time in vain, against the windmills of legalism and laxity: apathetic citizens, powerless police authorities, crooked politicians and unduly lenient judges. His task is never finished, as we are reminded by the films' credit sequence: a panoramic view of the urban jungle at night, taken from a helicopter, which circumscribes the arena where the passion of Harry is played and played again, like a ritual. In *Sudden Impact* he compares himself to the finger plugging a breach that threatens to sweep away a crumbling dike. He might as well have been invoking Sisyphus and his rock.

This crusader may stand on the front line against the barbarians' assaults, but he remains an untouchable. He endures a perpetual nightmare where the criminal has more rights than his victim; where the torturer, released after three murders, can whine, 'I have a right to a lawyer!', while the policeman is rebuked 'for excessive use of blunt force'. In truth, the renegade detective has more in common with a psychopath like Scorpio (Andy Robinson) than with the spineless technocrats in authority. What they share, for instance, is their solitude, a fetish for firearms, an immense resentment and the ability to target a child if need be. But unlike Scorpio, Harry is no racist; he is only 'politically incorrect' in jest, to provoke his colleagues. Siegel's film even makes use of a certain physical resemblance between Eastwood and Robinson, as if it behooved the hero to bring down his demonic double. Hence this quasi-fantastic finale where both men fight to the death in an implacable ordeal. *Tightrope* will offer a variation on this parallel by transposing it to the sexual plane: the cop with a dirty mind finds an alter ego in a killer of prostitutes, who happens to be a former cop. Later, the motive of the doubles will be re-orchestrated one more time in *Blood Work*, where Buddy the serial killer boasts that he is to investigator McCaleb what Cain was to Abel.

The mirror effect that fascinates Eastwood the most is the one that compels the detective to recognize himself in his antagonist. In *Magnum Force* Harry finds himself outflanked on his right by a death squadron that executes criminals in cold blood and claims to be following his example. Shocked, he dissociates himself from these radicals by paraphrasing the pragmatic arguments of *Coogan's Bluff*'s police lieutenant: 'I hate the goddamn system, but until someone comes along with changes that make sense, I'll stick with it.' On the other hand, *The Enforcer* repositions the character in his rightful place: at equal distance from the terrorists and the authorities. Callahan is back on the warpath, more uncompromising than ever, ostracized as 'the Neanderthal Man' by the paper-pushers. His combat against revolutionary militants, led by a veteran of the Special Forces in Vietnam, is so dubious that a black activist commiserates with him and encourages him to change uniform in order to fight on the side of those who want to overturn the system. Harry denies serving the privileged of the white élite, but is incapable of saying why or for whom he risks his life: 'If I told you, you wouldn't believe me.' Again, he prefers to throw away his badge and carry on alone in his hopeless quest.

In some instances, the criminal is the protagonist instead of the antagonist, and may even lay claim to our sympathy. Such is the case of Jennifer in *Sudden Impact*, who takes her revenge for a gang rape by eliminating the culprits one by one. Harry understands her rage too well to arrest her; she is his undeclared disciple. Her violence cannot be separated from the denial of justice she endured initially. The environment offers no moral counterbalance; it is the very source of depravity. Everywhere, the law of the jungle prevails. The corrupt notables of *High Plains Drifter* deserve the humiliations inflicted upon them by the Stranger. In *Escape from Alcatraz*, the 'hero', a hardened felon, is all the more sympathetic because the warden of the penitentiary is utterly evil. Little Bill (Gene Hackman), the sheriff of *Unforgiven*, is more obnoxious than the outlaws because he abuses his authority with sadistic relish. Jonathan, the mercenary of *The Eiger Sanction*, works for a US agency headed by a former Nazi who plays perverse games with the 'enemy'. In *A Perfect World* one cares more for the escaped convict (Kevin Costner) than for the sheriff whose ill-considered severity led him astray. In *Absolute Power*, yet another variation on the struggle of the individual against the organization, the good part goes to Luther, the burglar who steals only from the super rich. The political paranoia of the 1970s is reignited in an over-the-top scenario where the debauched is none other than the president (Gene Hackman, again). The case plays out like a Watergate of sadomasochism. And who can better purge the White House than our old cat burglar?

A film noir in color: Eastwood directs Sondra Locke in *The Gauntlet* (1977).

On that theme of betrayal at the top, Eastwood's most eloquent film harks back precisely to the 1970s. In *The Gauntlet* the conspiracies of the 'paranoid thriller' (*The Parallax View, Three Days of the Condor, All the President's Men*) reach apocalyptical proportions. A slightly obtuse cop, who has always obeyed orders, is manipulated by an administration in league with the Mafia. As he loses all illusions about his superiors, Ben learns to respect Gus (Sondra Locke), the person he despised most, a prostitute better educated and more informed than him. (Gus may be his Breezy.) What he discovers is the inconvenient truth that tormented Harry so much: there's no worse enemy than the one within, no more hateful an adversary than the system itself. The conspiracy justifies on all levels Gus' terror. Rogue policemen in uniform behave like gangsters or terrorists. The centurion who thought he belonged to the last legion comes to understand that the barbarians have already infiltrated the fortress. Having been turned into an outsider, he finds the guts to carry his mission to the bitter end. If one warrior remains on the ramparts, it will be him. Eastwood conveys his determination through an unexpected, facetious reference to Dirty Harry: without good reason, Ben rashly lashes out at a group of Hells Angels, at the risk of provoking a confrontation ... one lone man against a wild bunch.

Such erratic behavior would soon be out of season, the extremism of Inspector Callahan no longer justifiable once victims found recourse within the system. Thus *True Crime* can re-examine the issue, but from the reverse angle. Reporter Steve Everett's predicament is not to capture a monster that has escaped justice, but to save a wrongly convicted innocent by the name of Beechum. Like Harry, he has made unfortunate mistakes, but in the opposite direction: he torpedoed his journalistic career by taking up the cause of a rapist that he had prematurely deemed innocent. His failures have shaken him and made him a cynic who has stopped believing in anything: 'The pitiful truth is all I care about.' Yet this man who has seen it all before is still capable of risking everything. Everett even resurrects his former self, a passionate crusader for justice. The obstinate muckraker who had exposed the mayor of New York's transgressions and brought him down comes back to life. Whereas Siegel accented the many correspondences between Harry and Scorpio, Eastwood weaves them between Everett and Beechum: the victim of the system has found a champion in our Don Quixote of the pen. Does the reporter redeem himself? Or does he fall prey to wishful thinking? The film's happy ending – the vision of Beechum reunited with his family *after* the execution – is another *trompe-l'oeil*. We can't tell if this conclusion is told in the present or the future tense, in the indicative or the conditional. The interpretation is left to the viewer: is it a miracle, a vision or the fantasy of a sinner seeking absolution?

Lost Innocence

With Eastwood, the authorities are generally the ones that most seriously compromise the values that they are supposed to uphold. Calling institutions into question is a constant in his work, whether he tackles the police or the church, the army or the government. 'I have always hated corruption within the system', he stated early on, at the time of *High Plains Drifter*. Coupled with anti-authoritarian streaks, Eastwood's individualism sometimes borders on libertarianism. Far from advocating some kind of anarchy, it stresses the responsibility of the individual; calls for a reduction in the tentacular hold of the government on the citizen; and evinces a strong aversion for unwieldy government agencies and the military-industrial complex. Note, for example, the unflattering role imparted to the CIA in *The Eiger Sanction*, the FBI in *A Perfect World* and *Absolute Power*, NASA in *Space Cowboys*, the Treasury Department in *Flags of Our Fathers* or the LAPD in *Changeling*... *Firefox*, suffused with the sectarian rhetoric of the Cold War, seems to be the one exception. Mitchell Gant's mission is never examined critically, but it is noteworthy that the pilot gives his Soviet counterpart a fair chance to return fire; they are connected by the instinctual camaraderie of professionals. More importantly, the ace is haunted by the vision of a young Vietnamese girl incinerated by a napalm bombing; he too is one of the living-dead. The suspense revolves entirely around his mental vulnerability.

If authority is corrupt, if it is responsible for distorting and perverting the values of the community, what is left? Friendship, sometimes, when it is unconditional, as indivisible as the body and its shadow. At the end of *The Eiger Sanction*, that is what survives as Jonathan abstains from killing Ben (George Kennedy), the friend who was blackmailed into betraying him. For Bronco Billy, it prevails over his political convictions as it prompts him to protect a deserter. In *Bird*, it creates an indissoluble bond between Charlie Parker and the one he calls 'the other half of my heart beats', Dizzy Gillespie. Camaraderie is the Marines' main motivation in *Flags of Our Fathers*: 'They fought for their country, but died for their buddies.' Friendship doesn't survive the tragedy in *Mystic River*, but it can be a rare beacon of light in a darkened world, as suggested by the role of companion and confidant played by Morgan Freeman in *Unforgiven* and *Million Dollar Baby*. This confraternity is all the stronger for not being verbalized. It transcends the racial divide so well that the color of the skin is practically never addressed. One recalls that the escapee from Alcatraz befriended a black convict who had killed two white supremacists in self-defence. Harry himself, in *Sudden Impact*, was obsessed with avenging the murder of his partner, a black man who was his only companion.

In the darkest hour, religion is of no assistance. Has it lost all credibility because it fossilized into an institution? Because it rarely practises what it preaches? Or always ratifies the abuse committed by the mighty and powerful? Already, in *Hang 'em High*, Jed rejects the notion of Providence when he recounts his miraculous survival: 'God has nothing to do with it.' Later, revolted by the spectacle of the pastor reading the Bible and the populace singing a hymn during a public hanging, he breaks away and meets up with a prostitute. In the churchgoing town of *High Plains Drifter*, the priest equals his parishioners in villainy. The preacher of *Thunderbolt and Lightfoot* is an impostor; the chaplain of *True Crime* a sanctimonious hypocrite; the pastor of *The Enforcer* a Judas used as a front by terrorists. In *The Beguiled*, a pious image – the Descent from the Cross – inspires the headmistress of the boarding school with the strangest erotic fantasies. If there is a martyr in *Dirty Harry*, it is Harry himself, who is tortured under a monumental cross, while Scorpio the Antichrist fires his gun at the neon sign 'Jesus Saves'. This sardonic humor crackles again in *The Gauntlet* where one can catch, amid the flashes of a monstrous shoot-out, a glimpse of religious slogans such as 'God Makes House Calls' or 'God Gives Eternal Life'. Such a god can only have the insensate gaze of a funeral statue.

In *Million Dollar Baby*, the Christ-like iconography is passed on to young Maggie (Hilary Swank), martyred in the ring by 'The Blue Bear', a female Scorpio. (The hood falling on Lucia Rijker's eyes is reminiscent of Andy Robinson's ski cap.) At the beginning of the film, Frankie questions Father Horvak – who is afflicted with the wooden tongue of organized religion – on the mystery of the Trinity, to no avail. He doesn't know yet that he is about to re-enact this holy triad with Maggie and Scrap, his partner. As usual, sinners, heretics and blasphemers are much closer to true sainthood than the cloth. Notice at the hospital how Frankie embraces Maggie lying on her torture rack in a heart-wrenching *pietà*. Or how the Holy Spirit, through the gentle, one-eyed Morgan Freeman, dispenses his solicitude to all, including a retarded young boxer. A small town diner, lost somewhere in Missouri, takes the place of a sanctuary, but at the outcome, when the world is plunged into darkness, its misted windowpanes suggest it was an illusion, an unattainable mirage. The impalpable community of wounded souls is the only church that offers sustenance in this life. Such was the gospel according to Josey Wales, the messiah of the humble and the offended, with his convoy of apostles in rags: an old Cherokee, a Navajo maidservant, Mexican vaqueros, a grandmother from Kansas with her granddaughter, a buxom harlot and a mangy dog.

In Eastwood's universe the notions of salvation and redemption remain strictly secular. They are the concerns of the individual conscience, particularly when the psyche is pierced by an ancient guilt. The Frankie of *Million Dollar Baby* cannot forgive himself for allowing the match in which Scrap lost his eye to go on. By taking charge of Maggie, he is grasping for a second chance, which fate will eventually deny him. In *Unforgiven* it is William Munny's ghastly past that stands for original sin. The reprobate mended his ways, but is tempted by the prospect of a last 'contract' into leaving his purgatory (which is, literally, a pigsty). The shame is just as overwhelming in *A Perfect World*: Butch relives his youth through the child he has kidnapped, especially the violence he suffered first in his mother's brothel, then in a reformatory. He is the sacrificial lamb of the drama and pays for the sins of the imperfect world in which he had the misfortune to be born. In *Mystic River*, young David is such a sacrificial lamb. The crime perpetrated against him by pedophiles affects all the characters, ricocheting from one period and one generation to the next. If the camera seems in several instances to call the heavens to witness, it is not to implore the Almighty, but rather to identify the *fatum* that leads humans to tear one another to pieces.

Do not look for religious or patriotic hymns in Eastwood's films. Most often, antagonistic ideologies mirror each other, like the North and the South in *Josey Wales*. The opportunism of the ferryman, who sings 'Battle Hymn of the Republic' or 'Dixie' depending on his passengers being Unionists or Confederates, epitomizes the logic of survival. The only Lincoln-like figure in the film is the old Cherokee who has observed first-hand the duplicity of white politicians in Congress. In *The Eiger Sanction*, spies from the East and from the West fight mercilessly, with the same dirty methods. Jonathan's only loyalty is to his collection of paintings, which grows with each 'sanction'. The debunking of values is even more blatant in the fantastic fable of *Absolute Power*. A president who thinks he is above suspicion turns the White House into a house of infamy. His excesses are such that an FBI agent, horrified by the orgies, ends up committing suicide. As for Luther, an artist and a thief, he too is an aesthete for whom the end justifies the means. It is only when he discovers the crime committed by the president against the wife of a rich philanthropist that he experiences a fit of moral indignation. The burglar actually returns his loot to the husband and helps him take revenge. Once again, personal retribution prevails over the judicial system. And the story's twists and turns find their resolution in a semblance of poetic justice.

'The Craziest Idea in History'

Eastwood's work cannot be surveyed without a salute to its irreverent vein. Observe, for instance, the indignities poured on the American flag in *Bronco Billy*. The patients of an insane asylum are sewing it to serve as a tent for the circus troupe. The Vietnam draft dodger will be performing his lasso routine under the stars and stripes he deserted. When Billy pretends to scare the children, the flag that hangs behind him participates in the trickery. The flag is mistreated again in *A Perfect World*, where it decks the trailer of the sheriff, an inept lawman, yet lucid enough to confess his shortcomings. At the end of *Heartbreak Ridge*, it is waved by Marsha Mason upon the return of her man, and is so minuscule that it reduces the Grenada expedition to its true dimensions. The flag of *Space Cowboys*, planted on the surface of the moon next to Tommy Lee Jones' body, is but an insignificant speck in the cosmos. In the last scene of *Mystic River* the banners of the Columbus Day parade throw a veil over the crimes of the community. In *Flags of Our Fathers* finally, the flag becomes a propaganda tool, used as a symbol for victory but forged by multiple deceptions. The first victims of these lies are the solders who raised it on Mount Suribachi. The survivors will even come to regret that they were identified on Joe Rosenthal's historic photo, one whose impact resulted from a series of accidents rather than through its subjects' heroism.

The diptych formed by *Flags of Our Fathers* and *Letters from Iwo Jima* attacks straight on the masquerades of patriotism, the discrepancy between the combatants and the brass behind the lines, as well as the abuses committed by governments (whether democratic or totalitarian) in the name of the state. Eastwood's relativism exposes all the clichés concocted for both the right and wrong reasons by military staffs, politicians and the media. This time, disillusionment hits young conscripts, American and Japanese alike, rather than the veterans of inglorious wars (Korea, Vietnam, Grenada) who populate *The Eiger Sanction*, *Firefox*, *Heartbreak Ridge*, *Absolute Power* and *Gran Torino*. In *Flags of Our Fathers* particularly, Eastwood dissects the American dream with his cinematic scalpel. It is a story of lost innocence, first shattered on the battlefield, then crushed beneath the wheels of an illusory celebrity. The protagonists are the 'forgotten men' of the greatest generation, those who confronted the Great Depression and World War II. They gave everything so that the country might prosper again, but were repaid for their sacrifice with mere crumbs: a few medals, a memorial, but not the relief of a helping hand. René Gagnon was denied a police job. Nobody stopped for hitchhiker Ira Hayes. Doc Bradley, the most stoic of the three, carried on his dealings with death as the manager of a funeral parlour.

A choral, polyphonic piece, *Flags*... transcends the behaviorism of the classic war film to paint a global vision of the nation and its myths in an era when 'the craziest idea in history' was tested. The truth that the film uncovers, layer after layer, is both simple and complex. The three survivors are not the heroes fabricated by propaganda, but become heroes as one shares their discomfort, their reticence and their resistance – even if it remains mostly passive. At the center of the canvas Eastwood places Ira Hayes: the Native American is the outsider *par excellence*; he is also the one who hasn't learned to shield himself against grief. Yet the storyteller avoids the pitfalls of melodrama by 'deconstructing' the fresco as it unfolds. In a counterpoint almost as elaborate as that of *Bird*, the editing intermingles the event and its re-enactment, past atrocities and present nightmares. This structure is supple enough to allow for a constant weaving of the battle and its subsequent exploitation. The most emotional flashbacks hinge first on Ira's character, who can't overcome the guilt of having survived, and then on Doc, who does manage to cope but will remain haunted by the horror. The height of absurdity is reached when the editing intercuts the trio climbing the real Mount Suribachi and its replica in papier mâché at a Chicago football field. And the depths of sadness are plumbed when Ira, back in the squalor of his reservation, poses for a family of tourists and receives a few pennies for his effort. The worn flag he has kept for such occasions is no bigger than a handkerchief.

One of the skinny kids of the Depression dear to Eastwood appears to have sneaked into *Letters from Iwo Jima*: Sam, an Oklahoma boy. Wounded, he has been captured by Baron Nishi, the 'Pale Rider' of the island. The Japanese attempt in vain to save the prisoner's life. It is the only moment when a direct contact is established between the two sides. After Sam's death, a letter from his mother is found on his body, and Nishi translates it for his men. It expresses with a mother's simplicity the prayers that they all whisper in this hell-hole. A singular communion takes shape and reaches across national barriers. The distress of a suffering humanity is the only voice that is heard. 'Do what is right because it is right': these are the words that Nishi quotes to his men before committing suicide. He knows that there are more similarities than differences between them and their foes. This intuition will survive in Saigo, the recalcitrant baker, who makes a very poor soldier, but is the closest, paradoxically, to General Kuribayashi. Nobility is not the prerogative of a class, a race or a tradition. Nor is heroism. By focusing on emotions stronger than any ideology, deeper than any culture, the diptych demolishes the very notion of war to affirm the unity of mankind and its interdependence. At the end of *Letters*..., when the stretcher carrying a bleeding Saigo is dropped next to that of a bleeding Marine, Eastwood taps very naturally into the sublime humanism of King Vidor and *The Big Parade*. Which of the two is 'one of ours'? Which is the 'enemy'?

In turn visceral and reflective, analytical and poetic, the diptych is an important and precious testimony, especially at a time when the media fosters a jingoistic rhetoric petrified in its unreality. It should be ranked, along with *The Battle of San Pietro*, *The Story of G.I. Joe*, *Objective, Burma!* and *Paths of Glory*, among the rare films that are impervious to ideology and force us to look war in the face: far from danger, leaders pull the strings in all good conscience, and combatants are always their victims, even when they come out alive. Appropriately, the war machine and its manipulation of images are disassembled by a filmmaker who is himself an expert on the art of images. No one knows better than Eastwood the illusory nature of show business and the double-edged sword of celebrity. And for a very good reason: he has survived it all. Like his favorite characters, he belongs to an endangered species, the creator free to do what he pleases. He is also one of the last cineastes to make meaningful films for mature audiences in Hollywood, and probably the only one to follow in the footsteps of the old masters: Ford and Walsh, Capra and Wellman. More vital than ever, he is still following his own path... unpredictable, unclassifiable, indispensable.

The Formative Years

This page: Clint's childhood in Northern California during the Great Depression: enjoying the beach with his parents, Clinton and Ruth Eastwood, and his sister Jeanne. 'They were tough times, but a kid like myself, who didn't know anything else, didn't think of them as terribly tough.'

Opposite page: Clint from the 1940s to the 1960s (clockwise from top left): as an adolescent; when he started working as an actor; in uniform at Fort Ord (1951–2); learning about photography in his room (1962). 'I wasn't trying to prove anything. My gut just told me to go in that direction.'

Eastwood's first breakthrough came with the television series *Rawhide* (1959–66). He learned his trade while shooting some thirty episodes a year. He played the part of ramrod Rowdy Yates, the second in command to trail boss Gil Favor (Eric Fleming). He would soon call his character 'the idiot of the prairie'.
Opposite page: on the wagon, one recognizes Paul Brinegar as the cook *Wishbone*.
Below right: in the episode 'Incident of the Widowed Dove' (Ted Post, 1959), Rowdy defies his boss: 'I don't need a wet nurse!'

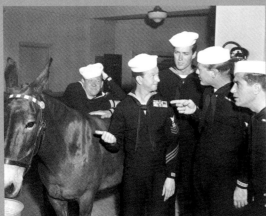

Eastwood's early days in Hollywood:
Top: Marlon Brando visiting the acting school at the Universal studios where Clint was trained: 'We would philosophize endlessly on our trade, as young actors so often do.'
Above and right: Two of the small parts the young actor landed when he was under contract at Universal: a sailor in *Francis in the Navy* (1955), starring Donald O'Connor, and a pilot in *Escapade in Japan* (1957), both directed by Arthur Lubin.

Top: Clint got a better part in William Wellman's last film, *Lafayette Escadrille* (1958), starring Tab Hunter. 'During the three weeks we spent shooting on the Santa Maria airfield, I watched everything Wellman was doing.'
Above: He was to make his mark in television first, as cowboy Rowdy Yates in *Rawhide*.
Left: A command performance with two young starlets for some publicity event: 'The studio system was on its way out'.

Following pages: Working abroad with Sergio Leone was a beneficial estrangement for Eastwood, who discovered another approach to film. With Eli Wallach in *Il buono, il brutto, il cattivo* (*The Good, the Bad and the Ugly*, 1966).

1

'Whether I succeed or fail, I don't want to owe it to anyone but myself'
From *Play Misty for Me* to *Honkytonk Man*

Interview conducted on November 19, 1984

The first meeting takes place in the offices of Malpaso at the Warner Bros. Studios in Burbank. The modesty of Clint Eastwood's surroundings comes as a surprise; so does the relaxed affability of the star that welcomes you in jeans and sneakers. You are not facing Dirty Harry, but rather Bronco Billy. Everything in his bearing suggests that he is exactly where he chose to be. Bolstered by thirty years in the business and a career in full bloom, he could easily echo Bronco Billy's statement, 'I am who I want to be.'

The time for critical kudos has arrived. The first significant tribute in the United States was a Clint Eastwood Day at New York's Museum of Modern Art in December 1980. 1985 will be the year of his European consecration, which comes courtesy of three prestigious institutions: the Cinémathèque Française in Paris, the National Film Theater in London and the Filmmuseum in Munich. The stakes are important, for this signals a change of identity as well as a change of image: the superstar is about to be knighted as an *auteur*. But this doesn't mean that he holds forth with any pretensions. His sense of humor would forbid that. As he is fond of repeating, only the work deserves to be taken seriously.

The immediate pretext for this first dialogue is the release of *Tightrope*, a thriller credited to Richard Tuggle, but directed for the most part by Eastwood himself; it is impossible not to feel his presence behind the camera. This sombre tale of doubles confirms a desire for renewal already hinted at by some bold choices on the part of the actor (*The Beguiled*) or the director (*Breezy*). With *Tightrope* he is subverting his mythology, as he has been doing in a more melancholy vein with his offbeat chronicles, the ones he calls 'my little detours', *Honkytonk Man* and *Bronco Billy*.

Sergio Leone compared Eastwood's gait to that of a cat. The image also applies to his career. Our subject moves like a feline, progressing by leaps and bounds. He won't let himself be locked in any cage, in any kind of system. He probably has nine lives. And he's already spent a few... To free himself from the *Rawhide* television series he crossed the Atlantic and shot an Italian–German–Spanish western (1964). Back in Hollywood, he established his own fiefdom, Malpaso Productions, to escape the dictates of producers and studios (1967). With *Play Misty for Me*, he stepped behind the camera to circumvent the traps of the star system and retain greater control over his image (1971). Avoiding the humdrum of proven formulas, he has since been alternating between commercial vehicles and labors of love.

Whenever it strikes his fancy, Eastwood the filmmaker can now venture resolutely off the main road, even if Eastwood the star sometimes chooses to confine himself to it. He can simultaneously pursue genre films and art films, just like the old masters did. This he does by sticking to his golden rule: only choose projects that would intrigue him if he were a regular filmgoer.

'I tried to avoid over-analyzing the material.' Clint Eastwood's first directorial effort was *Play Misty for Me* (1971).

Right: 'It's someone who fantasizes a love relationship.' Dave and Evelyn (Jessica Walter) in *Play Misty for Me*.

Below: The dramatics of the chiaroscuro: Donna Mills and Jessica Walter in *Play Misty for Me*.

What do you think you've learned from filmmakers you collaborated with before you became a director?

I learned a lot, but wouldn't be capable of distinguishing the contribution of each one. The films of Don Siegel, like those of Sergio Leone, were models of economy. They never went over their allotted budget. That was my school. I've made very few pictures where the money was spent without counting, and even when it was, the lesson was useful because I learned what not to do. Each of the filmmakers I worked with taught me something new, or at least helped me to define myself.

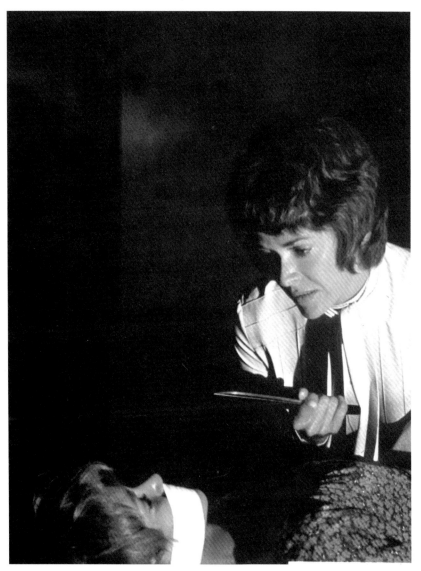

When others were directing you, were you conscious of the production work that was going on around you?

I don't think I was conscious of it, but I suppose my subconscious assimilated it all. I recall that since the time of *Rawhide* I have wanted to try my hand at directing. My contract with CBS even provided that I would direct several episodes of the series. But after they had some trouble on other series where some actor-directors went over their budgets, CBS changed policies from one day to the next. It didn't do me any good to make a fuss – at the time I didn't have a choice. They never honored their contract. I did trailers and a few little things here and there, and I fumed, but I convinced myself to wait for a better chance.

Let's go back, if we may, to your first steps in film production. Under what circumstances did you form the Malpaso company at the end of the 1960s?

I had come back from Italy, where I had just filmed *The Good, the Bad and the Ugly*. My agent was urging me to do *Mackenna's Gold*, a big, spectacular western, but this wasn't the kind of thing I was looking for. I aspired to something more mature, more probing. That was when *Hang 'em High* came along, a much more modest project. I liked the idea of weighing the pros and cons of capital punishment in the setting of a western. That gave me the idea of starting my own company to share in the production of this small film.

Were you already thinking of directing films? Wasn't the formation of Malpaso a step towards directing yourself?

Not really … or maybe subconsciously. After *Hang 'em High* I acted in several pictures without being actively involved in their production. Then I found myself making my directorial debut directing the second unit on a picture of Don Siegel's, *Dirty Harry*. Don had the flu and I replaced him in the sequence where Harry tries to convince the would-be suicide not to jump from the roof. That turned out OK, because, for the lack of space on the window ledge, the only place to perch me was on the crane. I shot this scene, then another one, and I began to think more seriously about directing. One of my friends, Jo Heims, had written a script I was fond of, *Play Misty for Me*. I'd even taken out an option on it. I had just been offered *Where Eagles Dare* when she called me to ask for my advice. Universal was offering to buy her script and she had scruples about dealing with them, although I wasn't in the position to renew the option. Of course, I encouraged her to sell them her script. And it was only some years later, after I had a contract with

Universal, for three movies, that I could tell them, 'By the way, you have a project on your shelf that I would like to do. I also want to direct it.' Because it wasn't a very costly production, I got the green light.

Why choose this project in particular for your first movie?
It was the subject. I had lived through a similar experience, though it was less dramatic. The character played by Jessica Walter, which was suggested to Jo Heims by an acquaintance of hers, was also familiar to me. It's someone who fantasizes a love relationship. For my character, the disc-jockey, it's a one-night stand, but for her it's a devouring passion. This misunderstanding interested me: exactly when do you become involved in a love affair? To what extent are we responsible for the relationship we establish?

Weren't the people you were talking to at Universal surprised that you chose a story in which the dominant character is a woman?
Yeah, sure. They kept asking me, 'Why are you so eager to make a picture where the woman has the best part?' Their second argument was that the situation wouldn't be believable: 'How could a big strong guy like you be threatened physically by a weak young woman?' I thought, on the contrary, that the obsessive dimension of the relationship would only make the dynamic between the two more interesting and would actually work out better. Besides, it is a type of behavior that you can observe in either sex. I've known men who were as possessive as women about the object of their passion.

Was the story originally situated in Carmel and Monterey? Or was it your personal attachment to this region that dictated your choice of locations?
In the script, the setting was in Los Angeles, but a friend of mine, who had some features in common with my character, was a disc-jockey for a Carmel radio station. And in a small town like Carmel, a disc-jockey is more likely to become a celebrity than in Los Angeles. Besides, this region is spectacular, and I happen to live here and be familiar with it.

Did this first experience present any technical problems for you?
No, none, except for the challenge of directing oneself while also taking charge of the whole production. The most nervous person was Don Siegel. I had cast him in the role of the bartender and he kept saying, 'You've made a big mistake, you should have gotten a real character actor. I'll never be up to it.' To which I answered, 'Don, you'll be sensational. And

it will give you a better appreciation for what actors go through. Besides, if something goes wrong, I'll have a director on hand to get me out of it.' In fact, that night after the first day of filming, Don confessed to me that he had had a terrible case of stage fright and would have been completely incapable of helping me out!

How did you prepare for your directorial debut? Did you draw storyboards before filming?
No, *Firefox* [1982] is the only picture on which I used storyboards. The last fifteen minutes required some special effects and I made a set of sketches, which I gave to a professional designer for retouching.

Visually, some of your action shots imply a complex choreography. Even in those cases you didn't draw your shots beforehand?
I hate to be the prisoner of a diagram. The best ideas come to me when the camera is in place, ready to shoot. That's when I am all wound up. Of course, I have a general idea of the sequence, but I try to remain as flexible as possible. I'll always try to leave an actor the latitude to modify one of his movements if he has a good reason. If I am doing exterior shots, I always take into account the light and the way it evolves during the day, because it might entail changing camera positions.

Left: 'Exactly when do you become involved in a love affair?' With Donna Mills in *Play Misty for Me.*

Below: 'The stronger the female role, the stronger the drama.' With Jessica Walter in *Play Misty for Me.*

Following pages: 'Don, it will give you a better appreciation for what actors go through.' Don Siegel as a bartender witnesses the first encounter between Dave and Evelyn (Jessica Walter) in *Play Misty for Me.*

Right and below right: When the flights of the heart prevail over masculine reticence: William Holden is transformed through his encounter with Kay Lenz in *Breezy* (1973).

Opposite page: *Yojimbo* (Akira Kurosawa, top); *A Fistful of Dollars* (Sergio Leone, bottom).

Visually and thematically, High Plains Drifter *evokes Sergio Leone's westerns, but I suspect that you wanted to go even further into excess and cruelty.*
In the Leone films, the story was more fragmented. It was a series of vignettes that were rather loosely linked. In *High Plains Drifter* all the elements overlap, even though there are several sub-plots. Everything is related to the lynching that haunts the protagonist. And there's a moral perspective that only appeared episodically in the Leone films. I am thinking of the scene in *A Fistful of Dollars*, where the hero helps the family get away and pays for this rare moment of compassion with a beating… after which he's got to return to take his revenge on the town.

High Plains Drifter *is a baroque allegory that shatters all the rules of the classic western.*
I decided to do it on the basis of a treatment of only nine pages. It's the only time that happened to me. The starting point was: 'What would have happened if the sheriff in *High Noon* had been killed? What would have happened afterwards?' In the treatment by Ernest Tidyman, the sheriff's brother came back to revenge the sheriff and the villagers were as contemptible and selfish as in *High Noon*. But I opted eventually for a somewhat different approach: you would never know whether the brother in question is a diabolic being or a kind of archangel. It's up to the audience to draw their own conclusions. Tidyman wrote the script from this perspective, but a certain number of elements were missing and I rewrote it with the help of Dean Riesner, who had collaborated several times with Siegel.

You like characters that form part of the system, or at least appear to form part of it, but don't play by its rules and end up by revealing its corruption. The Stranger of High Plains Drifter *exerts his power in a subversive way, like a Caligula of the West.*
I'm aware that this type of character attracts me. Why? Maybe because I have always hated corruption within the system, no matter what it is. In this respect, *High Plains Drifter* goes further than *High Noon*. When the hero helps them get organized, the townspeople believe they can control and manipulate him. As soon as he leaves, they fall back into the error of their ways. Their failure is obvious, their villainy hopeless. In the end, they've learned nothing, but they're forever traumatized. In *Pale Rider*, the western I've just finished, the situation is similar, but this time the hero is really an archangel. He helps the small community of miners to organize themselves against a trust; he inspires them with the courage to resist and defend their rights.

Do you feel affinities with a filmmaker like Kurosawa?
I like his films a lot, especially those of his earlier period, from *Seven Samurai* to *Red Beard*. It was *Yojimbo*, as you know, that prompted me to make *A Fistful of Dollars*.

There is a hellish quality to the palette of High Plains Drifter, *a tonality of blood, fire and scorched earth.*
That's due in part to the place where we filmed it, Mono Lake in California. The town in the script was situated in the middle of the desert, like in most westerns, but this convention bothered me because, even in the West, a city couldn't develop without the presence of water. I discovered Mono Lake by chance, while I was driving around, and I

was immediately taken with the strangeness of the site. The saline content is so high that no vessel can venture a trip on its waters. I spent two hours walking around in the area. Not a boat, not a living soul, only the natural noises of the desert. From the nearest town I immediately called my art director [Henry Bumstead] and had him jump on the first plane. When he arrived, he blurted out, 'You'd think you were on the moon!' And I replied, 'It's a weird place, but that's exactly what I want this story to be.'

The cinematography of Bruce Surtees was extremely elaborate, especially the chiaroscuro for the night scenes. How did he become one of your faithful collaborators?
He'd been the camera operator on several of Siegel's pictures, particularly *Coogan's Bluff*. When we were filming *Two Mules for Sister Sara* in Mexico, Don recruited him because he had communication problems with Gabriel Figueroa [his director of photography]. Figueroa's forte is lighting; Bruce's is composition. His help proved invaluable. So one evening, Don and I resolved that we would promote him to director of photography as soon as the opportunity came up.

At what stage of the preparation do you discuss the style of the cinematography?
In general, I only give Bruce a script when it is finished. Then I explain to him what I want. For instance, the light and the colors of autumn were the determining factors in *The Outlaw Josey Wales* and again in *Pale Rider*. I have a predilection for exteriors; I feel more at ease there than in a studio. There's nothing like the atmosphere of a real location to inspire you and your crew. That's where we make most of our decisions.

With Breezy *you probably surprised a number of your fans. You couldn't conceive a film more remote from the type of movie the public at large identifies you with. Is this a project that was hard to put across?*
No, not especially. It was a very inexpensive picture and shot on location [in Los Angeles]. I liked a lot the script by Jo Heims, her second I believe. It was about the regeneration of a cynic, an older man, divorced, who's a successful professional but doesn't have an emotional life any more. It's about how he's rejuvenated, thanks to a naive teenager who proves to be not so naive after all.

You feel a particular sympathy, it seems, for those of your characters who learn something in the course of their adventure.
The audience follows a story by adopting the point of view of one of the protagonists, whether it's an adult or a child. And if this protagonist learns something, you'll identify with him even more when you feel that you're maturing with him. In *Breezy* I wanted to say that even a middle-class man of substance has something to learn from someone who doesn't have anything. This girl hasn't got much of anything, but actually, she has a lot. She sees and feels what he's stopped seeing and feeling, all those things in life he doesn't take time to enjoy. It's a very simple fable and it's true everywhere. All of us go past something and fail to appreciate all the colors of the prism.

In The Eiger Sanction, *friendship is stronger than the corruption of the system. Indeed, it's the only value that survives in a world of Machiavellian schemes and plots. Your character and that*

Left, below and
opposite page:
Is he an
archangel or
a demon? The
Stranger of *High
Plains Drifter*
(1973) raises
terror and the
arbitrary into
a system.
Derision is his
most devastating
weapon. He
spares only
pariahs such as
the dwarf,
Mordecai (Billy
Curtis).

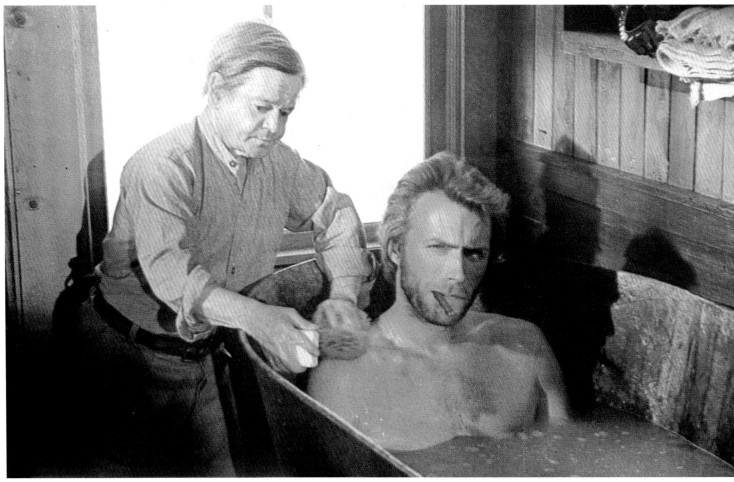

of George Kennedy make up in the end, foiling the agency. In The Outlaw Josey Wales, *the friendship that binds you to John Vernon appears in spite of everything to be stronger than partisan passion.*

Yes, it's an important value, friendship, especially a friendship that doesn't have any other basis than friendship for its own sake. In *The Eiger Sanction* the pressures of the agency compromise it, while in *The Outlaw Josey Wales* it succumbs to the psychoses of the war. Josey Wales is like a haunted man. The ghosts of his past, even when he thinks he's starting a new life, beset him. Even the wounded soldier and the women in *The Beguiled,* who are consigned to the periphery of the war, don't escape from this corruption of feelings.

Isn't the strangeness of The Eiger Sanction *the result of the odd structure of the plot? It develops in three distinct stages, nearly independent of each other.*

There were, in fact, three stories in one, and it was a very difficult picture to make. It was a good thing that our gadgets were limited in number; we were running the risk of heading in the direction of the James Bond movies. And the mountaineering sequences, especially, posed enormous problems. We had to shoot with two crews: one crew of technicians and one crew of mountain climbers. Every morning we had to decide, depending on the weather report, which one to send up the mountain. The three actors and myself had to undergo intensive training. On the seventh day of filming we lost one of our mountaineers, and believe me, I asked myself repeatedly if it was worth it.

Once again, in The Eiger Sanction, *you short-circuit genre conventions by means of black humor.*

The humor was frankly sardonic, but I believe it was inherent in the story. I couldn't have considered handling it otherwise.

But on the other hand, this type of humor is nearly absent in Firefox. *The film would probably have benefited from a tongue-in-cheek treatment.*

Firefox was more 'square', more traditional. It wasn't about bad guys with pink eyes, but ordinary characters faced with an impossible mission.

By its naturalism, Firefox *also contrasts with* The Eiger Sanction, *which has the baroque, flamboyant quality one finds in* High Plains Drifter *and* The Outlaw Josey Wales.

I probably stand somewhere between the two. I don't believe you can label me, pigeonhole me in one style or another. My films all have a different 'look'. It depends on the story, on its structure, on the relationships that develop among the protagonists, and probably also on the way I feel about the subject.

When Josey Wales says, 'We all died a little in that damn war', one can't help thinking about a contemporary war, Vietnam.

You can interpret it like that, but it's a feeling that isn't specific to today's wars. In the case of the Civil War, there had to be something particularly traumatic there. Americans were fighting other Americans. You had one people, but

Opposite page and above: In *The Eiger Sanction* (1975), only friendship survives the corruption of all other values. Jonathan spares Ben (George Kennedy) even though he was betrayed by him.

Following pages: An exile in his own land, Josey can only coexist with Ten Bears (Will Sampson) and his Comanches on 'the trail of tears'. *The Outlaw Josey Wales* (1976).

split in half. And according to the state or the county where you were living, you were recruited to join one camp or the other. It is the same absurdity today in Northern Ireland, where a single community is killing itself in the name of God and religion.

You took over the direction from Phil Kaufman after a few days. What happened?
I was the one who'd hired him to rewrite the script and direct it. His work as a writer was excellent, but when it came to shooting it, it turned out that our points of view were completely different. I had invested my own money to buy the rights to the book, I'd spent a lot of time developing this project, and I'd conceived a precise vision of what the film had to be. Phil's approach was probably solid, maybe it was better, but it wasn't mine, and I would have been angry with myself if the result hadn't corresponded to what I'd hoped for.

Josey Wales, like the 'archangel' of High Plains Drifter, *sympathizes only with the marginal, the underprivileged, the disenfranchised…*
The irony is that Josey Wales inherits a family. After he has fled from everything he was tied to because everything he ever loved has been destroyed, he finds himself picking up these outcasts along his way: the Indian, the grandmother and her granddaughter, some Mexicans and even a stray dog. And soon this heterogeneous group becomes a kind of community.

In The Gauntlet *the relationship is even more unexpected. For the cop, the discovery of human solidarity happens by way of his prisoner, who also happens to be a prostitute. Was it the improbability of this romance that attracted you?*
It was that aspect and the contrast with the *Dirty Harry* series. Inspector Callahan was always on top of the situation and he was in permanent conflict with the bureaucratic system. The cop of *The Gauntlet* is a guy who just follows routine, not very sharp, easy to manipulate. All he expects from life are simple things: to do his job well, find a wife, settle down. And when he confesses his longings, it happens that he is talking to a woman he would have ordinarily treated like a whore, but who is much cleverer than him. She is the one who opens his eyes, because he is too regimented to understand what is going on. He can't imagine that his superiors could deceive him deliberately.

In The Gauntlet, *which is a film noir, you were reworking the theme of betrayal that was already at the heart of* High Plains Drifter, The Eiger Sanction *and* The Outlaw Josey Wales.
Betrayal is everywhere, isn't it? And it's universal. Since Judas, hasn't this been one of the great themes of literature and most kinds of drama?

You declined the part played by Martin Sheen in Apocalypse Now, *a film that explored that very theme in a provocative way. Why?*
Mostly, I didn't want to spend month after month on location. I liked the character and everything that was connected to Conrad's book, *Heart of Darkness*. There were impressive action scenes. But I wasn't sure that it would justify my spending two years shooting in the jungle of the Philippines.

No film would justify that. It would have to be the most beautiful screenplay, the most beautiful book ever written, and even then … I don't like long shoots. I like to work hard and fast, without letting up, twenty hours a day if needed, but over a period of six weeks rather than six months. It's when you have an adrenaline rush that you give your best. Otherwise, you rack your brains, you doze off, and there is a strong chance that the audience will be doing the same in the theater.

Is it possible to see in Bronco Billy *a commentary on your activities and responsibilities as a filmmaker?*
I had a really good time. When Dennis Hackin sent me the script, at first I thought it was about Bronco Billy Anderson, the silent movie star. I devoured it in one sitting and immediately thought it was the kind of film Capra would do today if he were still making movies.

Once again, there was this micro-society we were talking about…
Yes, but in a contemporary version. Of course, you could also say that in a certain way these misfits belong to a bygone era. There aren't a lot of people who are really interested in a 'Wild West Show' today.

Bronco Billy allows his fellow players to interpret the role of their choice in a world of illusions, to express their truth by becoming whatever they choose to be. The circus tent is like a metaphor of filmmaking… or even of Malpaso Productions?
I hadn't ever thought of it from this angle, but maybe you're right: after all, it isn't so different from the movies! I'm always moving on, and I can't analyze what I do as consciously or objectively as an observer who's outside the project.

You supervise the casting very closely. You often say that it's the key moment in your preparation.
If the script is good and the casting is right, you've only got to stay on course. On the other hand, if the casting is wrong, you don't have a chance to achieve your goal. I don't mean that there's only one way to cast a role, but I have too much respect for actors, I'm too sensitive to the particular dimension they can give a part, not to control the casting myself from beginning to end.

Bronco Billy gives the impression of being a film of family and friends. You're celebrating a certain lifestyle.
The actors had almost all worked with me before, many times. They formed a very homogeneous group. The fact that we had this common experience meshed well with the story. The relationships of the characters with Bronco Billy were not very different from those the actors had with me. I think this helped the film. On the other hand, for *Escape from Alcatraz*, we took the opposite approach: we hired only people who had never worked with us. On some films, I surround myself with my family; on others, I search for new faces.

In Bronco Billy, *as in* Honkytonk Man, *you offer us splendid scenes of provincial life, but the picture is often ambivalent: this rural America is far from being idyllic; it, too, is badly tainted by corruption. Let's take, for example, the episode with the vicious sheriff in* Bronco Billy.
When we were shooting the sequence, someone suggested, 'Why not add a scene where Billy returns to town and takes vengeance on the sheriff?' I answered, 'You can't do that.

It would be another movie.' Billy endures the sheriff's insults in order to get his young team member out of jail. This voluntary humiliation says everything about his character. Maybe it's even the message of the picture. If he returns to take vengeance, you're going back to *Dirty Harry*.

How involved are you in establishing the definitive script for your films?
Formerly, I'd often make changes during the filming itself. Now, I try to make them beforehand in order not to waste time and be completely organized. If the original writer isn't available, I do the work myself. But on *Pale Rider*, for instance, the screenwriters [Dennis Shryack and Michael Butler] wanted to be involved until the end and they took care of the modifications I asked for. For *Bronco Billy*, I added a number of scenes myself – for instance, the hold-up at the bank. I'd attended a fight with Muhammad Ali, and after his victory, while reporters were bombarding him with questions like, 'How did you place that lightning left hook in the last round?', all he would say was, 'I just want

to say hello to my pals. And I'm eager to thank my father, my uncle, the reverend so and so, etc.' That gave me the idea of the sequence where Billy is asked about the hold-up [which he stopped], but his only thought is to promote his circus. I also wanted to show that this anti-hero was still capable of accomplishing a heroic action.

In your selection of projects, you seem lately to be observing a rule of alternation: a small, intimate, personal film that challenges your image, and a more important production with an assured commercial potential. Thus, after Bronco Billy *you turned to* Firefox, *and after* Honkytonk Man *to* Sudden Impact.
Maybe that's only a coincidence. I don't believe it's a conscious process. Even if I had been certain that they wouldn't be big successes, nothing would have stopped me from making *Bronco Billy* and *Honkytonk Man*.

What attracted you to Firefox? *Of all your films it's the one where the confusion of values and ideologies is least marked.*

I liked the story and the script. It started out like a classic spy movie, but then there were some pertinent reflections on the arms race and the imbalance of strengths caused by new technological advances. What worried me a little were the special effects. Luckily, they came up only in the last part of the film. The problem, in particular, was that these special effects played out against a background of the atmosphere of our planet, and not in some faraway galaxy off in the future. I must confess, I'm not crazy about special effects. I prefer a thousand times over to have to deal with human beings and their problems.

It's often been said that the film drew on the Cold War climate that followed President Reagan's taking office.
It was only a hypothesis: 'What would happen if...?' I don't believe we manipulated the public's paranoia. We only noted that the Cold War was there. And even if it hadn't been there, you need an antagonist or a certain kind of conflict. And as for conflicts, if it isn't the one that opposes the United States and the USSR, there are enough of them everywhere on the planet.

The hero doesn't call into question either his mission or the system. Not even when he discovers that the Russian dissidents must sacrifice their life for him.
He's a professional, and he doesn't have any idea, before he goes over there, of what his mission implies for the dissidents.

He doesn't know anything about the behind-the-scenes political machinations. And over there, he doesn't have a single moment when he's at ease. Except when he takes command of the prototype, because then, at last, he's in his element.

You suggest a possible friendship between the American pilot and his Soviet counterpart, a friendship of two technicians as opposed to the infamous games of politicians.
It's a little like *The Outlaw Josey Wales*: these two men could have been friends in other circumstances, if they hadn't belonged to different types of society.

In logistical terms, was Firefox *as difficult as* The Eiger Sanction*?*
Yes and no. We had to find a substitute for the Soviet city – Vienna, as it turned out. The Russian base was set up in the Austrian Alps. The London scenes were shot here, and so forth. The shot when I head to the hangar was filmed in Austria, but the reverse angle shot was done here, because we weren't about to transport the contraption from one continent to another.

Honkytonk Man *is the only one of your movies, other than* The Beguiled, *where you die at the end. Did you have any difficulties pitching to Warner Bros. a project that contradicted your traditional image so decidedly?*
No, none at all. It was a small inexpensive picture, but since *The Beguiled*, I knew exactly what kind of risk I was taking.

I liked the story and thought it deserved to be told. I hoped that the audience would sympathize enough with the young boy to be interested in it. There is a big part of my public that expects heroic actions from me, and perhaps they were disappointed with *Honkytonk Man*. I can't make all my pictures for a specific segment of society, nor can I defend the same values constantly. A filmmaker worth his salt can't keep making the same picture all the time. I need some new variations, or some completely new themes. Otherwise, it doesn't interest me, it's' not a challenge any more. If there's some advantage to being a 'star', or rather passing for a 'star', it's being able to make projects that normally would never see the light of day … pictures that can only be done because you're interested in them, as was the case with *The Beguiled*, *Bronco Billy* and *Honkytonk Man*. On the other hand, take the example of *Every Which Way But Loose*. No one wanted any part of it. The script had been refused forty-six times! Finally, I shot it and it made a fortune. What the studio lost on one film, it got back on another, and so forth. Today when you make a movie, you have to really want to make it. You can't think about the box office. I never think about it; I never did, even when I had some of my greatest hits. I am not arrogant enough to think that the public is going to rush to see any of my movies. Every time, I knock on wood, up to the last moment … because you never know.

Your core audience would probably have recognized itself in Honkytonk Man, *but that audience doesn't go to the movies to be faced with its daily problems.*
Unless it is a case of pure fantasy, as in *Every Which Way But Loose*. But the story of a dying musician like Red Stovall in *Honkytonk Man* is not necessarily one that they want to see on the screen. But I do.

Did a real-life singer inspire Red Stovall?
No, he's a collage: a mixture of Hank Williams, Red Foley, Bob Wills, basically all of those country singers who drank hard, burned up their life on the road and ended up by self-destructing.

What are your own connections to country music?
I discovered it at the age of nineteen when I was working as a lumberjack in Oregon. At that time, I only liked jazz, particularly the West Coast jazz of Dave Brubeck and Gerry Mulligan. I was looking for girls and I landed in the town's only nightclub. Bob Wills and his band were playing there. Since I didn't know anybody and didn't know how to dance to this music, I spent hours listening to the band, while forgetting to try to pick up girls! After that, I started listening regularly to the small local country radio stations.

On Honkytonk Man, *did you draw from your childhood during the years of the Great Depression?*
Yes, I was raised during those dark years. I had some contact with families like that during my wanderings from city to city, and I certainly met characters like Red Stovall. That probably helped me to re-create the atmosphere. But as you know, for me it was love at first sight for the book by Clancy Carlile, and although we pruned it a little, we remained very faithful to it.

Since Bronco Billy *and* Honkytonk Man, *you seem increasingly interested in family and community relationships.*
You can only do so much with the lone hero. If you give him some family ties, you give him a new dimension. You build conflicts that enrich the story. In *Honkytonk Man* he has a family, but he is doomed to destroying himself. In *Tightrope* he seems to debase himself and drag his family with him. In *Pale Rider*, although he doesn't belong to the community, he gets close to two of its members unwittingly because they become attached to him.

Isn't it the fact that you've become your own director that has allowed you to change your image like this?
That's right. It's allowed me to widen my register and control my career better. I recall a picture I made in Yugoslavia called *Kelly's Heroes*. It was a very fine anti-militaristic script; one that had some important things to say about war, about this propensity that man has to destroy himself. In the editing, the scenes that set the debate in philosophical terms were cut and they kept adding action scenes. When it was finished, the picture had lost its soul. If action and reflection had been better balanced, it would have reached a much broader audience. I don't know if the studio exercised pressure on the director or if it was the director who lost his vision along the way, but I know that the picture would have been far superior if there hadn't been this attempt to satisfy action fans at any cost. And it would have been just as spectacular and attractive. It's not an accident that some action movies work and others don't. What makes the difference is the quality of the writing.

Honkytonk Man *is a picaresque journey through a forgotten American South. Was it familiar ground?*
No, but I've had many opportunities to cross the country by car, observing little towns and storing these scenes in my memory. For *Bronco Billy* I criss-crossed Ontario, Oregon, Washington and Idaho. In the first script the setting was in Oklahoma, but I made it in the Boise area of Idaho because you can capture there the 'Mid-American' atmosphere that I was looking for. For *Honktonk Man* I preferred Central California to the flatness of Oklahoma, where the Dust Bowl had vanished anyway.

Bruce Surtees' cinematography sometimes evokes the photographs of Walker Evans. During your research, did you consult photos and documents of the time?
Sure, I browsed through piles of books on the 1930s and the Great Depression. Photo albums of my own family also inspired me.

Unfortunately, this kind of 'Americana' seems to be vanishing from the screen. You are one of the few to remain faithful to that genre. Would you like to carry on with your explorations of the heartland?

Yes, I'd like to come back to it from time to time. Regularly, if I can! Today the only thing that Hollywood swears by are its space adventures, because that's what goes over well. For my part, I trust my instinct and I make the films that I believe in. If the public follows me, that's wonderful. If it doesn't, *c'est la vie.*

Can one describe Sudden Impact *as a black comedy?*
Sure. There are a lot of comic elements in all of the *Dirty Harry* series, if only because Inspector Callahan's cynicism calls for a cynical type of humor.

Some American critics blamed you for discrediting the judicial system, for advocating vigilantism and individual justice.
I can't help it if my sense of humor escapes some people. One of my favorite restaurants in Carmel is called the Hog's Breath Inn. When I asked the owner why he had chosen such an ugly name, he told me, 'We want to make sure we only serve customers who have a sense of humor.' A few months before his death, I had lunch with Hitchcock and afterwards we speculated together about the movies. Suddenly he concluded, 'Don't ever forget that it's only a bloody movie!' He was sure as hell right about that. No movie can ever change the world or make it a more just place, even if it contains an important message. *Dirty Harry* touched a nerve because the country was up to its ears in bureaucratic inefficiency. But that character is a pure fiction. In today's society, no cop would be capable of assaulting the system while remaining so uncompromising. Even if some of them would like to have such power and if need be, go beyond the law, they just can't. After all, Harry Callahan never deliberately set out to go beyond the law; it was only under the pressure of time or when forced by the urgency of the situation. To come back to your question: I can't worry about these kinds of problems. I do the best I can. I can only hope that the audience will like the film and the critics will be more receptive to the positive than to the negative aspects.

You were unpleasantly surprised by the accusations of racism brought against Dirty Harry.
When I hired blacks, I did it to give them work. Before filming the hold-up sequence in *Dirty Harry*, a scene that had been written for whites, I told Don Siegel, 'I'm tired of always seeing the same stuntmen in this kind of role. What if we got some new faces?' A group of black stuntmen had just been formed and they were the ones I suggested. That they were all blacks was logical: there are as many black gangs as white or Asian gangs. It's absurd to conclude from it that only blacks commit crimes. Again, in *City Heat* we have changed all the casting and blacks have now taken two-thirds of the roles written for whites. That fits the real atmosphere of Kansas City, which was dominated by the jazz scene in the 1930s. Lord only knows what some critics are going to conclude from that!

A number of your movies, Sudden Impact *in particular, express the frustrations of today's America and the resurgence of populism.*
Maybe I can be accused of being old-fashioned, of dreaming of an era when things were simpler, more obvious and more honest. The power of bureaucracy is increasing as our planet is shrinking and the problems of society are getting more

A picaresque journey through a forgotten America: *Honkytonk Man* (1982). 'I was raised during those dark years and I certainly met characters like Red Stovall.'
Above: With his son Kyle (top) and the young Alexa Kenin (bottom).
Right: 'An unvarnished America where it is not always easy to sort out the righteous from the sinners.' Thanks to Uncle Red, Whit (Kyle Eastwood) learns the facts of life.

complicated. I'm afraid that individual independence is becoming an outmoded dream. Paperwork, administrative red tape, committees and subcommittees overwhelm us. It has reached such a point that in order to get elected, our politicians have to promise they'll keep their interference into citizens' lives to a minimum. That's the rhetoric that's dominated the recent presidential campaign. What *Dirty Harry* was saying is, 'If you have to fill out fifteen copies of every report, the felon will have time to commit another crime before you've finished. There comes a time when you have to stop stalling.' It's an extreme position, but that's where you get back to the irony: without it, the audience wouldn't go along. That's something I felt by instinct. For my part, I've succeeded in remaining pretty much independent, but to reach this stage I've had to fight. And I continue to fight every day.

In your movies, irony is most often tied to something excessive, whether it's an improbable situation or the hero's extreme reactions. The Gauntlet *is a good example.* I had seen on television the barrage of gunfire that followed the abduction of Patty Hearst by the Symbionese Liberation Army. It was a tremendous shoot-out, right in the middle of the city. Bullets flew in all directions and at least three buildings caught fire. I imagined what would occur in a city of middling importance like Las Vegas, where the police don't have anything to do but arrest a drunk from time to time. If it were suddenly announced that Public Enemy Number One had seized a bus and taken a police officer hostage, all the cops in town would want to be part of the action. It is most likely that their reaction would be excessive. Life offers you examples every day of the bizarre excesses you mention. The real is sometimes surreal. And anyway, as a filmmaker, excess is good dramatic material. What interests the public is the extraordinary, isn't it?

Tightrope *is based on the transference of guilt, a theme dear to Hitchcock. Was this what attracted you to Richard Tuggle's script?*

What attracted me was that this cop has been abandoned by his wife, that he's got custody of the children, that he's intrigued by Geneviève Bujold, but doesn't want to get involved with her because he's got enough problems in his life. He may be more efficient than the hero of *The Gauntlet*, but he is not the type of man to attack the system head-on like Dirty Harry. He just wants to do his job well. But as crime follows crime and the crimes get closer and closer to him, you begin to wonder, 'Could it be him? What is his connection to the criminal? Who is his alter ego?' And it does turn out that the criminal is also a police officer. The interaction of all these elements interested me.

Why didn't you direct the picture yourself?
Richard Tuggle was anxious to direct it. He had written the script, which was excellent. He's the one who wrote *Escape from Alcatraz*. Why not let him direct it? I have enormous respect for anyone who can write a book or script. That's where the real work of creation takes place. The rest is in the interpretation or illustration.

Have you ever written a first treatment and then given it to a professional screenwriter?
Not a complete treatment, but sometimes I may call a screenwriter and tell him, 'Here's the idea. It's up to you to develop it.' That was the case with *Pale Rider*. The writers developed the story, and then I added a few scenes that I wrote myself.

It's to be hoped that Pale Rider *will contribute to the resurrection of the genre, but isn't it a gamble to film a western today?*
I don't know if the genre has really disappeared. There's a whole generation, the younger generation, that knows westerns only from seeing them on television. And I notice that audience ratings for *High Plains Drifter* and *The Outlaw Josey Wales* continue to be excellent. When someone asks me, 'Why a western today?', I'm tempted to answer, 'Why not? My last western went over very well.' It may be that *The Outlaw Josey Wales* was the last western to have been a commercial success. Anyway, aren't the *Star Wars* movies westerns transposed into outer space?

Beyond the western genre, are you interested in the West and its history?
In a personal capacity, of course, but in my pictures the approach has mainly been in the realm of mythology. *Pale Rider* is no exception; it's got numerous biblical references. However, since it's about the miners, I had to read a lot of works about the topic and the Gold Rush era. Again, we filmed it in Idaho, in the Sawtooth Mountains region. It's magnificent country, some of the most beautiful in the United States. As we did for *High Plains Drifter*, we built a whole town, from the ground up.

Which of your films have given you the most satisfaction so far?
The Outlaw Josey Wales, *Bronco Billy* and *Honkytonk Man* were the most satisfying because they were small films.

Were they more personal too?
These films were more personal, better managed and more independent because they were filmed in remote areas, far from Hollywood.

What is the most exciting stage for you? Writing? Shooting? Editing?
Editing. It's the time when you're subject to the fewest constraints, because you are alone with your editor, putting together the pieces of the puzzle. While you are shooting you have to deal with some sixty or eighty people, who are bombarding you with questions; at every moment you have to find an appropriate answer. There is no chance to stall for time. It's exhausting and exciting, of course, because it's there that everything is being played out. You know that if the pieces aren't correctly shaped, you'll never be able to put them together. When I think about the number and the complexity of the elements that enter into play, I'm astounded that good movies exist.

In the light of maturity and of the experience you've acquired as a filmmaker, how do you feel about your character's evolution?
I don't see my characters as one entity. Rather they are a series of variations. It's true that on screen, from film to film, it's the same face, the same physique, but with the coming of maturity, you change your perspective. This is especially true in the selection of subjects. It's probable now that I am choosing scripts that wouldn't have attracted me fifteen or twenty years ago, or that I wouldn't have had the audacity to make then. I can't imagine constantly redoing what used to work for me. Maturity has to be an incitement to progress, to develop and, you hope, improve.

In the course of your career, you've succeeded in altering your image profoundly. You challenge it again in almost every film. But isn't it difficult to live with this alter ego who sustains a whole mythology, who has been the subject of innumerable commentaries and analyses, and about whom books are now being written?
I know it's not about me. I know there is what I am as a person and what I am as an actor. And this image exists only in the mind or the eyes of the audience. I am very careful not to think about it. When I am editing a picture, I don't think about protecting or favoring myself. I think only about the character and his role in the story. Otherwise, everything would be off-center. And I suppose it is the same thing in life. When people write about me, I don't take it personally. If the article is positive, I tell myself, 'Perfect. He understood what I was trying to do.' If it's negative, I live with it by telling myself that it takes all kinds to make a world.

But when you approach a new project, aren't you forced to take into account what your image was in the previous films?
You mean, how do I avoid repeating myself?

Either repeating yourself or consciously embroidering variations on a pre-existing image. For example, Red Stovall, in Honkytonk Man, *is a completely new character for you, whereas the policeman in* Tightrope *seems to have grown from some of your previous roles.*
I don't think so. In the case of *Tightrope*, I was influenced neither by *Dirty Harry* nor by *The Gauntlet*. With that character, I started out again from square one. Even though some general character traits, such as my professional behavior, might appear similar. Of course, it is still me; I can only disguise myself up to a certain point. I can't appear all of a sudden as Quasimodo. But, internally, I approach every new character in a distinct way. That is true with the

Dirty Harry series too. When I was preparing for one of the sequels, I forbade myself to watch the first one again. Even Dirty Harry has changed in fourteen years. He's changed as I have changed. I wouldn't want to reach the point where I am imitating myself. You and I know some filmmakers and actors who are reduced to that. I don't have this problem, but sometimes I wonder if the day will come and I'll tell myself, 'Gee, I don't know what to do any more. Maybe I should go back to doing the things that worked so well for me back then?' That would be sad. When I started work on *Pale Rider*, for a minute I was tempted to see *Josey Wales* again and my first westerns. Then I told myself, 'No, I can't do that. There isn't any connection. The only connection is that it is a western and there's a certain mythology associated with that genre. But I don't want to repeat myself, I don't want to be influenced by the past.'

The mythology that you play with in your pictures resonates with the core values of this country. As a result, they are sometimes treated as sociological phenomena. Does that make you uncomfortable at all?
I don't think about it … I would be afraid to think about it! I don't like people who take themselves too seriously and I especially wouldn't want to be categorized in that way. If I

started analyzing the impact my pictures produce or what I represent in today's America, I would be paralysed, incapable of functioning. It's not for me to dissect myself because I could never have the requisite objectivity.

What is the best antidote against the spirit of seriousness? Black humor perhaps?
There is nothing like it!

How do you see the future of Malpaso? Would you consider developing and producing projects in which you wouldn't be involved either as the director or as an actor?
It's a possibility. Maybe it's what I will do later, but right now I am anxious to keep Malpaso to its modest dimensions. I don't want to serve as a front man. I'm keen on putting my personal touch on everything I do. The reason for Malpaso was originally, 'Whether I succeed or fail, I don't want to owe it to anyone but myself.' It remains my motto.

Above and left: A Hitchcockian transference of guilt: *Tightrope* (1984), with Geneviève Bujold. Signed by Richard Tuggle, it was partially directed by Eastwood.

Opposite page: as indestructible as the Road Runner or the Terminator. *Sudden Impact* (1983).

Following pages: Inspector Harry Callahan in *Sudden Impact*, a Don Quixote of urban crime, fighting against the windmills of legalism and laxity.

2

'The film must speak for itself'
Pale Rider

Interview conducted on April 1, 1985

'…And I looked, and behold a pale horse; and his name that sat on him was Death, and Hell followed with him' (Revelation 6:8). This is how the Preacher manifests himself to the young girl who conjured him up. This wandering soul was simply awaiting a human prayer to appear in the flesh.

Eastwood, as we well know by now, expects an emotional experience from the cinema: 'It's not an intellectual art form; it's something visceral, animalistic', he is fond of repeating. In his case, that creed applies to the creative process itself. *Pale Rider* confirms that his instinct, or intuition, always serves him well. With total disregard for market research and audience polls, he is revisiting the western, his genre of predilection. He is not interested in bringing it into line with current tastes; what he wants is to rekindle its original fervor in order to celebrate the unlimited power of dreams and myths.

Opening under the sign of the phoenix, the film is evidently a rejuvenating experience for its maker. By returning to his sources, by reviving the noble inspiration of the 1950s westerns, which ranged from Allan Dwan to Anthony Mann, Eastwood undergoes a new metamorphosis at the same time that he resurrects a vanishing genre.

Some may have concluded that the actor's persona was tense with bitterness or derision, but what a challenge the mystical figure of the pastor brings to that cliché! Eastwood has shed the poncho dear to Leone's mercenaries. His Preacher has more in common with Shane than with the Man with No Name of *A Fistful of Dollars*. He is also the opposite of the High Plains Drifter, an angel rather than a demon, even if it is an angel in exile, tarnished by an infamous past. (Under his collar, he bears its scar, a pentacle drawn by the impact of five bullets.)

From the outset, the film immediately stuns you by its visual splendor; the majesty of the natural location in the Sawtooth Mountains has a lot to do with it and the mysterious half-light of the interiors does the rest. The director, who had to endure the flat lighting of *Rawhide* for so long, encouraged his cinematographer, Bruce Surtees, to be as creative and sparse as possible. He reputedly told him to use as a model *The Third Man*, in which Orson Welles' face emerged only intermittently from the shadows. *Pale Rider* proves, at any rate, that a western can accommodate the ambiguities of chiaroscuro as well as an urban thriller like *Tightrope*.

My second encounter with Eastwood is taking place five weeks before the Cannes Film Festival. To everybody's surprise at Warner Bros., *Pale Rider* has just been selected for the competition. He himself is slightly incredulous that this invitation has been extended to a western. This first visit won't be his last.

A characteristic ambivalence: the providential savior of *Pale Rider* (1985) is a former desperado.

Right: On the side of the oppressed and have-nots: *Pale Rider*, with Sydney Penny and Carrie Snodgress.

Below: *The Naked Spur* (Anthony Mann, top); *The Man from Laramie* (Anthony Mann, bottom).

Since the Rawhide *days, your image has been identified with the western. What is your emotional bond with the genre that's played such an important role in your career?*
I feel very close to the western. That's where my roots are. It certainly was a big factor in the early part of my career, both in television and the Italian-made westerns. In recent years they've been out of fashion quite a bit. I'd hate to see the genre completely disappear, though that's not really why I made *Pale Rider*. When I'm asked why I decided to do a western at this time, I have to explain that there really isn't any correlation to a time or place. I just liked the story and wanted to tell it. Maybe there were other motivating factors in me, but at the onset I liked the script and felt moved to do it. I don't believe in market research or popular wisdom. I trust my instincts.

How was the project developed? I understand you had been contemplating it for quite some time.
I started on it about four years ago. Michael Butler and Dennis Shryack had written *The Gauntlet* for me. They often talked of their love of westerns, so one day we sat down and tossed around various ideas. They came back with the concept for *Pale Rider*. I ended up making it a little more supernatural than it was written, getting into parallels with the Bible.

Could you be a little more specific about your contribution to the writing process?
They came up with the conflict between the independent miners and the big corporation, as they had done some research on the Gold Rush era. Proceeding from there, they wrote a treatment. When they brought in my character of the Preacher, I felt he needed a prior relationship with an antagonist, the

marshal. That would give the *Pale Rider* an added dimension. It also tied in with the image of the horseman from the Apocalypse. I am no biblical scholar, but I've always been fascinated by the mythology of those biblical stories and how they relate to the mythology of the western.

Did you do some research yourself on that period?
I'd been raised with a little bit of the history, having lived in some of the smaller California towns that had been affected by the Gold Rush. Naturally, I had read a lot of stories about pioneering in this particular part of the country. My grandmother used to live in Angels Camp, the center of the Gold Rush country. In fact, it was right near where we filmed. I had also done some episodes of *Rawhide* in the area, and that's where we filmed the train station, in Sonora. Then I went up north to scout locations in Idaho, where hydraulic mining had once existed. You can still find pieces of old equipment there, but we ended up building our machines from scratch. Fortunately, California outlawed that process shortly after the period of time depicted in the picture because it was so hard on the land.

Pale Rider *is also a piece of Americana, an epic dealing with the quintessentially American experience of the pioneer.*
It was an important moment in American history. We don't have the cultural legacy that Europe has. There are not too many American art forms that are indigenous to this country; most are derived from European art forms. Other than the western, jazz and blues, that's all that's really original. On the other hand, there are parallels between European and Oriental mythologies. My first Italian picture was taken from a samurai

story, Kurosawa's *Yojimbo*; when I first saw that Japanese film I thought I was watching a western! So there's really nothing new on the planet.

When you were a youngster were you already fascinated by westerns? Do you think some of them may have influenced your own approach to the genre – for instance, Anthony Mann's westerns with James Stewart?
I liked them a lot, but I wasn't totally obsessed by them. I don't really recall one particular director that stood out. In those days, filmgoers weren't very conscious. You went to see movies because you wanted to see John Wayne or Gary Cooper. You didn't know who directed the picture. Maybe there were some film buffs, but I didn't know too many young people who were really educated as to the whole background of films. Maybe Hawks and Ford were the ones who got the most recognition as directors, the name above the title sort of thing.

Did you find it more difficult in 1984 to implement a project like Pale Rider *than you did ten years ago when you undertook* The Outlaw Josey Wales?
No, maybe because *The Outlaw Josey Wales* did really well. It wasn't like the last picture I'd done had been soft at the box office. I have to give the studio [Warner Bros.] credit … they liked the idea, or maybe it just grew on them.

But then why didn't you make it when you were approached originally? Were you committed to other projects, or did you feel that the moment was not quite right?
I'd like to say I picked the moment, but I am not that smart! I did it on instinct. At that time I had other projects and I put *Pale Rider* aside. All of a sudden, a year or so later, it just hit me that I'd like to see a western. Everything I've ever done has been that way, something I'd like to see. I thought, 'Gee, I'd like to see a western, it's time to make the script I've got in this drawer here.' I hate to play to a preconceived idea of the audience. I just like to make the project. I've done this all the way along. If you go with a preconceived idea you get in the bind of guessing the audience, which is dangerous. It will affect the film and the way you make it if you try to second-guess the public. I am sure if I wanted to make *Bronco Billy* a more commercial picture, I could have found all sorts of ways. I could have tossed in action scenes, but that would have ruined the film. Somewhere down the line I would pay for it, since it wouldn't be as good in quality. I guess the studio feeds stuff into computers and polls people, but that's nonsense. If I approached *Pale Rider* that way, with bigger shoot-outs and thousands of extras, I would be sacrificing the story, the feel and the soul of it, for pseudo-commercial reasons. Audiences are not going to be fooled if you start throwing artificial things out to them like that.

Below: The Preacher of *Pale Rider* and his magic wand: a cinematic illusionism dear to Eastwood.

Following pages: In *Pale Rider*, sheriff Stockburn (John Russell, center) and his deputies sounded the death knell of the Man with No Name and his amoral ways.

Weren't you going against the tide in dealing with the subtleties of mature relationships when it came to the Preacher and Michael Moriarty's family? The rich emotional texture of the film isn't necessarily geared to the younger segment of the population.

Yet, they were my second reason for doing *Pale Rider*. There is a whole youthful audience that hasn't seen me in a western for nine years, and whose only exposure to the genre has been through television re-runs. I've had very good luck: *High Plains Drifter* and *The Outlaw Josey Wales* keep getting good ratings every time they are on. So someone out there wants to see westerns. Look at the so-called space movies. Aren't they really just spin-offs of westerns? In *Star Wars* they talk about 'the Force', but westerns all used that theme before. Now the question is, if the audience is a more mature one, will they step outside of their homes and come visit us, or wait with their beer can in hand for it to go on TV? I think if a picture is good on its own merit, the audience will come. If it's no good, maybe they won't. I'd like to think that, whether it's true or not.

Going back to the supernatural elements you stressed in the narrative, was it your intention to suggest the young girl might have dreamed the whole story?

Maybe it's a dream, maybe it isn't. She says a prayer, and the Preacher is sent down from the mountains. There are a lot of ways to interpret that. To me, it's just the spirit. Whether the hero is a supernatural being or an emissary from a higher plane, he brings spirit to these discouraged people, who are ready to leave the camp. But it turns out that the Preacher has another reason for being there as well. He had a whole other life there with the antagonist that has to be settled. As the struggle between the big corporation and the miners develops, you witness the basic confrontation of the forces of good and evil. The hero comes to the aid of the underdog and maybe the meek will end up inheriting the earth…

A common thread in the three westerns you directed is a feeling for people who have banded together in some sort of informal community. Disenfranchised from society and unorthodox in his methods, your character seems naturally sympathetic to the underdogs, the outcasts and other marginal elements of society.

I feel that it adds to the drama if the hero is not just a loner, if there are other conflicts and relationships. I also think that the bureaucratic workings of nations and corporations have encouraged people to form counter-societies. It seems that the growing complexity of our lives has made us wonder if there isn't some way to cut through it all. Unlike *High Plains Drifter*, where the hero lets them all fend for themselves, the Preacher in *Pale Rider* brings the people together in such a way that they are willing to resist and fight for their rights.

Being fairly similar in structure, with the hero as catalyst in a micro-society, High Plains Drifter *and* Pale Rider *offer an interesting contrast.*

They both have elements of the classic western, with mythological characters that drift into a situation and have an effect on the people they encounter. In *High Plains Drifter*, he is the bereaved brother who comes back and persecutes the people for their apathy and corruption. In *Pale Rider*, the stranger comes to the aid of hardworking people, who are trying to eek out a living while being harassed by the major

corporate concern. It's a classic pattern that's being played out hundreds of times, whether it's the cattlemen against the sheep men or the land barons against the settlers. Hopefully, it's new and different enough for people who like westerns, yet nostalgic enough to bring back some of the things they might have liked.

In High Plains Drifter, *as well as in Sergio Leone's westerns, moral values were totally confused. In* Pale Rider, *the line is drawn clearly, as it used to be in classic westerns, between right and wrong, the little guy and big business, or individuals and the establishment.*

It was a different era. In that period of the 1960s, cynicism was more prevalent. The westerns I made in Italy were strictly entertainment. But I hope people now are reaching beyond cynicism and are interested in ecological and other modern-day concerns.

Could Pale Rider *be seen as reconciliation between the baroque flourishes of Leone's westerns and the classical tradition that they had departed from?*

The westerns I made with Sergio Leone were great fun to do at that particular time. After three of them I felt it was time to move on and do something different. I don't think it would be good for me or anyone else to go back and attempt that kind of satiric piece unless they were something new and special. I like the more traditional western, but when we made the Leone films in the 1960s, that genre was in a dormant state. So his highly stylized westerns came back as a breath of fresh air. Then when I came back to the States, I was offered a part in *Mackenna's Gold*, which was a huge production. But I turned it down and went for *Hang 'em High*, which was a much smaller film while analyzing the pros and cons of capital punishment, an issue that concerned people on a much deeper level. I feel that now the time has come, if you are going to do a western, to revisit some of the classic mythology and the spirit of the genre.

The western is such a simple and stylized arena that it allows you to deal with any emotion or conflict. In that framework, archetypes become so powerful that you can cross over and reach a wider audience.

That's the key term – cross over – for people who would possibly shy away from the western genre. On a creative level, all the films I did offered some sort of challenge, whether they were westerns or detective stories. Sometimes you do things and you are not sure why you did them. But later, when you look back, you realize there was some kind of thought or statement worth putting on the table for discussion. In a western, especially, you can make any statement because it's a ritualized form.

Like the best classical westerns, Pale Rider *is affirmative and inspirational. You feel the power of human solidarity and you care for a community that is vibrant and alive.*

To me, in a film, whether it's a western or not, you have to be wishing for something to happen. Watching a film like *The Good, the Bad and the Ugly*, you just sit there like a voyeur and take in a lot of different ways of shooting people. It has great entertainment value, but in *Pale Rider* you really want someone to wipe out the villains, you build up steam. It gets you in the classic vein.

The dignity of the characters also puts you in that classic mode. Their emotions are understated, yet as poignant as they were in the cinema of John Ford or Anthony Mann.

Michael Moriarty's character evolves through his contact with the Preacher, eventually becoming a leader of the community. They all learn something, including the mother and daughter. These elements were not in the script, but I added them because I felt that the people in the community had to grow.

The power of a community is something you rarely experience in the western. Since High Noon, *many have been structured around a lone man trying to get an apathetic community to stand up for their rights. However, in* Pale Rider *one empathizes with the miners and their aspirations; you show that they are worthy of the help bestowed on them by the Preacher.*

That's a key point. I suppose when it comes to reality, worthy people have prayers that are never answered. Maybe they are only answered indirectly when the person picks himself up, moves on and tries to fight the best he can. In this case, the mythology is that someone comes down and helps these worthy people who are concerned about their land. He helps them. However, he lets them make their own decisions because he wants them to stand on their own two feet.

Would you rank Pale Rider *as one of your most satisfying film experiences? Can we include it among your small,* *intimate, more personal movies such as* Bronco Billy *and* Honkytonk Man, *movies that were shot in remote places, far from Hollywood?*

Pale Rider was filmed way up north, and nobody knew what we were doing. All the studio knew about was the script and the casting, and I liked it that way. I shot fairly fast, in about forty days, but I was well organized. It took a little bit of building to make the sets for the mine and the town. Once we had all that together, there was really nothing to it. Everything worked, we forged ahead, and I really enjoyed myself. How it rates is in the eyes of the beholder. To me, it will remain a pleasant experience because I put down what I intended, so I don't feel cheated.

Visually, Pale Rider *offers a striking contrast. On the one hand, you experimented with darkness, shooting with as little light as possible in the interiors. On the other hand, you expressed your love for the open space and the wilderness. It may be your most lyrical piece about the beauty of the land.*

Open spaces are one of my favorite visuals. But when you do go into the interiors, it shouldn't be lit like outside. Watch a television show and the interiors will look exactly like the exteriors. I saw a western the other night where everything was tremendously lit and yet there were just a few coal lanterns in the room. On *Pale Rider* I tried to get the mood of how it would feel to live with two or three little lamps lighting a whole house. They really just make pools of light.

Could one see an analogy between the struggle of the independent miners in conflict with big business interests, and the challenges you face as a producer/director working in a small, semi-autonomous unit?

I had my share of struggles earlier in my career. But I am lucky, I guess. After so many pictures, they leave me alone. If I turned out six or seven flops, they might say, 'Wait a minute, let's scrutinize him more carefully.' But usually I have no cause for complaint. They don't even go to the dailies. The president of the studio [Warner Bros.] just says, 'I want to see it when it's all done with music.' So it's a very good position to be in, one I've striven for my entire life. Those analogies you mentioned are not something I can consciously talk about; the picture must speak by itself. If the film stirs a person's imagination, it's doing the right thing. I don't know what I would want them to think. I would want them to think what they want to think.

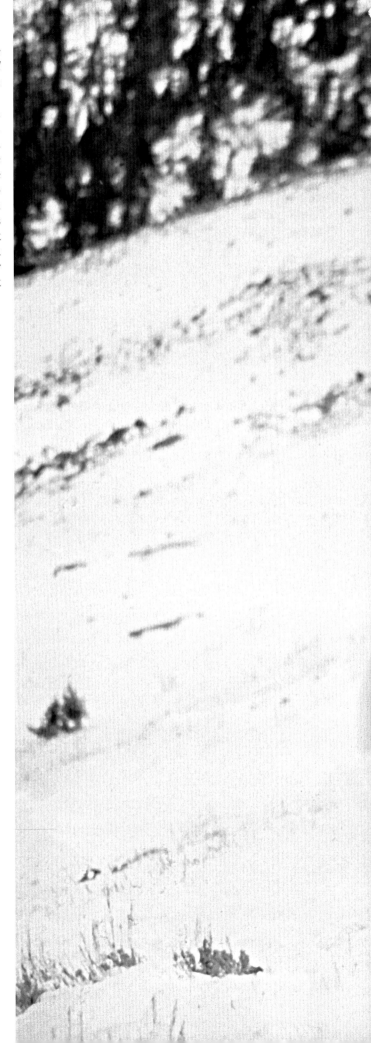

3

'I approach politics as a citizen, not as an ideologue'
Carmel: from movies to politics

Interview conducted on July 18, 1986

Eastwood has invited me to lunch at the Ramada Inn in San Clemente, which houses the production offices of *Heartbreak Ridge*. The conversation is not concerned with the film, which is being shot in the vicinity at Camp Pendleton, but with the filmmaker's new identity: he has just taken his first steps into the political arena. In April he was elected mayor of Carmel with 72 per cent of the vote, for a two-year term and a monthly salary of $200!

He takes this responsibility very seriously, but denies harboring higher ambitions, even though Norman Mailer encouraged him to do so as early as 1983 by remarking that his 'presidential' face and his 'iconic statute' would carry him to the top: 'My ambitions start in Carmel and stop there!' He is quick to add that he would be totally incapable of waging the type of campaign that is expected of a candidate for the White House, because that would mean making all sorts of promises while knowing there would be no way he could keep them. 'Let Reagan do his job, and I'll do mine!'

Carmel-by-the-Sea, with less than 5,000 inhabitants, is the Saint-Paul-de-Vence of California. Its growth has been rigorously controlled. Residences don't even display address numbers. Fast-food joints and neon signs are prohibited. As stated by a famous zoning ordinance of 1929, 'Business and commerce must be subordinated to its residential character.' An avowed enemy of state control and bureaucracy, Eastwood himself has suffered from its excesses. Brandishing the weapon of good sense, he has waged a 'centrist' campaign and vowed to loosen administrative shackles. Champions of the environment are keeping a close watch, fearing that he may promote the dreaded over-commercialization that has until now been kept at bay.

One of the problems awaiting him, a particularly thorny one, is the fate of Mission Ranch, an old dairy farm converted into a bed-and-breakfast resort. It features some twenty acres of wetlands along the sea. A developer threatens to build condominiums on the site. By the end of the year, Mister Mayor will have taken care of the issue with a grand gesture: buying the whole ranch out of his own pocket. He will eventually restore it, while preserving its rustic environment.

Eastwood won't seek a second term. The official reason is that he plans to spend more time with his children, Kyle and Alison. But as a man used to making decisions at all times and famous for leading his crew at a brisk pace, he quickly realized that presiding over a city council is much more complex than shooting a movie. Chances are he got tired of the bargaining and compromises involved with his position, whatever the issue might be: building a library annex for children, dividing drinking water more equitably or reauthorizing ice-cream vendors on the ocean front!

'A minimum of common sense will carry you a long way.' The new mayor of Carmel took the oath on April 15, 1986.

Throughout the years, Clint Eastwood has regularly called on his children.

Right: Daughter Alison appeared at his side as early as *Tightrope*. She would be seen again in *Absolute Power* and *Midnight in the Garden of Good and Evil*.

Below: Little Morgan had a magical moment in *Million Dollar Baby*, when Maggie (Hilary Swank) recognized in her the child she used to be.

Opposite page: His son Kyle contributed as an actor in *Honkytonk Man*, and later, starting with *The Rookie*, as a musician.

You were elected mayor of Carmel on April 9. What prompted you to campaign for the job?

I've lived in Carmel for fifteen years. I felt the need to give something back to this town that I cherish above all others. For some, politics is the road to power or money, or both at once. As far as I'm concerned, I'm not motivated by money; I don't need money. As to power, I have no desire for it. Before making the decision to campaign, I tried to find candidates among people I knew, who might be capable of instigating a change of course. But everybody told me, 'Why don't you run yourself instead?' I kept coming up with various excuses for not doing so. But I finally gave in to their arguments by telling myself, 'You may be doing something stupid, but if you can contribute to charting a new course, it will be worth the try.'

What did you think you could contribute to Carmel?

A little good sense and a firm will to act. I want to encourage everyone's participation in the council's debates and promote a healthier attitude towards business. Under the previous administration [of Mayor Charlotte Townsend], I witnessed the ill effects of bureaucratic meddling in the life of citizens. Everything was caught ever more tightly in a regulation grid that ended up discouraging people instead of stimulating their entrepreneurship. Actually, I was one of the victims. They refused me, under ridiculous pretexts, a permit to build offices next to my restaurant, The Hog's Breath. If the administration can do that to Clint Eastwood, imagine how far it would go against defenceless people … I'll give you another example. They had decided that each fiscal home would be allowed only one kitchen, and to enforce this, they sent inspectors at any time of day to check people's residences. For retirees who survive financially by renting a part of their house, this new regulation was a very tough blow. Locals even baptized it 'the Gestapo decree'.

Is this the kind of excess that you were targeting by centring your campaign on the theme 'Bringing the Community Together'?

Exactly. I took up Reagan's cry, 'Get government off my back!' After all, I was entitled to borrow it from him, since he stole one of my lines from *Sudden Impact*, 'Make my day!' He used it during a press conference at the White House to challenge Gaddafi [in reality, to defy Congress to raise taxes]. What we suffer the most from, I believe, is excess of government, at the local as well as at the federal level. Concretely, my first gesture after I was elected was to enlarge and diversify the council, notably by bringing in young people. Now, all together, we are going to try and clean up municipal legislation. We

Above: Mission Ranch has become one of the highlights of Carmel after being restored by Eastwood. The filmmaker has sometimes edited or composed the music for his films on the premises.

Below right: During the making of *Play Misty for Me*, Eastwood decided to film the jazz festival of Monterey, Carmel's sister city. Here with Donna Mills.

want to loosen the vice of regulations so that the law may help citizens instead of crushing them.

What do you think are the essential qualities required of a politician?
Good sense, essentially. It is a job that does not demand exceptional knowledge or intelligence. I even think that too much intellect can be harmful, whereas a minimum of common sense will carry you a long way. But of course, as you know, there is nothing less common than common sense! I would like to revive good old logic, and do so for the benefit of the entire community, not just for a well-heeled minority. I try to approach politics as a citizen, not as an ideologue. Ideologues are the most boring people in the world.

Have you been interested in political issues for a long time?
No, it came to me with maturity. Film contributed to it in no small part, but maybe not in the way people think. It's not in my scripts that I found my ideas, but in my travels outside the United States. In Europe, thanks to the distance, I started to look at the world globally. And I discovered that the rest of the world did not identify with America. You see, being brought up in America has some huge advantages, but also some drawbacks. One of these drawbacks is that you don't think you need to speak other languages or understand other cultures. The world is so much wider, so much more complex, than most Americans generally imagine. People are diverse. Some conclude too hastily that such diversity only provokes conflicts. In reality, it is the wealth of the world. The big question is, 'As diverse as we are, how can we all share this planet?'

Which are the major political figures that have impressed you?
They hark back to World War II – Churchill, de Gaulle and Roosevelt, but especially Churchill.

Which would you say are the most urgent problems that America needs to resolve today?
On the domestic front, we need to deal with the budget deficit. It threatens to jettison the tax reform. And it also affects our relations with the rest of the world. In foreign policy, I would say our relationships with the USSR and with our allies. There is no reason why we can't solve these problems with our God-given brains rather than with the weapons we keep manufacturing. Otherwise, we might as well give up on mankind.

What did you think of the American raid against Tripoli, a raid intended to punish Gaddafi for his support of terrorists?
How history will judge this event, I don't know. In my own humble opinion, once you have decided on a course, you should stick to it. When you are faced with certain powers that have become breeding-grounds for terrorists, there always comes a moment where it's not enough to say, 'No more!', and where you need to act. Reagan has a much better sense of that than Carter had. His strength is to be in step with the opinion of a majority of Americans. He's from the Midwest, so his style, his language resonate well with the American hinterland. It's for that reason that he communicates so easily with the country as a whole. And he does it in spite of the fact that his own world tends to be that of the privileged.

Isn't the Vietnam debacle still today a major trauma for America?
Certainly. It was the first war that people could watch every evening, at home and live, on television. Americans are an impatient people. If the Vietnam War had lasted six months, they could have lived with it. But it was never-ending. And the political class didn't know any more if America was supposed to win, to draw or to get out. That uncertainty has confused many people and even shaken those who held the reins of power. Nobody knew what to believe any more. It was a war that was waged with only one hand.

You took to heart the fate of American soldiers missing in action in Indo-China. It has been said that a few years ago

you helped an operation that purported to free prisoners of war still captive in Laos.
That's true. I had been approached by Lieutenant Colonel Bo Gritz, a Vietnam vet who was mounting a commando operation to rescue American soldiers missing in action. I helped him financially. Unfortunately, his information was inaccurate, and the plan failed. But my conviction was that you had to try something. You couldn't just sit idle when you knew that some of our guys were still alive over there.

During your campaign you have been likened to your character in Dirty Harry, *the man who fights crime with no holds barred.*
Bullshit! That's journalistic laziness. Of course, I could say that's almost flattering; fifteen years after its release, that film is still a reference. It's the ransom of success! Nobody, or very few people, would ever identify me with Bronco Billy. Mark you, the influence a film can have is not always imaginary. For instance, in *Sudden Impact*, when I proffered the famous line that Reagan borrowed from me, I knew that it would get a lot of play. But I could never imagine that it would end up qualifying as a title for legislative reform. I am talking about the new law on self-defence that is being called the 'Make My Day Law'.

How would you situate yourself on the political chessboard?
I am too individualistic to stand on the Left or on the Right.

You are nevertheless listed among conservative Republicans.
I disagree with that label. I am indeed an old Republican. The first time I voted was for Eisenhower in the 1950s. But I'm not sectarian. There have been instances where I voted for Democrats. On fiscal and economic matters, you can call me a conservative. I'm not for state control; I have always thought that the country's affairs should be managed more along the lines of a private enterprise. On the other hand, I am very attached to the defence of individual freedoms.

Isn't moral conservatism or strict Puritanism somewhat in contradiction to economic liberalism?
It can become a contradiction in some cases. You know the Meese Report on pornography, which advocates full-scale repression? Like everyone else, I detest excesses, in particular when they involve children. On the other hand, I fear the rule of committees that would decide for everybody what is acceptable and what isn't, based on a handful of people's criteria.

What is the worst threat facing the individualistic values that built this country?
The dictates of fashion! Ten years ago, young people walked about bare foot with garlands of flowers around their neck. Today, with this generation of so-called yuppies, the pendulum has swung back very far in the other direction. To them, it all comes down to making a lot of money straight away. They'd feel dishonored if they didn't have the best stereo system or were not driving a BMW. These are the young piranhas of materialism that have been running the show for the last several years. Their 'every man for himself' mentality has nothing to do with the individual values that I defend. Between the hippies and the yuppies, don't you think we should be able to find a middle way?

Left: Oscar night in March 1993: Eastwood, flanked by Kyle and Alison, has just won the trophies for best picture and best director with *Unforgiven*.

Among all your films, which ones do you think offer the best reflections of America and its myths?
Because of the exceptional success of *Dirty Harry*, I'm often identified with that particular character. I'm afraid I'll remain 'Dirty Harry Eastwood' all my life. But to me personally, *Bronco Billy* is a film as important, if not more important. The hero is an individualist, a dreamer who translates his dream into reality, at the risk of seeming completely crazy. He is a man determined to do what's right, and succeeds. Anyway, America itself is history's craziest idea! There exists an insane streak in American life, and that insanity, very often, is our main source of friction with the rest of the world.

Will your new position affect your choice of film projects?
No, these are two separate domains. When I choose a part, I trust only my intuition. It's my only guide. The Carmel people who elected me may dislike some of these film portrayals, but I can't let that stop me.

Politically speaking, what does your intuition tell you?
My ambitions start in Carmel and end at the city limits. I have no intention to run for the Senate. And I have no intention ever to transform Carmel into another Rodeo Drive [Beverly Hills' deluxe shopping area], contrary to what I have been accused of by opponents who portrayed me as an opportunist. Carmel should remain a small residential community; there will be no radical changes. One of the advantages of being an actor in politics is that you are used to unfair or malevolent critiques! I don't need publicity; Hollywood has served me well in that area. Besides, I'm going to be significantly less active movie-wise. For the duration of my term [two years], I intend to give Carmel absolute priority. I have to attend one council meeting per month, and it is my firm intention not to miss a single one!

4

'I like the dream that inhabits the idealist'
Heartbreak Ridge

Interview conducted on November 20, 1986

Exterior day: University of Grenada. At Solana Beach on the outskirts of San Diego, a Christian school stands for the Medical Faculty, 'liberated' by the Marines during the invasion of 1983. Some fifty students and teachers are working as extras. Sergeant Highway's platoon consists of about fifteen actors. Eastwood is easy to spot as he strides back and forth between his camera and the patrol, his face 'camouflaged' with shoe polish.

On that day, cinematographer Jack Green will get through no less than thirty-one set-ups. Yet some of them involve crowd reactions and special effects, such as the dance of a skeleton machine-gunned by a Marine in one of the classrooms. None of the shots will require more than four takes. In most cases, one or two will do. Entirely male, the crew runs like a well-oiled machine. Among these veterans of Malpaso shoots, even the 'rookie' already has seven of them under his belt.

Eastwood, perfectly relaxed, starts tinkling at the piano in the music room while the scene is being set up. He could be a coach in a summer camp, albeit one who would never need to raise his voice. He compares his role on the set to that of Sergeant Highway: he is the platoon leader, the officer who must inspire and guide his men while relying on the talents of each individual. His young actors seem delighted to play along. After six days of intense drilling during real Army exercises in Puerto Rico, a military walkover such as the Grenada invasion must feel like a picnic to them.

It is not a war film, insists Eastwood, but a character study, the portrait of a grizzled career soldier who owes his stripes to his numerous decorations (Korea, Santo Domingo, Vietnam), but will never be promoted to the higher ranks. Too pigheaded to fit into the military bureaucracy, he sticks out like a relic of the past in the technocratic army of today. Yet he has a few lessons in survival to pass on to his young recruits. If the language wasn't so profane, one might conjure up John Wayne's double face in the classic *Sands of Iwo Jima* directed by Allan Dwan (1949): a master warrior in the heat of action, but a pathetic lost soul in daily life.

The shoot will wrap seven days ahead of schedule. Eastwood won't have missed any meeting of Carmel's city council. But several months later, claiming that the unflattering film doesn't paint the Marines accurately, the US Department of Defense will withdraw its support. Unlike *Top Gun*, *Heartbreak Ridge* is not considered to be a proper recruiting tool. The advance screenings scheduled at Camp Pendleton will have to be cancelled, and all mentions of the US Marine Corps' participation in the credits deleted.

A man at war with his own demons: Sergeant Highway in *Heartbreak Ridge* (1986).

When you became interested in Heartbreak Ridge, *what was the main attraction?*

The project was brought to me over a year ago. I wasn't immediately enthralled, but I liked the main character. I've always been intrigued by the premise of a man who is told, 'Your job is over, you're going on mandatory retirement.' What can a soldier like Sergeant Highway do in a case like this? He has devoted his adult life to fulfilling his duties as a non-commissioned officer and, in the process, his marriage and everything else have gone by the wayside. Then all of a sudden it's over. As his ex-wife Aggie says when he returns to their town and the unit where he started his career, 'Are you just coming back because you know it's ending?' He may have wanted to be with her but I suspect he was selfishly motivated. He's got nowhere to go.

Didn't you expand the emotional spectrum of the story considerably?

The script evolved in the rewriting process. The relationship between Highway and Aggie hadn't been resolved and none of the platoon members was drawn out adequately. Stitch simply played the guitar, and then disappeared; he wasn't even in the military. Aponte, the Marine who is trying to support a family, and most of the other characters, didn't even exist. I felt that these individual stories were very important to the overall story, so I set about rewriting it with writers Joe Stinson [*Sudden Impact*] and Dennis Hackin [*Bronco Billy*]. Although the Writers Guild wouldn't let them take screen credit, they made a major contribution.

It is truly an impressive ensemble piece, one of the best casts you've put together.

Joe, Dennis and I worked very hard to get a wide spectrum, to assemble the many pieces and still tell the story in a reasonable amount of time. The next important step was to find actors who would enhance the characters and contribute more shadings of their own. The casting was much easier than I had expected because everyone liked the story so much, including Marsha Mason, who was my first choice for Aggie. The members of the platoon were just as enthusiastic. There were a lot of good actors who could have played those parts, but I was very pleased with the ones I cast. Everyone worked together and these interactions reflected the spirit of the film itself.

Caught in a web of conflicting situations and relationships, Sergeant Highway is at odds with almost every other character. But it seems that he is essentially a man at war with his own demons.

He is fighting the enemy within him and that is the probable cause of his inability to function outside the military. At first he appears to be out of control; the judge, the cops and his superiors chastise him. But as one is slowly exposed to the people he's known in the past, and as his relationships with Stitch and Major Powers unfold, the perspective shifts. Highway ranges from the ridiculous to the sublime. A good example is when he discovers that Aponte is raising a family and helps out by giving the man some of his own money. Ten years earlier, Highway might have said, 'Deal with it yourself. I'm interested only in how you are as a Marine.' But now, maturity is causing him to look at life differently.

Sergeant Highway is a mass of contradictions. He is at once a hard-boiled professional and a self-destructive, vulnerable outcast. He may be a relic of past wars, yet he's more efficient than his technologically oriented superiors. A bullying drill sergeant, he is also capable of acting like Santa Claus with his platoon.

He is a strange paradox. Nowadays in the Marine Corps, recruits are represented as computer operators having a great time. Highway is from the old school. He's been in the trenches and fought in the jungles. He doesn't think the realities of war should be hidden or covered up; he strongly believes his platoon should be prepared. On the other hand, he feels tremendous anxiety about his personal relationships. The whole idea of reading *Harper's Bazaar* or *Cosmopolitan* to learn the secrets of a relationship are really naive, but he actually is naive about women. He has never been understanding or emotional his entire life, even though he may have wanted to be. He simply never took the time. His love life probably amounted to a gal in Bangkok or a woman in Taiwan now and then. His only serious relationship had been with Aggie, and he didn't know how to handle her. Actually they didn't know how to handle each other.

You had Marsha Mason's part developed significantly. Ever since Play Misty for Me, *you have repeatedly demonstrated that a strong female character enhances the male lead.*

Aggie is in her mid-forties, and a woman at that point in her life would realize that she had wasted her prime years with a man like Highway. I like the fact that she stands her own ground. In general, movies in the 1930s and 40s endowed women with strong characters. This set up more conflict, which was better for the leading man as well. In the case of Aggie, she can't just fall into Highway's arms. Maybe she's still intrigued by him, but there is a lot of bitterness on both sides. I carry this ambivalence all the way to the end. They don't even hug or kiss each other. One senses that there's still going to be hard times ahead, but hopefully the audience is rooting for them to be reconciled.

She's a woman of the 1980s, whereas he still has one foot in the 1950s.

She has moved along with the times, although if they got married when she was eighteen, she probably spent her twenties and thirties waiting for him, at a point when many other women were developing their careers and getting out of the house. Highway might also feel guilty that she had been

a cocktail waitress in a saloon. He'd have been more relieved if she had a better job or a happier life with someone else. He knows she has wasted her adult life on him and it probably rides hard on his soul.

On the surface he appears to be an emotional cripple, a victim of his own machismo.
The picture is actually anti-machismo. Machismo is part of what ruined his personal life and stifled his development with the females of the species. But at least he's not what I call 'pseudo-macho', someone who speaks loudly, is full of bravado and brags endlessly about all the chicks he's had. 'Pseudo-machos' are insecure men who are always trying to prove themselves. They take their 'man pills' and sit at the bar, talking tough as if they were in a John Ford movie, although John Ford might not have approved of their behavior! Highway is not that 'pseudo' type. He can fend off fights by getting people confused and catching them off-guard. He does just the opposite of what his opponents expect him to do, like in the case where the guy becomes so disoriented that he doesn't hit back with a club and just wanders off. Highway is a street psychologist who has learned many things, but there's still so much he doesn't know about.

He is also a rebel and an inveterate insubordinate; a man who stands on his own and sticks to his values, whatever price he may pay for it.

He doesn't approve of many things in the system he is part of. For instance, he doesn't like an officer misusing his position. He feels that Powers is playing at war and not dealing with it seriously. He'd love to smoke a contraband Cuban cigar but won't, simply out of principle. When he is in Grenada, he takes one from a Cuban soldier because it's a different situation and another country.

Early on, you suggest that Highway never could be a commissioned officer because he is too honest and too idealistic about the Marine Corps.
He is innocent in a scarred up kind of way, even though he shouldn't be innocent at all. I like that quality in him. It's possible that he attained the rank of sergeant only because of his heroics in past wars; he isn't political enough to work the system. A real political animal would be more manipulative and further his own career like Powers and his ilk do. Highway is not that type because he sees people and situations in black and white. He doesn't say, 'This guy's an opportunist, but I'll work with him anyway because I want to keep or improve my rank.' He says, 'This guy's a jerk and I'm going to deal with him on a jerk's level.'

He knows he is part of a corrupt system. And because he is uncompromising he carries the logic or the ideal of that system to its extreme consequences, not unlike Dirty Harry.
Dirty Harry was raised in a system and believed in it. So when he saw it had been corrupted, he was enraged much more

Above: 'He's one of the last of his kind': *Heartbreak Ridge.*

Following pages: As in *Pale Rider*, the hero becomes a source of inspiration. *Heartbreak Ridge*, with Mario Van Peebles.

than the average person would be. *Heartbreak Ridge* is similar in that Highway is totally devoted to the Marine Corps and is thus deeply upset by Powers' incompetence.

Oddly enough, Highway becomes a symbol of individualism in an institution where individuality is not generally regarded as a virtue.
All of the branches of the military have one thing in common: they are police states within themselves. One is pretty much at the mercy of their rules and regulations. It takes a certain mentality to live within a police state, which is the antithesis of a democratic society, at least in what we call the 'free world'. Highway has managed to live in the military because he believes in the idea of serving his country and honoring the memory of his friends who have been killed in action. But he is still naive about life and people, and what it means to be part of a democracy.

His brand of honesty is at the heart of American culture, yet Highway as a veteran is maladjusted in today's world. Are the character's inadequacies a reflection of America's evolution from the 1950s to the 1980s?
He's still in the running, but he's one of the last of his kind, along with his friend Choozoo. In every branch of the service there are a few like Highway and, when they're gone, it leaves the type of people one sees in commercials nowadays. A big question is whether we'd be better off with the 1980s type or if the dinosaurs of the past will be sorely missed.

It seems that Highway feels betrayed because the institution he serves is not flawless. His experience is strangely similar to that of the spy in The Eiger Sanction *or of the cop in* The Gauntlet. *People in charge are the ones endangering the system's code of values. The tragedy is that the enemy is not another ideology, but some negative forces entrenched within the system itself.*
That is true, just look at the political system. People get into positions where they could actually help, but instead move in the opposite direction. They become corrupt and lose track of the people. Just as this happens to many politicians in civilian life, members of the military political structure can also veer off track. One of the great virtues of the democratic system is that if they go too far, we dump them. Unfortunately, sometimes they cause a lot of damage before they can be stopped. The Highway character represents the kind of man who can't stand by and do nothing.

Your heroes are often the last of their kind and they are fighting a lost cause. The trials of the idealistic warrior, isn't that one of your favorite themes?
It's difficult to be an idealist today, but I still like the dream that inhabits them. That quest for 'doing it right' is something I liked in the Bronco Billy character and the *Dirty Harry* movies.

The upbeat note is that the younger Marines carry that dream. Highway's idealism is not dead once he's out of the scene. He started by antagonizing the platoon, but ends up becoming an inspiration to the kids. There's an interesting parallel with Pale Rider, *where the Preacher brought a new spirit to the community of independent miners.*
In the beginning, the members of Highway's platoon think he's crazy, but they eventually realize how dedicated he is.

Suddenly they understand that his way is more fun than just being some sort of flunky and hanging out. There is a parallel with *Pale Rider* because Highway does infuse spirit in the men. When they finally go to war, which is just a minor skirmish, Highway is confident that they will perform properly. He watches the platoon with a certain satisfaction; he can see the results of the solidarity he has built between them.

Do you think that the virtues Highway embodies have become obsolete?
In some areas maybe, but they shouldn't be. Bureaucrats like Powers and Webster may be hopeless, but that's not true of the young recruits. When the platoon goes into action, it is clear that it can function well on its own. There are certainly more genteel and civilized ways of accomplishing what Highway does. I can think, for instance, of a professor who sees his students take what he's taught them and go on to do something with it.

Were you in some way addressing the past traumas of America's unresolved wars in Asia?
Wars like Korea and Vietnam forfeited thousands and thousands of human lives and, given their outcome, you may question their legitimacy. But there will always be those who are willing to fight those wars without questioning the rights and wrongs. Like Highway, these are noble types but very sad as well … willing to do what they see as their duty, yet sacrificing their lives when they could have devoted themselves to much more productive activities.

When Highway says in Grenada, 'We won this one', did you mean this was essentially a personal victory for him and his team rather than a nation's victory?
I don't know if the Grenada situation was a definitive military or political victory. The sergeant just wanted to do his job. The point is that Highway's group won out over political types like Powers. I'm sure it rankled Highway that in Korea the armed forces went to the 38th parallel and stopped, after losing some 40,000–50,000 men. The politicians would say, 'We've got to negotiate our way out, there is no conclusion here.' To a military man like Highway, however, the armistice had to be a defeat.

Isn't Highway the opposite of a Rambo figure?
Rambo is pure fantasy. It isn't that easy to go into a country, shoot 'em all up and come out alive, and I don't see Highway as a superman coming to the rescue. It's more realistic; he's lived through real battles where he's been shot at and wounded. He has not only lost wars, he is even lost in his own life.

Didn't you systematically choose to tone down the heroics in the Grenada episode?
Yes, he's already been a hero – in the past. In the first Grenada skirmishes he's active in leading his platoon. But after a certain point he lets them take over because they have become a well-oiled machine.

During the invasion, one of the Marines shoots at a skeleton in a science lab, while another one 'liberates' a naked girl in the shower. These moments stress the relativity, if not the absurdity, of such military action.

They enter the school, but there is nobody present except the students. There might have been hostile forces in the country, but there is no one to shoot up or to rescue. The Marines simply get the kids on the next plane out. There is no glory about it. There are sporadic actions, generally without man-to-man combat. In the black and white opening montage, you see how combatants in Korea fought in trenches; they couldn't see anyone. Nobody was running around spearing the enemy with a bayonet like John Wayne!

The confusion and fragmentation of the war scenes evoke newsreel footage. Did you ever contemplate shooting them in Grenada?
We thought of it, but there's nothing left in Grenada now; the Cuban and Russian equipment has been confiscated. The Marines and the Seabees happened to have detachments in Vieques, near Puerto Rico. Also, the Marines were holding a big military exercise, which they allowed us to film, so we went along. I had six camera operators who had covered this sort of event before. It was like doing newsreel work. You simply couldn't say, 'Please turn all those amphibious vehicles back, we need another take!'

In the Grenada episode, you adopt the young Marines' point of view. What do they learn?
They find that they can function together and improvise on their own. Highway has been in battle many times before; his scarred face gives away his background. So why show the conflict through Highway's perspective? This is a new battle, a real war. In the skirmishes, the Marines have to shoot at real people. They see men getting killed and even lose one of their buddies. It is no longer a game or play exercise, and it affects each one of them differently.

How does Highway feel when he lights up his cigar?
He has had the satisfaction of one last successful jaunt. After that, he's pretty lonely because he has no service any more. With only minimal retirement benefits, what is he going to do? Probably not much except drink tons of beer and sit around in bars.

Doesn't he learn something from his interaction with the kids and the very different life experiences that they represent – for instance, that everything does not necessarily fit neatly into right or wrong?
I think he'll be a better person for knowing them. It's fun to see younger people having enthusiasm about something you had at one time. When Highway's watching his platoon round up Cuban soldiers and being so excited about winning, he's probably seeing himself thirty years earlier. And in the last scene, when he watches them embrace their loved ones, most likely he is seeing himself in the distant past. But when Highway greets his wife, the feeling is, 'Here we are, what happens now?' And her glance is saying, 'I don't know, but here we are!' Their whole outlook is quite different from the younger people. Yet he does have something good to remember and he may start to feel better about his past.

There's a wonderful irony in Marsha Mason waving her little flag, which is quite a contrast to the huge flag under which Highway stood at attention earlier on.
We used the smallest one we could find. I didn't want anything pompous at the end. They had such a contentious relationship

Above: 'This is not a John Wayne picture': the invasion of Grenada in *Heartbreak Ridge*.

that she couldn't be waiting for him with a big flag. It has to be tiny, and she just says, 'Hi, there.' There is something sweet about it. It's almost like she's saying, 'You're my military man.'

The American flag was treated with a good deal of irreverence in Bronco Billy, *where patients in an insane asylum are seen stitching a huge banner…*
… and they're making a whole tent out of it. Exactly. When I read that the first time, I immediately liked it. It was fun for Bronco Billy to end up in this pseudo patriotic show when he was so much into patriotism. You had the same irony when he ended up defending the deserter.

Would you say that Sergeant Highway was your most challenging part?
It was challenging but not more so than some of my other roles. Maybe Bronco Billy was the most difficult because it was so out on the edge – the fantasy of the ultimate idealist. In that case, the risk was falling into the trap of winking at the audience. Josey Wales might have been easier because a character that experiences one great tragedy is simpler to grasp. But in *Heartbreak Ridge*, Highway's whole life is a tragedy. War has taken a toll on his soul and might have contributed to his deliberate callousness. His receiving the Medal of Honor at a young age screwed up his life because it distorted his expectations. As a young man he most likely experienced great highlights. Then, later on in life, he had to contend with little skirmishes and defeats; he's the result of many years of despair.

Did you draw upon your own memories of the Army?
I draw on my experience to some extent. I was in the infantry from 1951 to 1952, but I wasn't one to enjoy that lifestyle. I would never have been like Highway and stayed in the military. I was in the 6th Army at Fort Ord, California. I suppose I would have gone to Heartbreak Ridge or somewhere in Korea like most of my company, if I hadn't been involved in a plane crash. I had gone up to Seattle to visit my parents. In those days you could hop a Navy flight for free if you were in uniform. On the way back, the plane crashed into the ocean and was lost. Unhurt, the pilot and I swam ashore, but the Navy asked me to stand by in case there was an investigation. As I recall, it threw me out of the cycle with the people who

went to Korea. The hearing never came about and I had only nine months left. In such a case, they don't ship you overseas; it's not economically viable. So I missed the trip and stayed at the Fort. I can't say I regret it. Nobody was in a hurry to roll around the hills of Korea. It was probably different in 1941–2. Some were quite gung ho then. Later, when they discovered what was really going on, they were not so keen. Many a volunteer must have regretted raising their hand. As far as I'm concerned, I strongly believe in destiny. It determines in a large part what you make of your life.

Were you trained for combat at Fort Ord?
Yes, of course. I had sixteen weeks of basic training. After that, I was promoted to instructor. I ran a swimming programme and I also taught a class on military history, for which I screened films, notably *The Battle of San Pietro*, which was always a popular one to run. We had a lot of 16mm prints of it. It was supposed to be all actual combat footage, but I think John Huston was clever enough to stage some of it before and after the battle to make the film more effective.

Sometimes, producing and directing requires as much spirit and discipline as waging a battle. Do you see an analogy between Highway's handling of his platoon and the filmmaker's job?
As a director, you have to work with everyone's personalities, make them feel comfortable and maintain their interest in the project. The men in the platoon really worked as an ensemble; they cared about the film and liked each other. They were so enthusiastic that they would come to me and ask, 'What about if we did this or that?' Some of the suggestions I liked, others I didn't. But even if I didn't, I would always explain why it wouldn't work in the overall picture. I didn't want to suppress the kind of enthusiasm that their characters were supposed to have for Highway.

To what extent did you identify with the Highway character?
I've felt some of the things he's felt over the years. I'm not in a profession that has a mandatory retirement, but then again, that can happen if the public doesn't want you any more! It's not hard to identify with a man who's lost in his own life and has nowhere to go in his relationships.

As a character study, Heartbreak Ridge *revives a classic tradition of American films dealing with the psychological aspects of war, rather than its heroics. In the late 1940s and 50s for instance, you had William Wellman's* The Story of G.I. Joe, *Lewis Milestone's* A Walk in the Sun, *Samuel Fuller's* Fixed Bayonets!, *Anthony Mann's* Men in War …
I miss those films. I would like to think that *Heartbreak Ridge* is more in that vein than in the shoot 'em up genre. The point here is not which stunt can outdo the last. I could have staged battles where men blow up or fall off bridges, but I wanted the war episode to have the flavour of a documentary – not a lot of direct hits, but soldiers skirmishing, diving for cover, hanging out. Also, the pictures you mentioned were strong on psychology and that is what I tried to accomplish. On the surface, there is probably enough action and clever dialogue to appease the less demanding filmgoers. But most important to me is that the audience grasps and appreciates the broad tapestry of this character study.

Some of the classic war films that have impressed Eastwood (clockwise from top): *Men in War* (1957) by Anthony Mann; *A Walk in the Sun* (1946) by Lewis Milestone; *Fixed Bayonets!* (1951) by Samuel Fuller; *Battleground* (1949) by William Wellman; *The Story of G.I. Joe* (1945) by William Wellman.

5

'Jazz encourages you to be different'
Bird

Interview conducted on November 12 and 13, 1987

By composing his elegy to Charlie Parker forty years after discovering him playing live in Oakland, Eastwood accomplishes an act of faithfulness. More than ever he marches to his own drum. In combining his twin passions, jazz and cinema, he is giving us his most experimental work. Joel Oliansky's excellent screenplay frees him from linear narration. It is a time-space puzzle that interweaves flashbacks and flash-forwards to produce a subliminal biography, thankfully devoid of any convenient 'Rosebud'.

We talked a lot about jazz during the preparation of the film and also upon the release of *Round Midnight*, an outstanding picture by Bertrand Tavernier that Eastwood had championed around Hollywood (so effectively that he convinced Warner Bros. to contribute to its financing). As *Bird* is being shot mostly around Los Angeles, I can return to the subject by spending three days with the production, which is moving from one club to another. Thus, the Memory Lane stands for the Three Deuces of 52nd Street, while the Embassy Theater in downtown replaces the Salle Pleyel, where Parisians came to applaud Charlie Parker in 1949. Osco's on La Cienega will be 'dressed' first as an LA club, then as a New York joint, where Bird is partnered by Dizzy Gillespie and Red Rodney respectively.

At age twenty-six, Forest Whitaker looks ageless. Like Bird, he might as well have fallen from another planet. He was well prepared for the role by his musical training: he studied opera at the University of Southern California's music conservatory, played the trumpet, and was guided by Lennie Niehaus, who pulled his sax out of the mothballs to teach him the proper fingering technique. Says Whitaker, 'I am now capable of playing "Lover Man" and a few other pieces by Bird. It's not me that you'll be hearing, but I trust that my gestures will be right.'

Whitaker had the privilege of engaging in long consultations with Chan Parker, who agreed to serve as an adviser. Portrayed by Diane Venora in the film, Chan has also presented Eastwood with an extraordinary gift: more than three hours of private recordings made in New York, notably when Bird was jamming at the Rockland Palace in Harlem. The quality of the tapes was such that Niehaus was able to extract Parker's solos, 'clean them up' and re-record them with musicians of today.

Forest marvels that Bird and Dizzie could ever get on the same wavelength when their lives and personalities were as different as night and day. He sees in Bird a 'chameleon', a rare creature always tuned in to others, maybe too sensitive to bear the discordant symphony of the world. I sense that Forest is taken over by the part, and therefore deeply tormented; you cannot immerse yourself in such pain without being lacerated by it.

'It won't be a film on drugs and their dangers', repeats Eastwood as he joins our conversation. What he wants to capture in Parker is the contradiction between his genius and his despair – how the demon of self-destruction tore him apart even as he was creating his most innovative harmonies.

'There is the western, the blues, and jazz!' Charlie Parker (Forest Whitaker) triumphs at Paris' Salle Pleyel in *Bird* (1988).

Aren't these musicians still your favorites?
They are. We all remain attached to the musicians of our youth. Their music is tied to such and such memories. Take Nat King Cole, whom you heard a lot in my time. To me, he'll remain forever connected to my first romantic dates. As years went by, I became more eclectic. I started loving them all, the young and the old, from Louis Armstrong to Miles Davis. That was the 1960s, the period conjured up by Bertrand Tavernier's film *Round Midnight*, when the passion for jazz tapered off and American musicians emigrated to Europe, particularly to France and Sweden. Most teenagers were turning to rock 'n' roll; others got into the fusion of rock and jazz. But some ended up realizing that jazz, after all, was something to be reckoned with.

Isn't it ironic that jazz masters such as Charlie Parker were acknowledged earlier in Europe?
It's all the more ironic as jazz is our indigenous music. It is even, and I repeat it whenever I can, one of the only original artistic forms that originated in America. There is the western, the blues and jazz! When travelling and working abroad, I realized how much these specifically American art forms had counted and what influences they had exerted. On the other hand, when I sat on the Council of the National Endowment for the Arts in Washington, a federal organization contributing to the financing of the arts, I was the only champion of jazz. After each new proposal, I would add, 'And what about jazz?' I ended up wearing on everybody's patience. The society ladies preferred to raise money for the opera, which was more 'cultural'. The problem, in this country, may be that jazz is too familiar, that it is taken for granted, whereas elsewhere the grass is always greener.

Jazz has played a big part in your life.
Yes, I grew up with it. And I knew I was different because I liked that music rather than swing or rock 'n' roll. You shouldn't forget that jazz remains a popular music, though, paradoxically, it doesn't reach all audiences. It is the music of a minority, however large that may be. That endears it to me all the more. Today more than ever, a kid who likes jazz rather than rock is a rebel, a maverick, an individualist who has chosen the road less travelled.

How did you discover the world of jazz?
For me, it all started with Dixieland jazz. Growing up in the Bay Area, I used to listen to groups such as Blue Waters, the Yerba Buena Jazz Band or Turk Murphy at a time when Dixieland was making a comeback. Then I discovered Dave Brubeck when he was playing on Lakeshore Avenue in Oakland. Later, when I left the Army and found myself working as a lumberjack in Springfield, Oregon, I would sometimes stay up all night to listen to something other than country music on the radio, in this case a jazz programme broadcast in San Francisco. I was hooked, and it hasn't left me since.

Have you ever encountered resistance from the studios about your taste for jazz?
Hollywood is less timid. The studios never tried to prevent me from using jazz in my film scores. In *Play Misty for Me*, my first picture as a director, I added the scenes of the Monterey Jazz Festival that were not featured in the script. For the score of *The Gauntlet*, I brought in Art Pepper and Jon Faddis. Faddis is a protégé of Dizzy Gillespie; he's the one playing the trumpet solo. As for *Tightrope*, which took place in New Orleans, Lennie Niehaus [composer, orchestrator, saxophonist and Eastwood's long-time collaborator] and I incorporated into the film everything that was being played in the streets, from jazz to reggae.

You were hooked to the point that you started practising it yourself when you were still quite young.
At age fourteen I learned to play the flugelhorn, an instrument that was certainly not popular at the time, but has since become much hipper. Then I started on the cornet at school. After that, I got into playing the piano in bars. I played ragtime and blues at the Omar Club in Oakland, where they would feed me a free meal. In school, I also got into rhythm and blues. Then I began attending concerts in the 'Jazz at the Philharmonic' series, and saw Charlie Parker, Coleman Hawkins, Lester Young and other famous figures, which broadened my taste. The West Coast jazz scene was also starting to become popular. The Dave Brubeck–Gerry Mulligan tandem dominated the 1950s. Both of them had incited me to skip classes, even when they were only local luminaries. There was also Stan Kenton, who directed a huge ensemble; Woody Herman, whose Lemon Drop album I loved and whose contribution is not recognized highly enough; and the not-to-be forgotten bebop, which was thriving with Dizzy Gillespie and Kenny Clarke.

You pushed the international executives of Warner Bros. to help finance the production of Round Midnight. *What did you think of the film?*
I was very jealous of Bertrand [Tavernier] … His film made me envious! You are not too sure where it's going at first, but little by little you fall under the spell. It is much more than a piece of history. Bertrand leads us to the core of jazz; he offers us a film that is in itself a jazz experience. I particularly appreciated and admired that he used real musicians, including for the main part. That was quite risky. But the gamble paid off. It is fascinating to see how Dexter Gordon slowly brings to life his character. There have been quite a few films on jazz, but very few as sensitive as this one. Bix Beiderbecke, for instance, inspired the character played by Kirk Douglas in *Young Man with a Horn*, but they hired

Harry James rather than someone like Red Nichols. They had James dub Kirk Douglas on the trumpet. To studio executives, Harry James was jazz; they couldn't tell the difference between swing and jazz.

You are in the process of sponsoring the European distribution of Bruce Ricker's documentary, The Last of the Blue Devils. The film deserves support and I want to help. The history of jazz in America has been documented only randomly. We have limited archives, a handful of films and no centralized organization to preserve that legacy. Bruce's documentary struck me as a rare achievement; I thought it deserved a wider audience. It's a unique document covering three generations of jazzmen while focusing on one of their most creative periods, the golden age of Kansas City. The main innovators at that time appeared in an ensemble called the Oklahoma City Blue Devils. Their surname of 'Blue Devils' came from the guys who were sent to cut down barbed wire fences during conflicts between ranchers and farmers. Among these Blue Devils were Count Basie, Lester Young, Buster Smith, Eddie Durham and many others. They settled in Kansas City, which was a freewheeling town. It was there, in the early days, that cowboys ended their cattle drives; alcohol, gambling and prostitution started flourishing. It never stopped; the city prospered and provided work for many jazz musicians, particularly during the Great Depression. Kansas City also had its own geniuses, such as Big Joe Turner, Jay McShann, and, of course, the great Charlie Parker, who was only a teenager then.

When did you first discover Bird's music?
I saw him play live in 1946. It was in Oakland, during a concert at the Philharmonic's jazz series. Parker was appearing with Lester Young, who was already my idol. Coleman Hawkins, Flip Phillips, Howard McGhee and Hank Jones backed them up … I still remember it all. Can you picture that? Then I saw Bird again at Bop City in San Francisco. His first records were stunning. Many people didn't understand his music, and those who understood it didn't know how he produced it. He was really the avant-garde. His dexterity was a mystery and so was his confidence. It seemed as if he had fallen from somewhere else. He was different from all the others. You felt that he was elevating jazz to a completely new level of expression. He was a giant, and everybody wanted to imitate him.

Bird's musical pieces were recorded in a studio before the shoot. How did you proceed in order to re-create the dazzling intensity of Parker's performances?
On a film like this, the score is crucial. Someone suggested that I use an alto sax that could imitate Bird, someone like Charles McPherson. But I couldn't do that to a genius like Parker. Only Bird could play Bird! I told Lennie Niehaus, who is supervising the music, that I wanted to use the original tracks. Chan Parker had made, without professional help, remarkable recordings of Bird's solos. Lennie had them cleaned electronically in a laboratory. Thus they were able to lift Bird's solos and re-record them in stereo. Lennie created new orchestrations, and we lured the best musicians we could find

Following pages: 'Jazz taught me to remain true to what I admire.' Eastwood directs Forest Whitaker in *Bird*.

by offering them a unique opportunity – to play with Bird some thirty years after his death! Some, actually, had had the good fortune to perform with him, like double-bassist Ray Brown, who accompanied him in London, or trumpet player Red Rodney, who toured with him and is one of the characters in the film. Ray and Dizzy helped us select the musicians. We were lucky enough to be able to reunite first-rate talents such as pianists Walter Davis and Monty Alexander, alto sax Charles McPherson, double-bassist Ron Carter, vibraphonist Charlie Shoemaker … all living legends!

Joel Oliansky's screenplay has a particularly rich and complex texture. How did you unearth it?
It was languishing at Columbia, where it was intended for Richard Pryor. I discovered it one day when visiting my agency, William Morris. As soon as I started reading it, I wanted to shoot it. I asked Warner Bros. to make a trade with Columbia, where, by chance, Ray Stark desperately coveted a Warner Bros. script called *Revenge*. Stark believed that Warner wanted *Bird* for Prince, who had just had a hit with *Purple Rain*. When he was told it was for me, he exclaimed, 'What? Clint Eastwood will play Charlie Parker? That's never going to fly! That film will never get made!' When I was told that the transaction went through, I literally jumped for joy.

What were your main sources of documentation?
I talked a lot with Chan Parker, who, as you know, lives near Paris. Her book, *My Life in E-flat*, had been a source of inspiration for Oliansky's screenplay. Chan agreed to be our

adviser. In that capacity, she spent quite a lot of time with the actors. Red Rodney, who had lived through that period, helped us a lot too. Buddy Jones, a bassist who performed at the time and now lives in Carmel, told me a bunch of stories. I also had many conversations with Dizzy, with historian Leonard Feather and, of course, with all the musicians that we approached for this project.

You managed to mount the film without having to cast stars. That's quite a feat!
I admire Richard Pryor's talent, but it would have been a mistake to give him the part of *Bird*. I wanted practically unknown faces that would be accepted immediately as those of the characters. I had seen Forest Whitaker in small parts, like the ones in *The Color of Money* and *Platoon*. He'd always get the maximum out of them. We did a test with him and he was terrific. He's an actor of great sensibility. Besides, he had studied music and played the trumpet. As for Diane Venora, I discovered her when viewing her audition on a cassette. She was the first actress I was looking at. I was transfixed: she was Chan Parker! I also wanted each actor to be able to play his instrument. It meant quite a lot of work for them, but they all did fine. Forest learned to play the sax under Lennie's guidance. Michael Zelniker, who played Red, was actually trained by him. Dizzy was not available, but for his trumpet solos we had Jon Faddis, who plays like Dizzy used to forty years ago.

This story seems driven by a constant duality: it's at once a celebration and a tragedy, very much like Parker himself, an

*artist who self-destructed at the same time as he soared. Pain
and euphoria went hand in hand throughout his life.*
I don't want to do a propaganda film against drugs. That is
not the issue. What is important is that you feel what it meant
to be an innovator of genius. Red Rodney told me that when
Bird caught him doing heroin, he got mad and called him all
the names under the sun, 'I forbid you to do that! That will
never make you play better!' What Bird was saying was, 'Do
what I tell you, but please do not ever imitate me!' Why was
Bird hooked on drugs? We'll probably never know the truth.
The film show his excesses, but without judging them. It's up
to the viewer to form his or her opinion. Charlie Parker was
a mystery, and we don't claim to solve it.

*It seems that jazz is also an inspiration for you as a director,
whether you are staging a scene, building a mood or playing
with emotions.*
It is due to the very nature of jazz, which is an art of
spontaneity. Sometimes the rhythm of a scene comes to me
like the rhythm of a piece comes to a jazzman that is
improvising on a given theme. This happens to me on the set
and also in the editing. I like to be free to greet whatever fate
has in store; and free to incorporate what my collaborators
may contribute. A structure is needed, but it shouldn't be
rigid. Your story may have the most intricate construction,
but it should never prevent you from remaining open to the
invention of the moment, whether it's your own or that of
the actors or technicians.

How would you sum up what you learned from jazz?
Jazz taught me to remain true to what I admire, to never just
follow the latest trend or fashion, whether in music or film.

Even when I was doing the Sergio Leone westerns, I was
aware that I was involved with something out of the ordinary.
As soon as I started hitting piano keys, I knew that one
shouldn't be afraid to appear different, even if it meant
remaining alone. Maybe that's the price you pay. Musicians
such as Charlie Parker, Art Pepper or Bix Beiderbecke
destroyed themselves with alcohol and drugs. But it is not
specific to that milieu; there are many Van Goghs, many
suicidal artists, it's not just in jazz. You see that too in country
music, with Jimmie Rodgers, Red Foley or Hank Williams.
That's the story I tried to tell in *Honkytonk Man*, the story
of artists who waste their life and talent. If Parker hadn't died
at age thirty-four, he would still be playing for us. That may
be the final lesson of this jazz film – knowing that you rob
the others when you die.

6

'It was the perfect subject for the final western' *Unforgiven*

Interview conducted on July 22, 1992

With *Unforgiven*, Eastwood offers us an etching drawn with tender loving care, far from Hollywood, in total communion with its subject. He compares this jewel to a rare watch that he might have kept safely in his pocket until the right occasion to rewind it. In fact, he waited about ten years – the time it took him to age into the role!

David Webb Peoples' outstanding screenplay lays bare themes that have preoccupied Eastwood from the beginning: the trauma of injustice, the spiral of vengeance, the tragic cycle of violence and reprisals. It is also an itinerary across the western genre, from the melancholy romanticism of *She Wore a Yellow Ribbon* (see William Munny meditating on the grave of his wife) to the revisionism of *The Left-Handed Gun* (the journalist fabricating the outlaw's legend) and even to the *Götterdämmerung* of *The Wild Bunch* (the growing absurdity of the carnage).

In *Unforgiven*, too, the world seems to come to an end. The sheriff and the outlaw behave the same way, shooting people in the back or when they are unarmed. The sheriff is probably the worse of the two, as he takes advantage of his position to torture his prisoners. Instead of a noble showdown in the dust, we get only gratuitous cruelties and despicable executions. Violence has ceased being an entertaining ritual; it is an object of repulsion. And for the first time in his work, Eastwood dwells essentially on its effects, not just on the victim, but also on the perpetrator. The one who exerts violence will be as profoundly affected as the one who is victimized, because he remains forever marked by the indelible stamp of his actions.

When I interviewed him a year later for the documentary *A Personal Journey with Martin Scorsese Through American Movies*, Eastwood was to remark, 'When you think the western is worn out as a genre, there always comes a film that brings a new point of view. It is fascinating when that takes place.' And he gave us such examples as *The Ox-Bow Incident*, a seminal picture of the 1940s, *High Noon* for the 1950s and the work of Sergio Leone for the 1960s. He might have also mentioned – which Scorsese and I were quick to do – his own *Unforgiven*, which strips the West of its glory, its mythology and all shreds of romanticism, including the post-romantic nihilism of a Sam Peckinpah.

This rendezvous is taking place in New York, before the American release. Eastwood knows he has surpassed himself, but is far from imagining that such an uncompromising film, let alone a western, can be awarded an Oscar. Incredibly, the Academy won't be lacking in discernment this time. *Unforgiven* will receive nine nominations before winning Oscars for best picture, best director, best editor and best supporting actor (Gene Hackman) in March 1993.

The audacity to grow old with his characters: William Munny, the killer of *Unforgiven* (1992), who turned to farming.

How did you discover David Webb Peoples' remarkable script?
A reader at Warner Bros. called it to my attention when it
was under option from Francis Coppola. I liked it so much
that I decided to contact the writer and ask him to write
another project. When I called his agent, I found out that
Coppola's option had expired two days earlier. So I
immediately took an option for a year. That was around
1982–3. Other projects kept me busy, but I finally bought it
outright and just kept this little gem on hold. The years went
by and I simply aged into the role.

*Was the screenplay revised or touched up in any way during
those ten years?*
It wasn't necessary. The subject was timeless; it hadn't aged
and remained just as powerful as when I first discovered
it. I realized that I shouldn't fool with it. Besides, the fable
is even more pertinent today; it's more likely in these times
of recession, of [racial] riots in Los Angeles, and the whole
questioning of the judicial system following the Rodney
King beating [March 3, 1991].

*What was the main draw for you originally? Was it the
relevance of the fable, the complexity of the story, the realism
of the approach, or simply the unusual character of William
Munny?*
All of these… the story, its morality, William Munny of course,
but all the other characters as well. It had more dramatic
conflicts than most western scripts I'd ever read. I always
wanted to do something in that vein. Some of my favorite
westerns, like *The Ox-Bow Incident*, paved the way. I don't
know if it will actually be my last one, but it seemed to be the
perfect subject to do as a kind of final western. It really sums
up what I feel about the genre.

*How do you envision the historical context of the film? Was
this the transitional period between the anarchy of the Frontier
and the advent of the law? The four main characters – William
Munny, Ned Logan [Morgan Freeman], Little Bill Daggett
[Gene Hackman] and English Bob [Richard Harris] – seem to
belong to a vanishing species.*
This is Wyoming in 1880, and probably one of the last enclaves
where law and order are not yet firmly implanted. I have to
make clear, however, that this picture is not based on historical
events or characters; it was all fiction. And what fascinated
me was that the denial of justice triggers the whole story.
Because of his lackadaisical ways, the sheriff fails to apply
law and order. Little Bill may be very strict when it comes to
gun control, but he's totally permissive in lots of other areas.
He fines the cowboys a minimal sentence, which only benefits
the guy who owns the place. The women, who are the victims,
are treated like second-class citizens.

*Lawmen and outlaws behave the same way; one senses that
they share the same past, that they are all former killers.*
And in the end, they all get taken out, even the innocent
bystanders. The young deputies are good guys, but they get
caught up. When they see Little Bill kicking English Bob
around, they see violence for the first time and they go, wow!
The sheriff represents a generation, a mentality that they
don't understand.

*Fate keeps weaving and intertwining these destinies. The innocent
young cowboy is hunted down on the same grounds as his
companion, who is the guilty one. Later, Ned is captured and
tortured to death even as he has renounced the bounty. This is
a world where one becomes automatically guilty by association.*
Yes, and it's one of the elements that I liked about the story.
The reward sets in motion a chain of events that no one will
be able to stop. In the eyes of Munny and the rest of the people,
young Davey is just as guilty as his buddy. It's the same for
Ned, who is presumed guilty because he holds the evidence,
the rifle. Remember, Munny gives it back to Ned when Ned
decides to ride back home.

*There is an undercurrent of black humor, an absurdist logic,
which contradicts the concept of poetic justice inherent in the
classical western.*
To me, the humor is mostly in the opening. Then the story
takes a turn; I think it happens when they kill the young
cowboy Davey, and then it moves towards tragedy. What I
particularly like is that the humor doesn't come from
superhuman traits of the protagonist but, on the contrary,
from his frailties. He hasn't ridden in a while; he has trouble
with his restive horse, and even blames it on his past cruelty
to animals! He is fragile, both physically and mentally.

William Munny is haunted by his past turpitudes. As in Pale
Rider, *there is a strong biblical subtext that evokes the
original sin.*
He is like a man coming out of rehabilitation. When he is
asked about his past, he says he was drunk most of the time.
But he reformed himself, kept going even after his wife died.
But when he wants to get his kids out of the pig farm, this is
a man who is forced to do the only thing he is really good
at… shooting someone. As Ned reminds him, he wouldn't
be doing this if Claudia were still alive.

Does William Munny's abominable past refer to the Man with No Name, the anti-hero of the westerns that you made with Sergio Leone?
No, he is not like the Sergio character. Munny has more soul; he's detached but he is not cynical. Obviously, he is much more disturbed and obsessed because of his past, when he committed so many robberies and raised a lot of hell. He has no self-worth. And he is constantly reminded that he is not worthy.

Leone lovingly cultivated a baroque iconography that was dominated by an invincible bounty hunter devoid of all morality. Your depiction of Munny undermines that image.
Munny is not great with a gun, just OK. This is not one of those westerns where the hero shoots the hats off people or shoots the eye of a bird in flight. It's more like real life, where nothing is right on. These guys are killers only because they have done it before, not because they are a better shot than anyone else.

You show how difficult it must have been to kill someone in cold blood. One had to be in an inebriated state.
That's what Little Bill tells the journalist. It isn't easy to shoot someone. And he gives a good example when he tells him how English Bob could shoot his opponent because the guy had shot his own foot before by mistake! This was the crazy reality. All these killers that became legends were really just guys who shot people in the back, not standing face to face in the middle of the street as they used to in the old westerns!

Was the role of Ned written for a black man?
No, but I thought of Morgan Freeman because I liked his lived-in face and he was the right age. The fact that he is whipped to death harked back for me to the era of slavery. Ned probably escaped from the South, and like many former slaves set adrift, moved west, where he ended up riding with Munny and a bunch of wild guys.

Gene Hackman is particularly adept at carrying out sadistic acts as though they were totally normal and ordinary. What inspired you to cast him?
He is one of our best actors and I needed someone with a lot of strength for this complex role. In his mind, the sheriff is a good guy. He's building a house, hoping that he will be able to retire there and take it easy. He believes he is right in dealing with renegades and setting up an atmosphere of terror. He also has a certain amount of charm and sophistication. That's what makes the character so interesting.

In most action films today, death has no more reality than in a cartoon. Unforgiven, *on the contrary, delivers a very strong moral perspective. Each death is given a precise narrative and emotional context.*
Each time someone is killed it has an effect on somebody. Killing is nothing glamorous. That's what made the project so appealing, especially at this time in my career. There is so much gratuitous killing in the movies today. They almost seem to imitate what I was doing in the 1960s and 70s. At that time it was new, it was fun, but ever since, people have been trying to outdo the last one. Violence has reached such extremes that it is time to take a step back and analyze its morality. I started thinking about my own work: 'You can't be doing the same old thing. You've got to move on.' When I approached Gene Hackman, he immediately warned me that he turns down violent roles systematically, as a matter of principle. So when I gave him the script, I told him, 'Keep

in mind that this is completely different. It will be a statement about violence, what it really is and its repercussions.'

You do not indulge in pastoral myths of bucolic farm life. One can't help thinking about the Great Depression and the sadness of Honkytonk Man.
The Depression? I don't know. But Munny is in desperate straits. He has tried to put together a new life. Fate was unkind and took his wife; he tried to survive the best he could, but everything goes wrong. When the Kid comes along, it is a temptation, the lure of adventure; he thinks he may give it a try for a week or so. His going to see Ned is an attempt to reinforce his resolution.

Does the title Unforgiven *apply solely to your unredeemed character or to the whole community?*
It has a dual meaning. It is about William Munny, but it also refers to the feminist outrage, the relentlessness of the women's efforts to get retribution for the crime against one of their own.

When the young cowboy brings her a pony, you capture on Delilah's face the irony of the situation. One can tell that she would be satisfied with this gesture, but she is caught in the middle because of her companions' refusal to compromise.
Even though she was the victim, she would have wanted to avoid bloodshed. Later, when the bounty hunters arrive at Big Whiskey, the women start questioning what they started and you read a look of foreboding on their faces: 'Where is this going to end up?'

What is the fate of the prostitutes after William Munny's departure? Might the outcasts share a common destiny?
What they have in common is that they all sold their souls

to survive; we don't know what happens to the girls. It is up to the imagination of the audience. I cut out a little scene where William Munny returns to the farm and his kids and you learn that the Schofield Kid has given the reward money to the children. The boy asked his father, 'Did you kill anybody?' and Munny answered, 'No, son. I didn't kill anybody.'

In your westerns you always contrast the beauty of nature and the infamy of human behavior.
Well, mankind isn't always beautiful. We found the ideal location in Alberta, Canada. It was magnificent country. The town was entirely built there, under Henry Bumstead's direction. He had worked with me on *High Plains Drifter*. Munny's farm and Ned's were filmed east of Calgary, where the open plains evoke Kansas and Nebraska. With the exception of the train, which was filmed in Sonora, it was all shot within a hundred-mile radius. And we were even blessed with snow. God, it was beautiful up there after two days of snow!

Your interiors are as dark as in Pale Rider. *They are probably as dark as they were…*
… when all they had burning were gas or oil lamps! To me, lighting is essential. You don't tell a story with actors and words only. You have to set the right atmosphere. In the old westerns, interiors were sometimes lit as much as exteriors. You entered a saloon or a hotel, and they were broadly lit, the way our supermarkets are lit today! Where did all that light come from? Certainly not from gas or oil lamps… That was enough to pull me out of the movie. I would stop believing in it, even when this happened in good pictures. Fortunately, we have now more sophisticated equipment and faster film. It gives us a lot more possibilities. On *Unforgiven*, we were

able to work it out so that the light emanates from natural sources like doorways, windows and the few gas lamps that would have been there. I think Jack Green topped himself when he lit Little Bill's saloon. It's one of the best lighting jobs that I can recall on pictures I worked on.

John Wayne used to say that to retain the audience's attention, the eyes of the actors have to be constantly visible.
It probably worked for him, but I disagree. I always think of the film's overall effect. I don't feel you need to see everything that's going on in every scene. Sometimes, a shadow across a person's face is much more interesting. It's what you don't see that matters then. It's up to you to read into what the character is thinking. Seeing everything would get boring. Often it's better to show as little as possible.

Since High Plains Drifter *you have had a fondness for characters that appear and disappear like mirages. They seem to emanate from the scenery itself.*
That's one of the things that was appealing about the western genre, being able to play with space, with expansive landscapes. The lone figure on a large canvas always has something mysterious, whether it is in a painting or on a screen. It conjures up a lot of things in the imagination.

But your character is not a loner any more.
The mysterious stranger who comes out of nowhere and goes off in the sunset is dead and gone. I can play that mystique; I guess I did. I may play elements of it in one particular scene, but I am not sure I want to play it so much now. If the character is rooted somewhere and engaged in conflicts, whether they are conflicts with other characters or inner conflicts, the drama is made much more interesting.

You composed the music for the film, as you had done for Pale Rider.
I was sitting at the piano in Sun Valley, trying to figure out the beginning of the film. I wrote down some notes for the guitar, something super simple; it became Claudia's theme. Lennie Niehaus orchestrated it. Our guitarist Laurindo Almeida would have probably liked to embellish it, but I insisted on something as simple as possible.

Through the character of Beauchamp and the 'dime novels', you show how the reality of the West was distorted. The presence of the writer actually impacts people's behavior. Little Bill, for instance, tries to conform to the image he would like portrayed for posterity.

Below:
Winchester '73
(Anthony Mann,
top); *The Shootist*
(Don Siegel,
bottom).

Below right: The
communion of
the reprobate.
Delilah (Anna
Thomson) looks
after Munny
in *Unforgiven*.

Beauchamp embellishes reality to make it more interesting. We all put our spin on things. See how the rumour starts and expands, how the details of the crime become more and more gruesome. Many of the stories in which mankind puts faith, starting with the biblical stories, were written by chroniclers who had a very limited or highly personal point of view. The West is no exception. One of the best examples of this distortion is of course Billy the Kid. For my part, I've always been interested in the real story of the West. Over the years, I've read tons of books on the mythology as well as the reality of that period. My roots go back pretty far in the history of the western, all the way back to the 1950s. But we were very far from authenticity in *Rawhide*; the context was real with things like the cattle drives, but the stories were pure fabrication without any sense of realism. This is also true of the films I made with Sergio Leone, where violence became a spectacle that was staged like an opera.

Which were the westerns that were important to you?
I mostly remember those I grew up with: *The Ox-Bow Incident*, *High Noon*, and Anthony Mann's westerns with James Stewart, starting with *Winchester '73*. I don't really remember the messages they had to offer, but I know they were important to me.

In Don Siegel's The Shootist, *the old gunfighter died of cancer. Did that influence you?*
It didn't influence me consciously, but it was an interesting film at the time because John Wayne also had cancer. It was an important film for him.

Did you view John Ford as a master?
Ironically, my favorite films of his are not his westerns. They are his chronicles of the Great Depression era, like *The Grapes*

of Wrath. I did like *My Darling Clementine*. *The Searchers* is still a beautiful film, even if some of the sub-plots and minor characters don't hold up today.

What did Howard Hawks represent to you?
He was the first film director I ever met! It was in the summer of 1947 and I was sixteen or seventeen years old. I was driving around in a beat up '39 Ford, drinking beer, playing the piano and chasing chicks. One day, when I was visiting a friend up in the hills near Sepulveda Boulevard in Los Angeles, we saw three horses running free down the street. We managed to stop them and keep them corralled. Then out of a remote villa came a distinguished gentleman, who thanked us profusely, and I realized, 'That's Howard Hawks, the film director!' We were very impressed. It must have been before he made *Red River*.

Can the western genre still be a vehicle to reflect on today's America?
The western will always be a mirror. Today, our society has become incredibly permissive of violent behavior; our parents would never tolerate what we tolerate. We accept violence, at least as long as it is not happening to us. *Unforgiven* is a commentary about the effect of violence on both the perpetrator and the victim. In most westerns, including mine, the perpetrator never felt any remorse. He killed the bad guys and that was all. Here, my character thinks and has a range of feelings.

Does the western bear some responsibility in our becoming desensitized to violence?
I don't think so. The western hasn't had that much effect. We all grew up with the western; it didn't make society more

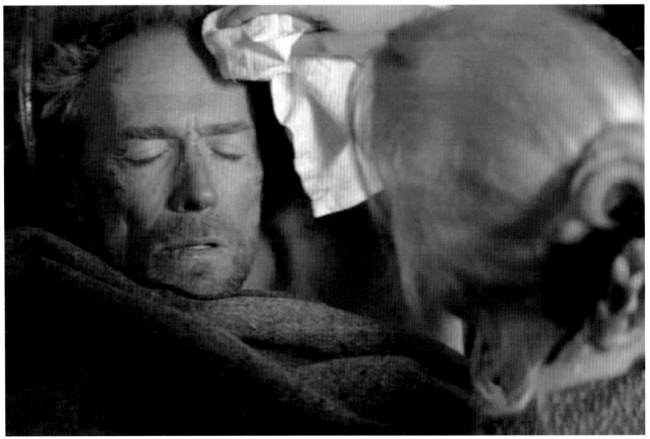

Left: How violence affects the perpetrator: William Munny in *Unforgiven*.

Below: *The Ox-Bow Incident* (William Wellman, top); Wellman and his cast, Henry Fonda and Anthony Quinn (bottom).

violent. The violence of the western has to do with its historical context. If someone were guilty, he'd be strung up; they didn't fool around. This was a society where people had to rely on their own judgement and were prone to taking justice into their own hands. It was a time where everything was more cut and dry, where moral values were clearer, where a lone individual might make a difference. Now, we are mired down in a bureaucratic society where the slightest dispute requires lawyers and legal battles. The simplicity of those times is what fascinates us.

In an era where mainstream movies, from Batman *to* Terminator, *are dominated by special effects, you hold your ground. You remain a maverick more than ever.*
I appreciate the technological developments brought about by these films, but it's not a genre I would want to tackle. I'm not interested in special effects. I want to do stories about people. That's why I made this film, which is a genre picture, but is different and unusual. I'll move on and continue in that direction.

The film is dedicated to 'Sergio and Don'…
I hadn't seen Sergio Leone in ten years. After the presentation of *Bird* at the Cannes Film Festival, I made a quick trip to Italy. He called me out of the blue and we had lunch; it was the first time we ever sat down together. We had such a good time that we decided to go out to dinner that night along with Lina Wertmüller. Sergio was completely relaxed and we had a really great time … lots of laughs and lots of wine. I'd never seen him that serene. A few months later he was

dead. I almost felt like it had been his way of saying goodbye. Shortly afterwards, it was Don Siegel's turn. He had been ill for a long time and I watched him deteriorate. Don was a friend. I loved his rebellious, cantankerous spirit. He was always supportive, and I think he would have liked to make *Unforgiven*. He would have loved that story. Most filmgoers won't even notice or know the difference, but I wanted the dedication. I stuck it in there for myself.

7

'Life is never idyllic'
A Perfect World

Interview conducted on December 10, 1993

Originally destined to Barry Levinson, who moved on to *Toys*, then to Steven Spielberg, who preferred wandering into *Jurassic Park*, John Lee Hancock's first screenplay landed at Malpaso as a 'writing sample'. This is the story of a loser who seemingly deserves a second chance. But Butch's desperate run is doomed from the outset. All the fugitive can do is to offer a wild adventure to his young hostage, while bestowing on him a paternal solicitude that he has never known himself. Raoul Walsh would have liked this outcast born under an unlucky star, who dreams of a new Frontier as mythical as the High Sierras… Alaska.

There was some talk of Eastwood playing the fugitive, but he decided he was too old for the part. It went instead to a star twenty-five years younger, Kevin Costner. Was the torch being passed from one generation to the other? Eastwood had appreciated Costner's ability to convey the inner life of his character, district attorney Jim Garrison, in *JFK*. That performance had reminded him of James Stewart's compositions in Anthony Mann's westerns: it suggested a fury simmering just under the surface and threatening to explode at any moment. This was also poetic justice since Costner had coveted the script of *Unforgiven* for a long time (seeing it as a counterpoint to *Dances with Wolves*) before it was stolen from under him by Eastwood.

If our filmmaker ended up on both sides of the camera, it was due to Costner's insistence. And it was also Costner who convinced the screenwriter to rework not his part of Butch, but that of Texas Ranger Red Garnett. This was a significant narrative turn of the screw as it assigned to Red a heavy responsibility in Butch's adverse destiny: the lawman had pushed the judge to send the young delinquent to a reformatory for a minor offence. The pathogenic environment finished the job.

Our ritual interview takes place in a Beverly Hills restaurant after a screening of *Dirty Harry* at the American Cinematheque, as part of a tribute to Don Siegel. A world separates Harry Callahan from Red Garnett. One couldn't think of a better opportunity to appraise the distance actor-director Eastwood has traversed within the criminal film genre.

In *A Perfect World* the worst violence is perpetrated by the system. Law and order are not what they used to be. Rage has given way to powerlessness. The Texan lawman screws up everything, including his possible redemption. After his fiasco, he is reduced to punching the FBI sharpshooter in the face and to confess with genuine anguish, 'I don't know nothing. I don't know one damn thing!' It is the last line of a film that lingers in our memory like a bittersweet ballad.

'The drifting of a lost soul': Butch (Kevin Costner) and Phil (T. J. Lowther) in *A Perfect World* (1993).

The violence
perpetrated by
the system: the
forces of law and
order in *A Perfect
World*. With Paul
Hewitt as the FBI
sharpshooter.

What was it about the screenplay of A Perfect World *that struck your fancy?*
When I read a script, the first question I ask myself is whether I would enjoy watching that story unfold on a big screen. When Bill Gerber, the vice-president of production at Warner Bros., gave me John Lee Hancock's screenplay, the answer was yes. I immediately wanted to direct it. It was another opportunity to experiment, to explore a vein that I hadn't mined before. In it were also concerns that are quite topical: family values, missing fathers, parental neglect ... And I liked that character of Butch, who tries to give the kid the childhood he never had, to become the father he himself had been deprived of.

Kevin Costner in a film noir, wasn't that a challenge in and of itself?
The fans of *The Bodyguard* may not appreciate this one, because the film goes deliberately the opposite way! When I heard that Kevin had committed to it, I thought, 'If he is prepared to work hard, it will be perfect. Otherwise, it will be a disaster.' Well, he worked very hard, and I'm glad we shared this adventure. He, too, was on unfamiliar ground. He had to create a much more tormented individual, a killer who is also a wounded soul. To his credit, he managed to render the complexity of the character.

There are two 'couples' in the film, the outlaw and the child on one hand, the outlaw and the lawman on the other.

The relationship between Butch and the kid was the most important. That's what I focused on; I preferred to sacrifice my character. There were more scenes involving Red Garnett, but I took them out, notably a press conference and a scene with a waitress that established him as a man without a family. It was too long. It's enough for the past relationship between Red and Butch as a young delinquent to be evoked obliquely as a subtext.

Did you ever consider retracing that early interaction of Red and Butch in a flashback?
No, but there was a flashback in the script. It was a scene where Butch as a child killed the man who brutalized his mother in a New Orleans whorehouse. I actually filmed it, but didn't use it. It seemed off-kilter. It was better to leave things to the audience's imagination.

One of the challenges is that the character of Butch is only revealed little by little, mostly indirectly, through his behavior towards mistreated children.
What makes him react is not violence against adults, but violence against children. Our perception of Butch changes as we go. We experience contradictory feelings towards him: one minute we feel hostility, the next minute sympathy. I hope the audience will follow us across the entire spectrum.

They followed you on Unforgiven, *which was similarly steeped in a disturbing ambivalence.*

In *Unforgiven* I liked the fact that the protagonist bitterly regretted his past acts of violence, and that for quite a while you didn't really know who that man was. It was not all black and white, like in the old days. Good and evil tended to get mixed up. The villains were not devoid of a certain charm and the hero carried a heavy burden of infamy.

In A Perfect World, *Butch's criminality is more the product of his environment than a reflection on his nature. You present him as a wounded character, traumatized by his past.*
Butch was abandoned by his father and exposed to a lot at a very young age. But I personally believe that we are only partially the product of our environment. This notion shouldn't be stretched to the point where it becomes an excuse. More and more you see felons claim as mitigating circumstances the fact that they were beaten or molested by their parents. There is no more horrible crime than physical or sexual abuse inflicted on children. But we live in an era where we are always looking for someone else to blame.

Doesn't A Perfect World *hark back to a more romantic tradition, to the figure of the sympathetic outlaw celebrated by a Raoul Walsh in* The Roaring Twenties, High Sierra *or* Colorado Territory? *In that tradition, the criminal was at once trapped by a certain social context and hounded by a contrary fate.*
There's no avoiding destiny, which I suggested in the scene where they are under the tree. The kid asks him what he's going to do, and Butch can only laugh. He's unable to answer. You see his fate carved on his face. You would want to help him change course, help him cling to life, but it's a lost cause. Cagney, Bogart, Garfield played that part in the old days, this absurd rush towards their own death. Garfield … I saw and liked practically all his films. Whatever the context might be, he was always the outsider. He would have been great in this part.

A Perfect World *is also another of your 'Americanas', a journey across the American hinterland.*
I have always enjoyed exploring Middle America. It is full of stories that haven't been told. When he came to view the film, Sean Connery made an interesting observation: 'It is a thoroughly American subject, but it gives the feeling that it was directed by a European.' I took that as a compliment.

This rural America is far from idyllic. It doesn't inspire any nostalgia.
Life is never idyllic, except in Disney's pictures!

Butch's encounters become ever stranger, more surreal. They recall the tone of Honkytonk Man, *a poignant mixture of the picaresque and the melancholy.*
Naturally the stories are quite different, but there is the same feeling of drifting across the American heartland, the drifting of a lost soul. Here, encounters become confrontations, some of them pretty intense, like the one with the black family, because Butch's underlying anger may explode at any time.

In your films, the hunter and his prey are often connected in a psychic bond. In Tightrope, *for instance, the policeman and the criminal were two facets of the same character. Do Red and Butch have something in common?*
They are both loners who have no family, no private life. Red could have been Butch. In life, there comes a time where you choose one direction, where you reach a point of no return. It's true for both of them. One chose the criminal path, the other the opposite.

Like Sergeant Highway in Heartbreak Ridge, *Red is a professional whose last illusions are shredded by the events. He's another 'dinosaur' whose breed is vanishing.*
Sergeant Highway was a lost soul. He was a real pro, but he saw the futility of his professionalism in a world dominated by technology. Red doesn't like bureaucrats and politicians either. And here he is, saddled with a young female criminologist! He could also do without the arrival of President Kennedy, who is expected in Dallas the week after. His future is probably just as bleak as Highway's. He is so disillusioned that he may have to settle for the quiet pleasures of angling.

Is it the end of an era when everything was simpler?
Yes. The world was about to change. And Butch has no more future in it than Red. When he talks about a 'last frontier', it's a mirage; it's Alaska, as though his father had been waiting over there for him all these years.

Do you feel it is more Kevin Costner's film than yours?
As far as directing is concerned, it's my film, but as far as acting goes, it's more his. Obviously, I have done more offbeat, unusual roles than him. I have often challenged my image in the course of my career. He may have done it too, but he has played it very safe over the last few years, whether in *Robin Hood* or in *The Bodyguard* … very successful films, but very safe from a performer's standpoint. *A Perfect World* was much riskier, and it's good that he dared to do it.

Did he resist the idea of interpreting a criminal who takes a child as a hostage?
I don't think so, but we talked about it at the beginning. I told him this would be his *High Sierra*. In their time, Cagney in *White Heat*, Bogart in *High Sierra* or even *Sierra Madre* weren't afraid to step out there and do something different. One easily gets caught in success and falls into a routine. Kevin was given the opportunity to break away from that, to stretch as an actor, and he seized it.

Both A Perfect World *and* Unforgiven *are essays on violence. They attempt to examine its roots. But here violence is perpetrated by the system more than by the protagonist. The police mobilization, for instance, is totally disproportional.*
I had already dealt with that in *The Gauntlet*: the excitement, the panic that leads to mass deployment and tragic excesses. The final shoot-out was inspired by the raid against the Symbionese Liberation Army, which destroyed an entire neighborhood in Los Angeles. Even recently, in Idaho, the FBI has been grilled about a raid against a white supremacist group, during which a sharpshooter shot from a distance a woman carrying a child in her arms. In such situations, there is always someone who fancies he is another Sergeant York.

In Dirty Harry *too, the story revolved around the kidnapping of a child. In the meantime, America has changed tremendously, and so has your perspective on the criminal film.*
Dirty Harry brought simple solutions to horribly complicated problems. If the character had such an impact at the time, it's because it struck a chord. What hasn't aged is the frustration

Below: John Garfield in *They Made Me a Criminal* (top); Humphrey Bogart in *High Sierra* (bottom).

of the professional who has a mission to accomplish in a given time but is thwarted by the government, the politicians, the civil servants, etc. Bureaucracy, on the federal as well as state or city level, has only gotten worse.

Did you ever imagine that the film's message would be so controversial?

It was a good story. Paul Newman turned it down for 'political' reasons. That intrigued me. I read the screenplay and didn't find anything political about it! I was never a politically oriented person, especially in those days. So I told Warner Bros. that I'd do the film, but I had to direct *Play Misty for Me* first. 'We can't wait,' they said. So they approached several screenwriters and directors, and such stars as Steve McQueen, Robert Mitchum and Frank Sinatra. The role was written for an older guy, a guy like me today! But when I finished *Play Misty for Me*, they hadn't made much progress and asked me again. I told them, 'I'll do it only if Don Siegel directs it.' Don and I went back to the original script by Harry Julian Fink, which was very exciting. Only the ending needed to be changed. It was a good story where there was more concern for the victims than for the criminals. Things have changed since; many organizations defend victims of violent crimes, which was not the case at the time. That a cop would expend such efforts to save a young girl who has been kidnapped and buried alive impressed the public. 'If something like that happened to me,' the audience wondered, 'would the cops be going for the doughnuts or would they go to extremes to save me like Dirty Harry does?' Some were shocked by the film, but I didn't care about the furor. The beauty in making movies, to me, is to try and make something different.

What is your next project?

I'm working on my golf swing. I have in the works an adaptation of *Golf in the Kingdom*, a book written some twenty years ago by Michael Murphy that has become a sort of cult book. It is about the game of golf, but as a mental and mystical discipline. It's the inner game that is important, in the sport as well as in life. I am hoping to be shooting in Scotland next summer. [That project never came to fruition.]

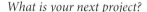

8

'Rules are made to be broken'
'Directed by'... Wild Bill, Sergio, Don and the others
White Hunter, Black Heart

Interview conducted on March 3, 1994

For its 400th issue (June 1994), 'Le cinéma vu par les cinéastes' ('The cinema as seen by cineastes'), the French monthly journal *Positif* asked some of the world's key filmmakers to write an essay on a seminal film, performer or director. One would have expected Eastwood to choose *The Ox-Bow Incident*, the Wellman drama that has become the password of our encounters, or his favorite Kubrick, *Paths of Glory*, 'a great film against war, which had something to say and remains true today' (see tribute to Stanley Kubrick in *Positif*, no. 464, October 1999), or maybe *White Heat*, Walsh's pulsating masterpiece, which he was to later pick as a milestone during an inquiry conducted by the Locarno International Film Festival (see Bill Krohn, ed., *Feux croisés: Le cinéma américain vu par ses auteurs*, Actes Sud, Paris, 1997).

Finally, Eastwood preferred to invite me to an informal, freewheeling conversation. For our topic he suggested the film directors he had worked with or wished he had worked with before stepping behind the camera. It would allow him to tell us how he served his apprenticeship in the Hollywood of the late 1950s and managed to carve a place for himself within a production system that was undergoing a complete transformation.

Eastwood actually devoted a film to that period, *White Hunter, Black Heart*, which remains to this date underrated. It was the chronicle, partially fictionalized, of the making of *The African Queen* in East Africa. Its protagonist, John Wilson, was loosely inspired by John Huston. The author, Peter Viertel, presented the director of *Moby Dick* as a sensation-hunter in search of novel and even sacrilegious experiences, such as the slaughter of elephants.

The rebellious adventurer, who comes truly alive only when he is roughing it far from Hollywood, was destined to captivate Eastwood, all the more so because the character is not without blemishes. (Huston, with his genius for self-deprecation, suggested that Viertel dramatize the story – and therefore paint a darker picture by having Kivu, the guide, trampled to death.) It was, after *Honkytonk Man* and *Bird*, another portrait of an obsessive artist. Yet it would be wrong to view it as a self-portrait. Our subject has always loathed hunting and is well known for his respect of animal life, even down to wasps and slugs.

Furthermore, as a filmmaker, Eastwood has never exhibited the sardonic offhandedness of Huston, nor abdicated his professional responsibilities to devote himself to an extravagant passion. His mentor, as we know, was the frugal Don Siegel, whose methods he adopted: meticulous preparation, swift execution, economy and simplicity in all things. Like Siegel, Eastwood knows exactly what he is going for when he arrives on the set. No elephant, whether alive or mythical, would ever divert him from his task.

'We were on the same wavelength.' Sergio Leone confers with Eastwood on *Il buono, il brutto, il cattivo* (*The Good, the Bad and the Ugly*), 1966.

According to Sergio Leone, who had noticed Eastwood in the *Rawhide* series, the Man with No Name evolved under the influence of Clint, 'who is like that in real life: slow, calm, moving like a cat …'.

In three films, Leone and Eastwood fashioned the character of the laconic, impassive pistolero with a heart of steel:
A Fistful of Dollars (1964), with Marianne Koch (3, 7).
For a Few Dollars More (1965), with Lee Van Cleef (1, 2, 4).
The Good, the Bad and the Ugly (1966), with Eli Wallach (5, 6).

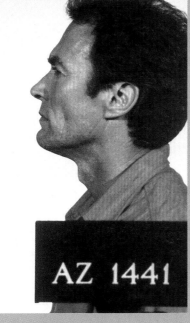

Previous pages: 'He was an original, which led me to think that we were meant to get along.' Don Siegel and Clint Eastwood on the set of *Dirty Harry* (1971).

The Siegel–Eastwood tandem in action: 'Don believed there were no rules; that rules were made to be broken. I feel the same way.'

Opposite page:
Top left: With Shirley MacLaine in *Two Mules for Sister Sara* (1970).
Top right: On location for *The Beguiled* (1971).
Bottom: With Geraldine Page in *The Beguiled*.

This page:
Above left: *Escape from Alcatraz* (1979).
Above right: Working with Don Siegel on *Dirty Harry* (1971).
Left: With Don Stroud in *Coogan's Bluff* (1968).

'Internally, I approach every new character in a distinct way. That is true with the *Dirty Harry* series too. When I was preparing for one of the sequels, I forbade myself to watch the first one again. Even Dirty Harry has changed in fourteen years. He's changed as I have changed. I wouldn't want to reach the point where I am imitating myself.'

Left, from top to bottom: *Magnum Force* (1973) by Ted Post, with Felton Perry; *The Enforcer* (1976) by James Fargo, with Tyne Daly; *The Dead Pool* (1988) by Buddy Van Horn, with Evan C. Kim.

Opposite page: Harry Callahan is so obsessed by monsters that he becomes one himself in *Dirty Harry* (1971), directed by Don Siegel.

Previous pages: When the mercenary questions himself, he takes the side of the victims in *Joe Kidd* (1972), directed by John Sturges.

This page and opposite: One film for them, one film for himself: Eastwood has alternated studio commissions with labors of love for years.
For them: *Where Eagles Dare* (1968), with Richard Burton (1), and *Kelly's Heroes* (1970), with Don Rickles (2), both directed by Brian G. Hutton.
For himself: *Hang'em High* (1968) by Ted Post, with Pat Hingle (3), and *Thunderbolt and Lightfoot* (1974) by Michael Cimino (4), two Malpaso productions.

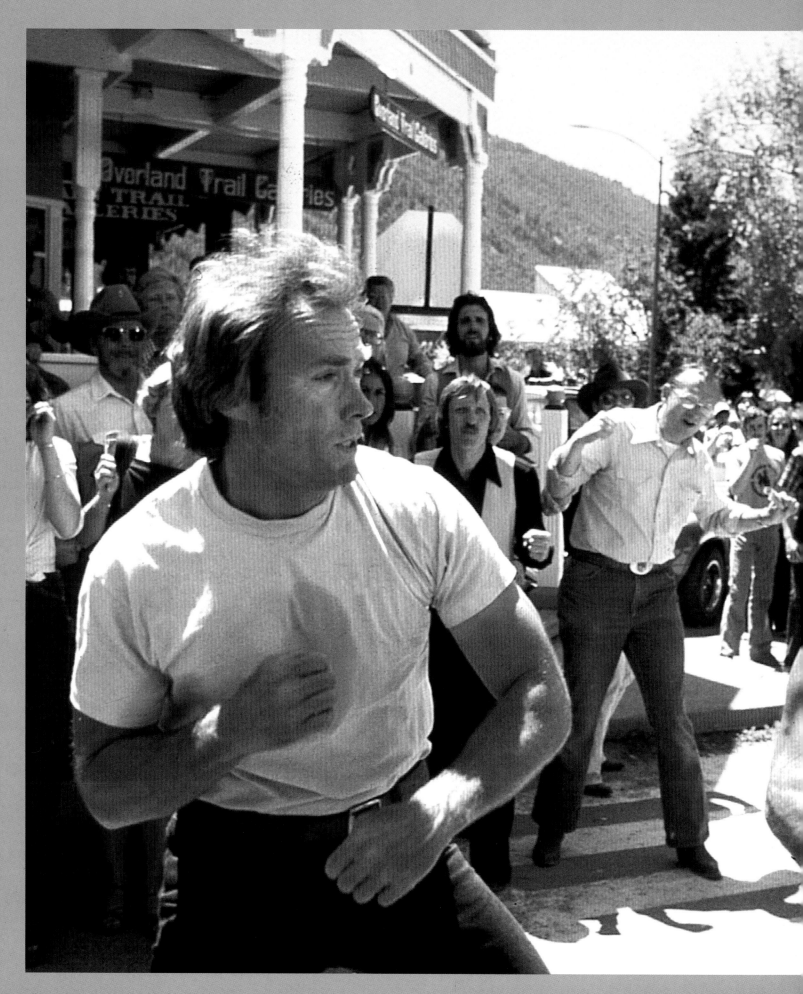

The screwball saga of trucker Philo Beddoe and his orangutan Clyde: 'All my advisors tried to dissuade me, "Don't do that picture, it isn't you", and I answered, "Well, what is me? Am I supposed to just run around and wield a gun for the rest of my life? Am I condemned to redo something that has already worked for me?"'

Left, top and center: *Any Which Way You Can* (1980) by Buddy Van Horn.

Above: *Every Which Way But Loose* (1978) by James Fargo.

I would like to go back to your experiences with some of the top directors you worked with.

What about starting with those I didn't get a chance to work with? Howard Hawks, for instance … I've already told you the very brief circumstance where I helped him round up his horses when I was sixteen or seventeen [see chapter 6 on *Unforgiven*]. Now, John Ford I never met, but he, too, is certainly one of those I would have liked to be directed by. I saw his pictures a lot when I was growing up. Frank Capra I knew when I was filming *High Plains Drifter* at Mono Lake, in the Sierras. I had rented a house nearby at Silver Lake, four houses down from Capra's, and I got to chat with him. Afterwards, each time I drove to the area, I'd go and visit him. He was always glad to see me, but I didn't get a chance to work with him.

Had Capra ever seen Bronco Billy?

I don't know but I would wish he had. When I read the script, I immediately thought, 'Capra could have made that one.' There was an underlying energy in Capra that was unique but not easy to pin down. Anybody can shoot a given scene, but with Capra, as with the greatest, there is something that is not written, not visualized, which nonetheless permeates the whole film. They all had that gift to some degree on such or such film. It depended on the material, their enthusiasm, and whatever problems they had to overcome.

Above and below, top to bottom: Frank Capra, Douglas Sirk, Alfred Hitchcock.

Right, top to bottom: *Sullivan's Travels* (Preston Sturges), *Sitting Pretty* (Walter Lang), *The Tarnished Angels* (Douglas Sirk).

In your youth were you aware of the importance of these great filmmakers?

At that time I couldn't care less about the name of the director. Like everybody else, I'd go and see the hit films, *The Grapes of Wrath*, *Gone with the Wind*, *It Happened One Night*, etc., but also genre films like *Sitting Pretty* or *Winchester '73*. If I go back to my childhood, I remember Preston Sturges' comedies. I liked *Sullivan's Travels*, and Joel McCrea in particular. He may not have had the aura of Gary Cooper, but he gave you the feeling that more was happening inside him than he expressed. Few foreign films were being imported at the time, but I do recall the Australian picture *Forty Thousand Horsemen*. It had a lot of action. It was the first movie I ever saw where actors cursed. You could hear 'damn' or 'hell'. It wasn't done here, the Hays Office saw to it! I can't remember who was the director [Charles Chauvel, 1941].

To escape the studios' demands, some Hollywood filmmakers, chief among them John Ford, created a kind of repertory company that they would employ film after film. Isn't that what you attempted at Malpaso?

At the time, they certainly had marvellous supporting actors. In the films of Sturges, as in Capra or Hawks, you'd always recognize a bunch of colorful characters. They all had interesting faces. It's a great comfort for a director to know he can rely on the same actors film after film. I tried to do something similar on *Every Which Way But Loose* and *Bronco Billy*, by surrounding myself with guys like Geoffrey Lewis, Bill McKinney and others. A director like John Ford preferred to be on familiar ground, amid known faces. When you are an admiral, you stick to your role; you don't challenge yourself constantly! He wasn't the type to analyze how he worked with his actors; he knew their range and what they could give him. Could I have been part of his clan? Maybe not, I'm not a man of clans, I'm not a joiner.

Did you cross paths with Alfred Hitchcock at Universal?
I did, but only at the end. When I was under contract at Universal, he was making his films elsewhere. I met him only once, years later, and a short time before his death. I got a call from his office: 'Mr Hitchcock would like to see you. His health is fragile. He may never do the film, but he wants to discuss the lead role with you.' We had lunch together at the Universal commissary. It took us a good ten minutes to make our way from the entrance to our table. He walked very slowly, very methodically. He ordered his ritual lunch: a steak and tomatoes. He was all there mentally. His conversation was brilliant and I was under the spell. His project took place in Finland or Norway, aboard a train. He knew my films a little, notably *Play Misty for Me*. I don't know if he had seen it or if he wanted to please me. I hadn't conceived it as a tribute, but it was a tribute, obliquely. We had a good time talking, but how could I ever be his man? I came a generation too late! It was the same with Ford and Capra, who were about to retire when I was getting started.

However, a new generation of directors – names like Anthony Mann, Nicholas Ray and Samuel Fuller – burst onto the scene by renewing classic genres: the western, the film noir, the war film…
I would have really liked to meet Mann and work with him during his heyday. I liked his films a lot, particularly his westerns with Jimmy Stewart. Nick Ray did some good stuff too, but I never got to meet him or Sam Fuller. Sam was preparing a western at RKO – I think it was *Run of the Arrow*. I wanted to be in it and I tried to get an appointment, but nothing doing. I met him only much later, in France. The same thing happened with André De Toth, a guy whose personality I liked immediately. At the end of the 1950s all these directors were looking for a second wind, so they'd go and shoot in Europe. The one who was riding high was Elia Kazan. Ever since *On the Waterfront*, he was the prodigy, the genius with whom everyone wanted to work. The problem was that he'd do his casting in New York or elsewhere. I never managed to make a film with him. The same holds true for Stanley Kubrick. I saw *The Killing* when it came out. I would have liked to work with him, but the opportunity never presented itself.

There is a photo taken at the Universal Studios' acting school where you can be seen standing behind Marlon Brando.
He came to meet with us and discuss his philosophy. He sang the praises of Stella Adler, but not of the Actors Studio. Rod Steiger, Dan O'Herlihy and many others also came to chat with us. It was part of our training. We would philosophize endlessly on our trade, as young actors so often do. With the old-timers, it was always simpler: 'You get up and you do your thing.' They didn't question everything. The studio system was on its way out. Not many people were left in our department; it was mostly starlets sent on publicity events – for instance, when a big store was being launched. Because television was growing, we didn't need acting classes as much. The real training was taking place in television.

You loved Sunset Boulevard. *Did you ever meet Billy Wilder?*
I managed to approach him when he was preparing *The Spirit of St. Louis*. As was the ritual in Hollywood at the

time, the press had reported in a series of communiqués that Wilder was looking for a young unknown to play Lindbergh. Every young actor, particularly the tall and lanky ones, coveted the part. I met him once … to shake hands, not even for an audition. His pictures made a big impression on me in my youth: *Double Indemnity*, *Sunset Boulevard* and so many others. I don't understand why he had to stop working so early or what were the circumstances, but it is incredible that a man of his talent wasn't more active during the past two decades.

A giant like Raoul Walsh was still working at Warner Bros. at the end of the 1950s. The film was called Band of Angels. *Were you able to approach him?*
I was one of his great admirers; I had loved *White Heat* in particular. I desperately wanted to be in *The Naked and the Dead*. My agent was unable to get a meeting with him. I came within about 20 feet of his office, but couldn't get through the front door, so I never auditioned for him. Small agencies didn't have power. Walsh was known as a terrific guy, plus he had been an actor. It's always pleasant to work with directors who have been actors first. They are always more receptive. When I gave Don Siegel a part in my first film as a director, *Play Misty for Me*, I told him that he would learn to be more tolerant with his actors, while I would learn to put myself in the director's shoes. Often, the performer is concerned only with his performance or with what his character does. He's not aware that the director can give him only five per cent of his energy, the other ninety-five per cent having to be spread out among the crew, the other actors and all the rest.

Right: The
adventurer
roughing it far
from Hollywood:
*White Hunter,
Black Heart*
(1990).

Below: *The
African Queen*
(John Huston,
top); John Huston
(bottom).

What were some of the opportunities available to a young actor under contract like yourself at Universal?

In my time, Universal was producing mostly B movies. They didn't have personalities such as John Ford, William Wellman or Raoul Walsh. They did have a stable of young actors under contract: Rock Hudson, Tony Curtis, Jeff Chandler, Rory Calhoun … But they couldn't afford major stars like Gary Cooper or Clark Gable. I played a small part in *Away All Boats*, for which Gable was approached. I was in the studio commissary on the day he made a regal entrance. It was an event. At Universal you were not used to meeting a star of that calibre. But in the end the part went to an in-house actor named Jeff Chandler, if I'm not mistaken. It was a good period, but Douglas Sirk was the only important director. Universal would entrust him with the prestige films, grand soap operas like *Imitation of Life* or *Written on the Wind*. I tried to get an appointment with him, but to no avail. I would go all the time on his sets to watch how he operated. When you were under contract you hoped that you could get in every door, at least when it came to in-house directors. You even believed you had an advantage over outside actors. But that wasn't true. You were considered as unimportant. Sometimes, directors wouldn't trust you precisely because you were under contract. Familiarity begets contempt; they could see you any time, whereas actors from elsewhere had the freshness of novelty. Given all of this, it wasn't easy to work with the great filmmakers.

But you did work with William Wellman at the end of his career. He directed you at Warner Bros. in his very last picture, Lafayette Escadrille.

He used to like me. He even approached me for the second male lead. Paul Newman was going to be the star, but after

The Silver Chalice bombed at the box office, he changed his mind and was replaced by Tab Hunter. To ensure a better contrast with Tab's complexion, they cast David Janssen and gave me a bone of a three-week part. I was a little disappointed, but I couldn't afford to turn down three weeks of work. It was not a great film, the script was not up to par, but it was a period of his life when Wellman was trying something different. What this eternal rebel wanted to do was probably what he was prevented from doing earlier. I remember that on the set we talked about *The Ox-Bow Incident*. It was one of my favorite films. He was surprised that I knew it because it had been a commercial disaster. 'It was Mrs Zanuck's fault', he would say. Everyone in the studio was very proud of the film, but the evening Darryl screened it at home, his wife hated it: 'But it's awful! How can you let them lynch Dana Andrews and Anthony Quinn?' The rumour spread that the film was a lost cause and it got only limited distribution. Only after the film was received enthusiastically by the French critics did Fox try to re-release it in New York. But it didn't spark any fire. Nevertheless, it's the model of a great film made for very little, in the corner of a sound stage. You can hear the sound reverberate against the walls, but the story has so much impact, it is so honest, so straight to the point, that you don't care. The film was shot very quickly, in less than thirty days, like a commando operation. That's how Wellman worked best.

Wellman liked to strip his stories of their more picturesque or spectacular aspects to focus on a bare reality that was often sad or painful. Did his minimalism influence you?

I don't know if it influenced me. Everybody influenced me! What I can tell you is that I really liked him. He had among his credits excellent war films like *Battleground* and *The Story* of *G.I. Joe*. He was a colorful character with a lot of history. He had had extraordinary experiences when he joined the Lafayette Flying Corps. On *Lafayette Escadrille* he took us up to Santa Maria, in Northern California, where he let us play with old French aircraft. They were antiques dating back to World War I. We had a lot of fun. During the three weeks we spent shooting on the airfield, I watched everything he was doing. To save time, he experimented with a method he had never used before: he would cover a scene with two cameras running simultaneously, one for that side, the other for the reverse angle. It made things a lot easier in the editing. His theory was that he wouldn't have continuity problems any more. He was right on that point, but I find that it entails too many compromises on the lighting and the camera angles. I've attempted it myself only on rare occasions, and solely for action scenes. I'd rather use several lenses than several cameras. After *Lafayette Escadrille*, Wellman retired, but I kept in touch with him and his family. He encouraged me enormously at the time of *Breezy*. He liked the film very much; he sent me a very nice note about it. As he was married to a much younger wife, I think he identified with William Holden's character. He had a great influence on me in the sense that he encouraged me to go ahead as a director.

In the meantime, the decisive breakthrough came to you not from Hollywood, but from Cinecittà.
You couldn't work every day with the Hollywood greats. That's why I worked with other unknowns or semi-unknowns like myself. Sergio Leone, for instance, had only one or two 'sandal and toga' epic films to his credit. *The Colossus of Rhodes*, I have to confess, didn't impress me very much, but I heard from many sources that Sergio had a strong sense of humor. This had struck me already when I read the script for *A Fistful of Dollars*. I started thinking that the project could be an opportunity to try a few new ideas. Worst-case scenario, if it didn't work, I could always say that I had a fun vacation in Spain.

You inherited the role of the Man with No Name in A Fistful of Dollars *because Leone couldn't get Henry Fonda or James Coburn.*
Sergio didn't have a choice. He was making the film on a shoestring budget. He chose me after watching an episode of *Rawhide*. When I was approached, an American who claimed to represent the producer even asked me, 'Can you provide your own wardrobe?' I was a bit disconcerted, but I went to equip myself in a shop on Santa Monica Boulevard. I bought some pants that looked period to me; I aged them by washing and rewashing them many times. I got my hands on boots and a belt that I had worn on *Rawhide*, packed it all in a tote bag, and there I went, off to Spain!

Sergio Leone was quite a connoisseur of the classic western. He insisted that he was striving for authenticity in every detail. Was his vision of the West very different from yours?
Sergio was a character. I didn't speak Italian; he didn't speak English. Our interpreter, Elena Dressler, was Polish; she could speak six or seven languages. She had been detained in a German camp that was liberated by the Americans. One of the assistants spoke a bit of English and gave me basic directions. After a while, Sergio and I got to understand each other quite well. The only time the interpreter was really asked to make a big contribution was when I wanted

to cut down the dialogue, which felt overabundant to me. At that point we did a lot of philosophizing on what we were doing, and finally came to an agreement. I played my character as I saw him, very internalized, with a minimum of gestures. I was hamming it up in reverse; hamming it up by betraying no emotion whatsoever! If I had tried to be as baroque as the rest of them, it would have been ridiculous. Sergio understood what I was doing, but when they screened the dailies, the producers thought I wasn't doing anything, and it was a catastrophe. Once the film was edited, they changed their minds.

Did Leone's visual choreography surprise you? Weren't his methods a total departure from what was done in Hollywood?
After *Rawhide*, where the stories were so conventional, it was fun to shoot with Sergio. I recall that when we started *For a Few Dollars More*, Lee Van Cleef thought Sergio was completely nuts. Sergio's ideas and methods may not have been quite orthodox, but they allowed me to discover another perspective. He was, as you said, a great admirer of the western masters; he was weaned on Hawks and Ford. But he had his own vision of what a western was, and some of his ideas were simply fantastic. Sometimes I had to intervene to straighten things up. But it was a good collaboration. We were on the same wavelength. Later, Sergio liked to claim there had been conflicts during our shoots, but that wasn't the case. I think he became a little jealous because I was more prolific than he was. It wasn't his fault, or mine. After the premiere of *Bird* at Cannes, I went to visit him in Italy and we had a good evening together [see chapter 6 on *Unforgiven*]. I think he had resented the fact that I declined the part played by Charles Bronson in *Once Upon a Time in the West*, and then later that of the Irish gangster in *Once Upon a Time in America*. Making *Once Upon a Time in the West* would have been fun if I hadn't done the three other westerns previously. It was time for me to engage in something new.

You then found a mentor and a compadre in Don Siegel. How was that special bond forged?
When *Coogan's Bluff* was being put together, Don Siegel heard that I had asked to screen some of his pictures. The only one that was more or less familiar to me was *Invasion of the Body Snatchers*. They let me screen *Madigan* and *Stranger on the*

Below: The sense of insecurity that haunts so many artists: *White Hunter, Black Heart*, with Jeff Fahey.

Right: 'You make the film in which you believe!' On the set of *White Hunter, Black Heart*.

Below: 'I'm still as eager as ever!' Shooting the film within the film in *White Hunter, Black Heart*.

Run, his two previous productions for Universal. So Don decided to do the same and asked to screen the pictures I had done with Sergio. He liked them, and that's how our partnership was formed. He was a character, an original, which led me to think that we were meant to get along.

Don Siegel had the reputation of being a grouch and a curmudgeon. But you made six films together.
We had only one brush at the beginning, because Don insisted on being on the location when he was writing. If he was preparing a story that took place in New York, he felt he had to live there. With me, it's the opposite. I'd rather focus on the story and then make the necessary adjustments. He liked

to go to the actual spots and plan everything accordingly. That's what happened on *Coogan's Bluff*, but then Don became so concerned with the geography that he sacrificed the story to it. When he came back, the script had to be rewritten, which we did together. In truth, Don always needed an antagonist, whether it was the studio or the producer. It harked back to his battles with Jack Warner. Most often, the enemy was the producer. When we were about to start shooting *Dirty Harry*, I told him, 'Now that you are your own producer, you won't have a whipping boy.' He laughed at the time, but it wasn't long before he took a dislike to the production manager! Don didn't like the people in charge of production. He had probably known them as assistants or secretaries, and he treated them as such.

Can we revisit the genesis of that remarkable film, The Beguiled?
The Beguiled? That was a lucky break for Don and I. Universal, which owned the rights to the novel, had a screenplay that I liked, so I gave it to Don. He saw in it an opportunity to escape from genre films and to attempt something a little different. It was about the Civil War, it wasn't a western. He liked that. We enjoyed making it tremendously, though it was not a commercial hit.

Were working conditions different at Universal and at Warner Bros.? How did they treat filmmakers?
Don hated the old studio system. You know, I'm the one who enabled him to get away from it. I'd climbed the ladder as a new system was shaping up, and my clout was not linked to any studio in particular. At Warner Bros. it was the era of John Calley and Frank Wells. They didn't claim to teach you how to make a film; they left you alone. But

Don had been used to constant interferences on the part of production executives. At the time, I was under contract at Universal, and I'd sneak in the back of the screening room where studio execs viewed the dailies, in order to listen to their comments. Generally, there were about twenty of them, and the poor director, sitting in the middle, was forced to listen to their bullshit. We had a bit of that on *Coogan's Bluff*, but afterwards we were able to elude it. At Warner Bros. it was completely different. When I brought in Don for *Dirty Harry*, they just said, 'It's your game.' Suddenly, Don found himself with more time than he ever had in his whole life. Seven or eight weeks, that was an eternity to him! Don was anything but extravagant. He grumbled all the time, but he was so efficient. He knew what he wanted and how to implement a decision. He was in control of his budget as well as of his schedule.

What are some of the lessons you learned from Siegel?
His frugality probably rubbed off on me. On *Escape from Alcatraz* I was the one who convinced him to shoot in the pipes through which the actual escape took place. Why spend $100,000 to build a set? Don knew exactly which shots he was going to get. But he was not rigid. He would change or add a shot at the last moment. I've worked with directors who become completely disoriented if you suggest a change in their set-up. During the shooting of *In the Line of Fire* I got hit on my forehead and arrived on the set with a bump. So that it wouldn't be visible, I asked Wolfgang Petersen if I could enter the shot from the right instead of from the left. Wolfgang had a hard time re-organizing the scene because he had visualized it using a certain angle. He became perplexed when he had one detail to change. That wouldn't have been the case

with Don. Sergio would have taken the time to reflect on it, and then probably said OK, but with Don, there wouldn't even have been a pause. He believed there were no rules, that rules were made to be broken. I feel the same way.

John Huston, too, loved breaking the rules. You portrayed him in White Hunter, Black Heart, *where he was seen pursuing an elephant hunt even if it meant jettisoning his own film. Did you get a chance to talk to him?*
I never met him, but I talked to his daughter Anjelica. He died when the project was still percolating. Not having known him personally gave me more latitude to create the character. We took certain liberties with Peter Viertel's book, particularly in keeping Katharine Hepburn and Humphrey Bogart out of the foreground. The book itself, as you know, is partly fiction. But I believe that the character of John Wilson is faithful to John Huston, at least to the John Huston of that era. Viertel, who took notes every day on the shoot [of *The African Queen*], drew a very precise portrait. He clearly showed how Huston had other interests besides film; how he sometimes looked for any kind of reason not to do the picture; how he was first and foremost searching for new sensations and experiences.

There is also in the Wilson character a streak of self-destruction.
Absolutely. He's a guy who cannot focus on just one thing. He has to be doing ten things at the same time, betting on a horse race, romancing a girl, embarking on something completely off the line of his current project. Huston was like that. This comes through in everything I've read or seen about him. On *The Misfits*, Huston would spend his nights gambling and ruining himself in the casinos of Reno. Some have said

Above: *White Hunter, Black Heart*: 'It's not a crime to kill an elephant, it's a sin.'

Opposite page: John Wilson in search of a sacrilegious experience, with his guide Kivu in *White Hunter, Black Heart*.

an audition at the Grand Ole Opry, but blew his chance because he had dissipated himself along the way. He had tuberculosis and did nothing to take care of it. He was constantly pulling himself down. You'd find that streak in the story of Charlie Parker. Why did such a genius self-destruct? Nobody could ever come up with an answer. There have been thousands of jazzmen like that, from Bix Beiderbecke to Chet Baker.

As a filmmaker, would you say that Huston's attitude – 'After me, the heavens can fall!' – is the opposite of yours?
He was determined to kill an elephant while he was in Africa. Everything else paled in comparison. It's that obsession that was the most interesting to me. Huston was someone who wasn't afraid of anything or anyone. That fearlessness is fascinating. Who hasn't dreamt of doing whatever strikes his fancy without worrying about consequences? We'd all love to enjoy boundless freedom. However, such offhandedness would go against my nature. I couldn't let down people who put their trust in me, financiers in particular. I always feel a responsibility towards them. This having been said, I agree with the character [of John Wilson] when he confronts his producer because the latter claims to know what the public wants. You can't make a film to fit the presumed tastes of the audience. You make the film in which you believe.

that Viertel was unfair to Huston, but that's not true. He portrayed Huston as he knew him, which was as a nice guy who was vulnerable because of his obsessions. When you are directing a film, you can't party all night and be sharp the next morning. Why did he behave like this? I don't know. Was it a feeling of insecurity? The fear of devoting himself totally to a project that might not be a success?

The sense of insecurity that haunts so many artists was already at the core of Honkytonk Man.
I have known quite a few guys in my life that you could call losers, or rather guys who didn't want to win. They had a certain talent, but couldn't help wasting it or sabotaging it. As soon as success was within reach, they managed to stumble. They were afraid to be winners; afraid of the discipline it takes to win. If you stay up all night, you have a built-in excuse for not being on top of your game the next day. I have observed that with several country singers, such as Hank Williams and Red Foley. The singer of *Honkytonk Man* was self-sabotaging. He strove to accomplish his dream,

Do you remember your first day as a director on the set of Play Misty for Me?
That was an eternity ago! I was certainly more tense than today. It was very exciting, but there was some apprehension, so I tried to remember my feelings when I read the screenplay for the first time. By referring back to my initial impressions, and relying on them instead of trying to change things, I avoided over-analyzing the material. I had to trust my instincts all the way, even in the choice of set-ups and camera angles. That impressionistic approach worked because it liberated me. I realized I could have faith in my impressions, in my gut reactions, in my inner voice, whatever name you want to give to that instinct. It encouraged me and, as you can see, after all these years, I'm still doing films, as eager as ever.

9

'Truth, like art, is in the eyes of the beholder'
Midnight in the Garden of Good and Evil and *The Bridges of Madison County*

Interview conducted on January 21, 1998

Based on a non-fiction bestseller, *Midnight in the Garden of Good and Evil* doesn't belong to any established genre. One might have earmarked it for a Robert Altman ensemble piece. Originally, John Berendt was going to adapt his own book, but he couldn't find a way to prune his abundant material: 'If I had written the screenplay, the film would have lasted twenty-five hours.' Eastwood therefore called on John Lee Hancock, his collaborator on *A Perfect World*, to condense this offbeat chronicle.

The film's Savannah is a Petri dish of a city where you can observe a rich human comedy. Writer Kelso's investigation immerses us in a little-known subculture that has developed in relative isolation and seems to be regularly visited by trickster spirits. He has to navigate without a map or a compass amid eccentrics who devote themselves to rituals so strange and decadent that they might as well inhabit a foreign land.

In fact, Eastwood finds in Savannah what Altman found in Nashville: a fecund microcosm where truth and fiction tend to blur together. The city threw its doors wide open for him; the production was able to take over the mansions where the story had unfolded fifteen years earlier, starting with the Mercer House, a Victorian museum put at the disposal of the crew by Dorothy Kingery, Jim Williams' sister. Some of the local protagonists were invited to mingle with the professional actors, notably black transvestite The Lady Chablis, pianist Emma Kelly, lawyer Sonny Seiler and a bevy of indigenous patricians.

One feels very strongly the pleasure the filmmaker took in composing his puzzle. It is the jubilation of a storyteller who is in no hurry to connect all the dots in his plot. As the voodoo priestess Minerva says laughingly, 'There are no answers!' Ambiguity reigns supreme. Its effigy is the 'Bird Girl', the inscrutable statue of the Bonaventure cemetery where the fable starts and ends. She could be an allegory of Justice since she holds scales that might symbolize good and evil. Or is it right and wrong, reality and illusion? Her face is that of a saintly innocent, but she could very well be smiling at the shenanigans she has in store for us. Such justice could only be 'poetic'.

This interview gives me a chance to revisit Eastwood's previous picture, *The Bridges of Madison County*, another provincial chronicle inspired by a bestseller. Although the book was nothing but pulp fiction, the film managed to strip away its sentimentality. The director's knife was as sharp as Douglas Sirk's, the 1950s master who had dissected the frustrations of the American heartland in such soap operas as *All That Heaven Allows*, *All I Desire* and *There's Always Tomorrow*. Eastwood's sobriety transcended all romantic clichés as it illuminated the truth of two lovers who must sacrifice their passion – the one thing that might have justified their entire existence.

When passion is the spark of life: Kincaid and Francesca (Meryl Streep) in *The Bridges of Madison County* (1995).

*Many American critics questioned your choice of a material
as ambiguous, ironic, polyphonic as* Midnight in the Garden
of Good and Evil.

What amuses me is the state of confusion this country's critics
are in. They keep complaining that we are not making
character-driven films like in the 1930s and 40s, but on the
other hand they rave about action-driven movies that are
devoid of any complexity. I think the influence of television
has transformed the way movies are perceived. There is a
whole generation, the MTV generation, which wants things
to keep rolling all the time. You never linger; you never revisit
anything. *Midnight in the Garden of Good and Evil* is not the
only film to have suffered from this syndrome this year; we

could mention several other examples. Whatever the case
may be, I can't worry about it. I filmed the story that I wanted
to film; it's as simple as that. That desire is what guided me.
When I undertook the film, I knew it wouldn't be for all tastes;
some would love it, others would hate it, and there would be
few reactions in between.

*John Berendt's book was not a piece of fiction, but an
anthropological essay disguised as a diary. What intrigued you
initially in the material?*
John Lee Hancock, the screenwriter of *A Perfect World*,
talked to me about it two years ago. The title itself sounded
interesting, and also the fact that it took place in Savannah.
I forgot about it, and then last year he called me back
because he wanted to submit the script he had been working
on for a long time. The book was reputed to be unadaptable,
but he thought he had found a solution. He also told me
that the studio would end up discarding him because they
preferred to treat the piece as an outright comedy. As I
didn't know the book, I read the screenplay without any
preconceived notion and I liked it. It prompted me to read
the book, so I was able to appreciate all the difficulties that
John had to overcome. Personally, I wouldn't have known
where to start! I then called Terry Semel, the Warner Bros.
honcho, to tell him that it was a good script and that I
wanted to direct it if nobody else had shown interest in
the project. Semel told me that they didn't quite know in
which direction to go with it. I told him it could be an
interesting character study because it involved an ensemble
of odd people. Soon after, on my way back from New York
City, I stopped over in Savannah. I looked around, met
some of the participants, got a feel for the city, and sort of
conducted my own inquiry. When I came back, I said, 'OK,
I'm ready to start.'

*Didn't your involvement trigger a revision or restructuring of
the screenplay?*
There was some rewriting. I asked John to reintegrate some
scenes from the book that he had deleted. One of them was
the episode when Jim Williams [Kevin Spacey] is in jail and
tells the narrator a second scenario of the killing. That was
one of my favorite scenes in the book, the idea that an
incident can be told from several points of view, like in
Rashomon. We either added or subtracted scenes. We
agonized, for instance, about the bridge club for married
ladies. Rather than eliminate it altogether, we kept a shortened
version. We could have easily dropped the black cotillion

Left: 'It is also about tolerance.' The Lady Chablis and John Cusack in *Midnight in the Garden of Good and Evil.*

ball, but for me, such details, the way they compose an atmosphere, are what makes the film more than a straight court drama. I like court dramas, but I didn't feel it should be the whole movie.

Were some episodes shot and then deleted in the editing?
Yes, and I miss some of them. I had enough material to do a three-and-three-quarter- or even a five-hour film. I had to suppress some good, very good scenes because we needed to preserve a certain rhythm. The relationship between the writer, Kelso [John Cusack], and the singer, Mandy [Alison Eastwood], was more developed, and so was the one between Mandy and her pianist friend Joe. Mandy was already a composite in the book, but John Hancock went even further by giving her some attributes of Nancy, Joe's partner, as well as of his first wife. He also made her younger to insinuate the sort of romance and charm that the town and its inhabitants exude. Minerva? She's a composite too. Several voodoo priestesses were the inspiration for the original novel, but the main one in the film, the one Jim Williams consulted, was based on a character that Hancock actually met. She lives seventy-five miles from Savannah and refuses to talk about anything. She is one of the rare participants who didn't try to capitalize on the success of the book.

Did you ever consider calling on the author, John Berendt, to adapt his book?
He didn't want to. He was approached, I don't remember when. He was convinced it couldn't be adapted. It was never conceived as a film, and he didn't see how it could become one. After seeing the finished picture, Berendt was very complimentary about both the screenplay and the direction. As I see it, one of the most inspired decisions was to collapse into one the four trials from the book. John Hancock managed

to distil the essence of the whole affair in one trial, whereas in reality, hung juries were unable to pronounce a judgement and it took years.

More than the book, the film focuses on the ambiguity of the main character, Jim Williams. His cunning recalls the infamous Claus von Bülow.
That's what was on our minds. That idea was more diffuse in the book, which is filled with anecdotes and digressions. We had to accentuate the dramatic points, whereas the book is all atmosphere. I wanted Jim Williams to be more alive, more present; the same held true for the journalist. In the book, you don't learn much about him. His is the voice of a detached observer. In the script, he became John Kelso, a vivid character who has more interactions with Williams, almost becomes his friend and is all the more disappointed when he is lied to. Kelso is the outsider with whom the audience can identify, as he enters into this world. John Cusack's performance has been underrated. It may be less flamboyant than Kevin Spacey's, but it is with him and thanks to him that you take this journey.

You managed to unearth a familiar theme: Kelso is a stranger who lands in a corruption-infested town and arbitrates the power plays between various clans. Midnight in the Garden of Good and Evil *can be seen as a quirky, laid-back variation on the premise of so many of your westerns.*
The difference is that this stranger doesn't really get into a conflict with the inhabitants of a sinful city, but harbors questions in his mind because the people with whom he interacts are so ambiguous. It is also about tolerance ... tolerating other lifestyles, learning to be less judgemental. It's an important aspect of the film, but surprisingly it was hardly mentioned by the reviewers.

Right: A
subculture visited
by trickster
spirits: John
Cusack, Irma P.
Hall and Kevin
Spacey in
*Midnight in the
Garden of Good
and Evil.*

*This is a world where everything turns out to be relative.
You have Kevin Spacey state, 'Truth, like art, is in the eyes
of the beholder.'*
We'll never know the truth, and I like that ambiguity. Williams
tells us two different scenarios [for the crime] with the same
conviction. It leaves Kelso in a quandary, but life is like that.
One of the detectives who conducted the initial investigation
told me that he didn't believe either scenario to be true. When
the police were called, an hour or so after the murder of his
lover, Williams was waiting for them with his attorney.
According to them, the boy must have stubbed out his cigarette
on Williams' ancient desk, and an enraged Williams must
have taken out one of his old Lugers, fired, then quietly dressed
the place so that it would look like self-defence. You are free
to choose your own version of the crime.

*Kevin Spacey's character is portrayed ambiguously as a
sophisticated gentleman, who is probably guilty of a criminal
plot. His elegance is reminiscent of Otto Preminger's heroes,
especially the dandy portrayed by Clifton Webb in* Laura. *As
in* Laura, *the grandfather clock serves as a dramatic and
symbolic device at a crucial moment in the story.*
In Savannah you hear a thousand different stories about
Jim Williams, but even those who interacted with him and
attended his parties concur with others in describing him
as a mysterious character. Those who liked him were
fascinated by this mystery; those who disliked him viewed
him as a dangerous pervert. He was an enterprising guy
who was clever, watchful and very observant. Berendt
suggests that very well when he compares Williams' eyes to
the tinted windows of a limousine; he can see you from
inside, but you can't see him when looking from the outside.
He remains impenetrable. You don't know what his smile
might hide.

*In the book, Jim Williams' death is told in a single paragraph.
In the film, it comes as a form of poetic justice. You conceived
a very elaborate sequence that forces us to reinterpret the
series of events.*
It's like a third version of the murder. Williams' machinations
come back to haunt and crush him.

*Kevin Spacey's portrayal is brilliant. Did you discuss his role
with him?*
Yes, at the beginning of the project. But we didn't rehearse
anything. He doesn't like to rehearse; he'd rather jump in.
John Cusack felt the same way. However, all the actors did
in-depth research. Kevin met Williams' family and friends;
he befriended his sister Dorothy. Jack Thompson, who is
Australian, spent a lot of time in the company of Sonny Seiler
to capture his Southern accent, his style as a lawyer, and also
to have his take about the case. Cusack had extensive talks
with Berendt. They all formed their own ideas of what
happened that evening in Jim Williams' house, just as the
inhabitants of Savannah did in real life.

*Savannah was bound to lure you with its lingering memories
of Johnny Mercer.*
Let's say it was one of its added charms. His great-grandfather
built the Mercer House on Monterey Square. But though
Mercer was Savannah's favorite son, he never lived in this
house and has no connections to our story. Except that Joe
and Mandy are blues musicians and that gave me an
opportunity to play Mercer's tunes throughout the film!

*John Berendt describes Savannah as a vestige of the old South,
'as remote as Pitcairn Island'.*
It's a little-known world, off the aerial grid. There are no direct
flights from New York or Los Angeles. Even the citizens of

Left: 'Like the tinted windows of a sleek limousine': Kevin Spacey is the impenetrable dandy of *Midnight in the Garden of Good and Evil*.

Atlanta view Savannah as alien to Georgia. Already at the time of the Civil War, Savannah had its own agenda. When the Union troops approached, the city's fathers quickly opened negotiations and dissuaded them from burning the town down by bringing them bourbon and throwing beautiful receptions. Thus Savannah was spared. General Sherman was even able to telegraph Lincoln, 'I offer you the jewel of the South as my Christmas present.' Since then, it has somewhat resisted changes and the waves of immigrants. That is particularly true of the old city, which was built around twenty-one plazas designed by James Oglethorpe on the model of Roman military camps. Some of its churches and synagogues are among the oldest in the country. Jim Williams was passionate about restoration. His popularity came from that. He did it his own way. When he wanted to restore an old building, the Pink House, to open a bar-restaurant and the city council opposed the project, he threatened to replace it with a parking structure and the next day positioned a crew of wreckers ready to bring it all down. He immediately won his case! To some extent, it is a liberal city that tolerates different lifestyles, but it is also a small provincial town where jealousies and gossip run rampant. Rumours are the inhabitants' favorite pastime. It's unbelievable, for instance, the tales they spread out, and the scenarios they built, about our movie production even before I showed up.

Throughout the film you take time to observe and appreciate the rituals of that micro-society. We are looking at a tribe threatened with extinction.
Today, most of the time, movies are content with shorthand. Maybe audiences are more impatient, or maybe it's the filmmakers, I don't know. Sometimes, I'd say I was making this film strictly for the people who are interested in detail. The others, the MTV generation, will doze off at times or be

bored throughout. What you call 'rituals' is precisely what I was interested in and wanted to spend time on.

Some have complained that you gave too much room to the transsexual, The Lady Chablis.
She was a colorful character, in life as well as on screen. Her outrageousness was part of the overall atmosphere of Savannah. Furthermore, I love characters that may have nothing to do with the final outcome but are still part of the story. The Lady Chablis forces John Kelso to see things a little differently. It's again the tolerance factor. I like very much how their relationship evolves. They are like the Cary Grant and Rosalind Russell of the 1990s!

For some time you have been more and more attracted to stories that rely on the development of a character, or even several characters like in Midnight…
The action-packed movie was fun when I started, let's say when I was in my twenties or thirties. Sometimes, the material had a good story; sometimes, it had great action, lots of movement and color. But at some point in your life, that's enough. You look for character studies instead, even if it's less commercial. When I was making *Unforgiven* I thought it was going to be unsuccessful. It wasn't a shoot 'em up like *The Wild Bunch* or the Sergio Leone westerns. It departed from the tradition I was part of. Gunplay was sad. You saw kids being killed for nothing. I thought the picture would be rejected for all those reasons.

In the meantime you surprised everybody by gambling on a 'woman's picture' like The Bridges of Madison County. *Was this another attempt at renewal?*
What can I say? Some forty years later, people are still trying to pigeonhole you. When I did the *Rawhide* series I was

identified with the TV western; when I did the Leones, with the offbeat European western; when I did *Dirty Harry*, with the urban cop drama. Later, when I tried to undertake an oddball project like *Every Which Way But Loose*, I remember warnings and even virulent opposition: 'There's no shooting. It's not your kind of subject. You're going to antagonize your fans.' But what is 'my kind of subject'? I don't know. I tell different kinds of stories; that's all. When I grew up, I liked all kinds, from *The Grapes of Wrath* to *Sitting Pretty*. Why should I still be making the same pictures that I started out with? Why should Dustin Hoffman have to play *The Graduate* for the rest of his life? I don't know if this is specific to America. But in the case of *Midnight in the Garden of Good and Evil*, no one else wanted to do it. The same thing happened with *Bird*; the script sat around for years. Nobody wanted to do *Unforgiven*. You may think that I was the least likely director for these three projects, but in fact I was the only one to find them appealing!

The rural Iowa of The Bridges of Madison County *is at polar opposites from the urban and slightly decadent microcosm of* Midnight in the Garden of Good and Evil. *But aren't there similarities between the two pictures, both adapted from bestsellers?*
Both pictures were very pleasant experiences. Thank God nobody was asking me to wear a sombrero in them! I have to say that John Berendt's book was much more intelligent, better written, than that of Robert James Waller, whose prose tended to be a little too flowery. But I was taken by the brilliant simplicity of the theme. There was no soap opera, no incurable disease, no *deus ex machina* like in *Magnificent Obsession* [directed by Douglas Sirk], only the encounter of two outsiders, one a globetrotting photographer, the other a frustrated housewife. They discover that their life is not over, that it can still bring them feelings that they didn't think they could ever experience again. The story had a sort of magic; it didn't resemble anything that was done then in film or literature.

You refocused the novel. It isn't any more the story of 'the last cowboy' that Waller had set out to write.
The novel was written from the man's perspective, that of Robert Kincaid. We preferred to tell the story through the woman's point of view, Francesca's. And we simplified considerably the protagonists and their aspirations.

You were the one who chose Meryl Streep as your acting partner.
She's like Gene Hackman and Morgan Freeman. She's always ready and gives you everything you might expect from her. She wasn't crazy about the book, where the woman wasn't in the foreground, but she liked the screenplay [by Richard LaGravenese] for its truthful depiction of behaviors and emotions.

In Midnight in the Garden of Good and Evil, *emotions are contained or hidden under beguiling appearances. In* The Bridges of Madison County, *they come flowing to the surface. We even see the hero shed tears.*
Jim Williams is not the kind of man who betrays his emotions. He has to retain a certain mystery. On the contrary, there's no mystery to Kincaid, who is very open and who, in spite of his sometimes flippant ways, gets pulled in deeply. It's a romantic love story. It starts out innocently enough. They

appreciate each other, until they become friends and later lovers, at which point they are obsessed with each other. You never question their sincerity.

Did you see aspects of yourself in the character of the photographer?
Maybe. A long time ago, I used to travel around like Kincaid in a pickup truck. In my early days as a director, on *High Plains Drifter* for instance, I would do that to scout locations. I'd get in a pickup truck by myself, drive up to the Sierras, come upon a location I'd like and make some arrangements to use it later for the production. So in that sense I was like him. I didn't run across any Italian housewives, but I could have. I will admit that there's certainly a bit of myself in Kincaid, whereas I don't identify with any of the characters in *Midnight* … even though I found them all interesting.

Despite its strong sensual dimension, you approach this brief encounter with a restraint that has become rare in film.
I wanted to tell the story without the explicit sexuality that is *de rigueur* today, more like they used to do. The housewife commits adultery, and you sympathize with her, but at the same time she has doubts, anxieties, like anyone caught in that situation. Francesca and Kincaid are both misfits. They are not 'liberated' types who are looking for a good time. As their relationship evolves, they realize they were missing something. For them, it's a unique experience. They have never known anything like it, and will probably never know it again.

Steven Spielberg, when he was considering directing the film himself, couldn't think of anybody but you to embody Kincaid.
That's true. But after *Schindler's List*, he wanted to relax for a year, so I inherited the film. I confess that I liked the character. I liked his independence, his integrity. He's someone who has a passion for what he does, but nevertheless is far from irresponsible. He is self-contained. Plus he has the good fortune to devote himself to a creative activity.

Men of action tend to disappear from your films in favor of artists, musicians, writers or show-biz personalities. Before the Kincaid of The Bridges of Madison County *there was the Red Stovall of* Honkytonk Man, *the Charlie Parker of* Bird, *the film director of* White Hunter, Black Heart. *In* Midnight in the Garden of Good and Evil, *Jim Williams collects and restores art objects. In* Absolute Power, *Luther devotes himself to painting. These characters all cultivate an artistic passion that sets them apart.*
You can add *In the Line of Fire*, where the hero is a music lover even though he's part of the secret service. And that's not all! In my next picture, *True Crime*, which is adapted from

Opposite page: *The Bridges of Madison County* or the slow modulations of a quiet lyricism. With Meryl Streep.

Left: 'They would also have jazz in common': *The Bridges of Madison County*, with Meryl Streep.

Below: *The Grapes of Wrath* (John Ford, top); *Of Mice and Men* (Lewis Milestone, bottom).

Following pages: 'There's certainly a bit of myself in Kincaid.' With Meryl Streep in *The Bridges of Madison County*.

a book by Andrew Klavan, I portray a writer/reporter who is covering criminal investigations and has lots of bad habits. At one time, he was demoted because he let out a guy he thought was innocent but turned out to be guilty. A similar situation presents itself and his past comes back to haunt him.

Can artists be viewed as the last individualists?
Sometimes, maybe. Yes, if you are talking about an artist like John Steinbeck. He always wrote about the individual and the individual's struggle. His were fascinating stories. Some great movies have been made out of them, such as *The Grapes of Wrath* and *Of Mice and Men*, the first version. They were stories that lent themselves to making good films because they were about the common man, about individuals fighting for their survival.

*Rather than using country music, you featured jazz in T*he Bridges of Madison County. *Didn't you even invent from scratch the scene at the Blue Note?*
In the novel, they would meet in the restaurants of Des Moines, but it seemed to me very unlikely that an illicit couple would show up so openly. As Waller's Kincaid played the guitar and was a fan of bluegrass, I thought, 'Why couldn't they go out to a small jazz club, to a roadhouse frequented by blacks, where no one would recognize them? They would probably be the only white couple. And they would have that music in common.' Given that background, I used recordings by underrated or forgotten jazzmen such as singers Johnny Hartman and Irene Kral. Why Hartman rather than Sinatra, Nat King Cole or Tony Bennett? Because you don't hear Hartman every day. Also his ballads are connected to memories from my youth. I heard him sing in San Francisco with Dizzy Gillespie's band. I also remember a dancing party with a girlfriend, where I was wearing a white tuxedo jacket and we were both under the spell of Hartman's unique voice.

Like Midnight in the Garden of Good and Evil, The Bridges of Madison County *has the feel of a novel. Its emotional orchestration implies a slow modulation. That slowness is essential to give the characters time to change and mature.*
These are films that don't work if you don't tell the story in real time. If you sped up the tempo on a film like *The Bridges of Madison County* you would be left with a skeleton. You would lose the inner conflict of the married woman, her hesitations, her contradictory yearnings, and there would be nothing left of what had interested me initially as an actor and a director. Those characters have to grow. Otherwise, you wouldn't care when they part. This brief encounter may be banal, it could happen to anybody, but I wanted the audience to root for them, identify with them, and see parallels in their own lives. It's harder to achieve because people who are looking for a fast pace always resent such slowness. These films are the most difficult to pull off.

Left: 'I used to travel around like him in a pickup truck': the photojournalist Kincaid in *The Bridges of Madison County*.

As he matured, Eastwood's empathy for outsiders deepened, and so did his taste for characters that cultivate an artistic passion.

Left: The Frank Horrigan of *In the Line of Fire* (1993, with Rene Russo) has a predilection for jazz.

Below and opposite: The Luther Whitney of *Absolute Power* (1997, with Laura Linney) dabbles in painting when he is not burgling posh mansions.

Following pages: As he confronts all the President's men, Luther comes off as a hero. *Absolute Power*, with Ed Harris.

10

'I need new challenges'
True Crime and *Space Cowboys*

Interview conducted on March 31, 1999

Deftly combining genres and experimenting with abrupt changes in tone, Eastwood is again walking a high wire. The reporters of *True Crime* could have come out of a black comedy like *The Front Page*, but the condemned man and his family stand in the foreground; their drama doesn't elicit many smiles. The situation couldn't be more serious for Beechum, a victim of ingrained racism, or for Everett, the disgraced journalist who attempts to prove him innocent. Nonetheless, the latter is allowed to get into several humorous exchanges with his colleagues and his young daughter. A lightning visit to the zoo, played for all its zaniness, precedes the race against the clock before the execution.

Like so many of Eastwood's films, *True Crime* deals with a miscarriage of justice. And just as in *Midnight in the Garden of Good and Evil*, truth remains elusive. Three *Rashomon*-like flashbacks, each shot from different angles, are necessary to elucidate what happened. There is no antagonist, properly speaking, with the possible exception of the smarmy chaplain who ignominiously tries to take advantage of circumstances. What is at stake is the blindness of the system. An innocent is presumed guilty only because appearances are against him: being young and black, he fits the stereotype. Ironically, it turns out that the real culprit is young and black.

A second paradox certainly seduced Eastwood. The most vulnerable character is not the condemned man, but the journalist who is fighting to save his life. There are numerous parallels between them and between the two families (Beechum's closely bound-together unit, and Everett's dysfunctional one). The editing keeps weaving them together, creating a real counterpoint that gives the story a rich emotional texture.

If the 'born-again' Beechum believes in a better world, Everett believes only in this one. He doesn't give credence to God any more than to Santa Claus ('I don't give a rat's ass about Jesus Christ'). But the idealist who fought against corruption in his better days needs to redeem himself, at least in his own eyes. He has to save Beechum in order to save himself. This disillusioned Don Quixote is to Dirty Harry what the Pale Rider was to the High Plains Drifter. The improbable finale, which contradicts the horror of the execution, could very well be a dream or a vision, unless it is a prayer that has been magically answered.

Space Cowboys, the following opus, does not deal with such complex issues, but it allows Eastwood to celebrate, once more, the triumph of individuals over the system. Comedy prevails this time, as the four musketeers are senior citizens. In the best Howard Hawks tradition, they are 'dinosaurs' that have a thing or two to teach their young colleagues. They also take great relish in defeating the technocrats of the military-industrial complex. It is *El Dorado* revisited in outer space!

'He violates every rule of our time': Steve Everett, the reporter of *True Crime* (1999).

Above: Suffering
from the
Casanova '70
syndrome: *True
Crime*, with
James Woods.

Is True Crime *one of those projects that you nurtured or coveted for a long time, like* Bird, White Hunter, Black Heart *or* Unforgiven?

No, Lili Zanuck brought the project to me. It was developed elsewhere, but the Zanucks had been having a hard time mounting it. They were told it wasn't commercial enough or that there had already been too many films about death row inmates. As far as I'm concerned, I don't care whether it's commercial or not. I liked the story, the characters, their relationships, so I said yes and the project found a shelter at Warner Bros.

Three screenwriters are credited. What were their respective contributions?

I have only read the latest version, drafted by Stephen Schiff. Because I liked it very much, I didn't feel the need to peruse the others to make sure nothing had been left out. However, I did refer to Andrew Klavan's book. The characters are similar, but our story is completely different.

In the novel, the protagonist is only thirty-three!

That's true, but it's the same kind of character. Actually, it works better if the journalist is older. We have all known reporters like him; veterans who refuse to retire and don't have a life outside their newspaper.

Once you were hired, was the part of Everett rewritten for you?

Not really. The Zanucks wanted Schiff to fly from New York and sit down with me to do rewrites. But I declined. I remembered that on *Unforgiven* I had had vague desires of rewriting. The more I was going in new directions, the more I appreciated the excellence of the original script! I ended up calling [screenwriter] David Peoples to tell him that we shouldn't touch it any more. And I even quoted him one of Don Siegel's favorite sayings: 'You can kill a script by trying to improve it'.

Why did you locate the story in Oakland rather than in St. Louis, Missouri, like in the novel?

I know St. Louis a little bit. It's very hot in the summer, and it's not as picturesque as Oakland. And you don't have a nearby penitentiary like San Quentin. You know what Gertrude Stein had to say about Oakland? 'The problem with Oakland is there's no there there!' She was from San Francisco, so she had to look down on that poor backwater of a town. Also, the proximity of a big city like San Francisco worked well with our story. Everett, who comes from *The New York Times*, should have been working for one of the papers there. If he's toiling at the *Oakland Tribune*, it means he's had problems.

Oakland also has a significant African-American population.

This was already the case when I was living there. It was the most important black community west of Detroit. It is due, I think, to the migrations that followed World War II and to the shipbuilding that flourished there.

There are several threads interwoven in True Crime. *There is the legal drama, which is really a pretext for a character study. There is also a sardonic comedy* à la Front Page, *but a painful gravitas sets in each time we enter death row and the issues of race and capital punishment are being raised.*

That's what immediately drew my attention. There were three or four different threads to weave. And there was one more element that I really liked: a race against time, like in *Dirty Harry* and *Play Misty for Me*. When you were reading the screenplay, you never knew where it was leading. Obviously, the reporter has a truckload of problems, but you can't tell what is going to happen to him. Obstacles keep coming up, red herrings keep presenting themselves, to such an extent that Everett starts questioning not only the guilt of the condemned man, but himself as well.

The connections with Dirty Harry *are obvious, not only because we find ourselves in the Bay Area, but also because Everett and Harry are both outsiders who confront the legal system when they try to rescue its victims. Naturally, Everett's methods are less radical; a certain form of humanism is allowed to seep in. Everett is more complex than Dirty Harry, and more quixotic, since he rescues victims to his own detriment. He sacrifices*

his career and even his family by conducting this investigation. He juggles with too many balls. In the end, you don't really know what he becomes. You can't even say that he's learned something. There's no happy ending for him. He's separated from his family, he lives in a hotel, he flirts with the girl selling toys, and he's lost none of his bad habits. A leopard cannot lose his spots.

However, the individual wins over the system, even if Everett is driven by his professionalism rather than by idealism.

He brings to my mind several of our presidents: Clinton, Nixon and even Lyndon B. Johnson. They all had a touch of the loser, a tendency to self-destruct. Once they reached the top, they couldn't help sawing the branch on which they were sitting. Everett, too, has an interesting job, but he suffers from the *Casanova '70* syndrome. Do you remember that film [directed by Mario Monicelli] where Marcello Mastroianni could only make love if he was in an exceedingly dangerous situation? If he has an affair, it can only be with the wife of a fencing master! Clinton probably experienced something similar at the White House, until his pursuit of the thrill of danger got him caught. Everett can't resist temptation either. He's very aware of the risks he's taking when he sleeps with his chief editor's wife. 'If I get caught,' he says, 'I'm finished', but he does it any way, as though he was asking to be caught.

Below: 'I'm trying to find new approaches': Frank Beechum (Isaiah Washington) and his wife Bonnie (Lisa Gay Hamilton) in *True Crime.*

You portray him as the most politically incorrect hero of the year. He violates every rule of our times. That's why it's such a great character and I enjoyed portraying him. I don't know if I'm like that in real life, probably not, but it quickly becomes a big bore to play the nice, sensitive type. We live in the era of political correctness. Such bullshit! Everything is filtered, censored. We all pretend there's no prejudice any more. We live in total denial of reality. As a result, you can't make a joke without risking losing your position or your job. It's a dishonest era. We owe it to the politicians. They would have prevented John Ford from shooting *The Searchers* because it was the story of a racist.

Some American critics have accused you of downplaying the issue of sexual harassment because Everett chases girls who are a lot younger than he is.
When he finds a girl sexy, Everett is not afraid to let her know. He's of another generation. In his days, you didn't think twice about flirting. He leaves good manners to his young colleagues. Besides, he is not always successful. At the beginning of the film, in the bar, Michelle, the young journalist who's killed that evening, brushes him off. The reason for the scene is to show precisely that he fails to seduce her. We don't know her reasons, but maybe she doesn't want someone that old.

One can't help thinking about Howard Hawks, and films like Rio Bravo *and* El Dorado, *where the ageing hero was a master in his professional world, but vulnerable and sometimes inept in his private life.*
I did think about Hawks, but it is the Hawks of *His Girl Friday*, because of the tempo. This is the reason why I cast James Woods and Denis Leary. They remind me of Cary Grant, Rosalind Russell or Fred MacMurray … a generation of actors I miss enormously, actors who had a perfect sense of repartee and timing. Today, each actor takes his time, quietly speaks when his turn comes. Maybe we should blame today's filmmakers. Hawks was the one who insisted that the actors cut one another short and let their lines overlap.

Was your confrontation with James Woods improvised? It has the spontaneity of a first take.
Most of it was on paper, but we added things here and there on the set. I did keep the first take, which was a long master shot of the whole scene. Nevertheless, I covered myself afterwards by breaking the scene down, shot by shot.

Going back to Hawksian behavior for a moment, wouldn't Everett prefer for his chief editor to punch him in the face or for the incident to end in a good fist-fight, like in the finale of Red River?
It would assuage his guilt. He knows he deserves a thrashing, but Findley, who's not stupid, won't give him the satisfaction. That, too, I had liked in the screenplay, the fact that the characters didn't do what was expected of them. Of course, it would be more 'commercial' if we had a splendid fist-fight in the desk room, if Everett and Findley imitated John Wayne and Randolph Scott. But this is not what the film is about.

In your typically facetious way, you deny the viewer the anticipated action set pieces. The car chase at the end violates all the rules of the thriller; it couldn't be less spectacular!
It's not meant to be a fire-on-all-4-cylinders kind of race. We have only a few cars honking. Car chases, I have done enough of them. It would be meaningless here.

Everett has something in common with Sergeant Highway in Heartbreak Ridge. *Both are survivors of a bygone era.*
Highway was more limited intellectually. He didn't have Everett's education and experience. Everett has great principles as a journalist, he's very proud of his intuition, but in his private life, he's too frivolous, too self-destructive, to keep a family together. He probably suffers from what psychologists call the impostor syndrome. Deep down, he doesn't believe he deserves what he has, so he is constantly sabotaging his career and wasting his life.

There are no 'villains' in True Crime, *except maybe the prison chaplain, a character whose vile hypocrisy is rather startling.*
He's an opportunist; he's trying to sell his wares. The irony is that the condemned man has another religion and his own pastor. One single individual does not embody evil. Witnesses are not malevolent, only fallible. The accountant is convinced that he faced the culprit; the district attorney is convinced that she did the right thing. Evil, as a matter of fact, is a combination of circumstances.

Like Altman in Cookie's Fortune, *you challenge the Manichaean morality that has been prevailing in the legal thriller since John Grisham and his epigones took it over.*
That black and white morality is too easy. In the old days, it was the staple of B films, at least of the worst ones! Are we going to go back to the simplicity of *Shane*, with the good Alan Ladd dressed in buckskin and the bad Jack Palance clad in black leather? Maybe this is what the audience favors, but it's worth trying something else. For instance, in *Unforgiven* I liked very much the fact that the antagonist, the sheriff played by Gene Hackman, had a point of view, a philosophy, even if it drove him to cruel extremes. This gives you a richer, more complex story. Little Bill was not a villain proud to be one, but a guy who had his own life, who was building himself a house for his retirement and who was convinced he was right. In real life, villains never see themselves as villains.

In your most personal films, from Honkytonk Man *to* Bird, *the hero is his own antagonist. This is again the case in* True Crime. *The conflict is within him; he is fighting his own demons. Isn't that what we do most often in real life?*

When it came to the re-enactment of the crime, did the screenplay feature three flashbacks in the style of Rashomon?
Yes, it had three different points of view like in *Rashomon*. That was a fantastic film at the time, and still is. Kurosawa was so ahead of his time.

To quote from Midnight in the Garden of Good and Evil, *'Truth, like art, …*
… is in the eyes of the beholder!' And this truth has many nuances. Beechum, the condemned man, is a victim of circumstances. The accountant is ready to swear that he saw him brandishing a gun. When you have such a heinous crime, in this case the murder of a pregnant woman, who can remain cool-headed? Take the recent case in Texas of white supremacists that tied a disabled black man behind

Opposite page: In Eastwood's films, justice is always in question. *True Crime*, with Frances Fisher.

Below: *His Girl Friday* (Howard Hawks, top); *El Dorado* (Howard Hawks, bottom).

their pickup truck and dragged him until he died. What can an attorney do? How could he take the heat out of such a case?

Do you believe in capital punishment?
Yes, for heinous crimes like this one. But there are cases where the truth is not so clear-cut and where you need to be extremely circumspect. Initially, in the script, the young hood that committed the crime shot the checkout woman in cold blood. But I wanted that shot to be fired almost accidentally, when the hood is startled by a voice coming from the room next door. Having said this, most condemned men are probably guilty. As it is said in the film, a convict always protests his innocence. That's why Everett cracks, 'Everyone lies, and I'm only here to jot down their lies.'

The racial divide is an underlying but recurrent theme in many of your films, from Bird *to* White Hunter, Black Heart *to* Unforgiven. *What draws you to that theme?*
I don't know. I have seen quite a few films on that subject, most of them unconvincing or even absurd. I'm trying to find new approaches. If I come back to that divide, it may be because it's ever present. We go and rescue some oppressed peoples, but we ignore many others. Today, our sympathy goes to the Albanian refugees from Kosovo, but who cared yesterday about the atrocities committed in Rwanda? Maybe it is impossible to rescue everybody. Maybe we should also care a little more about people who need help in our own country. We like to lecture other people, but we sometimes neglect what is happening at home.

The documentary approach, with its emphasis on the technical aspects of the execution, is like a brutal reality check.
I wanted, if not to educate the public, at least to show them the process in detail, the calculations needed for the injections, etc. For the prison employees, it's a job like any other. As to the warden, you sometimes get the feeling that he has doubts about Beechum's guilt, but is it really the case? It's up to the audience to decide.

How did you come to cast Isaiah Washington for the part of Beechum, the condemned man?
I noticed him when I was viewing the auditions on video. That's how he was chosen. I didn't even meet him. I prefer to rely on videocassettes to make my casting decisions. I have

the auditions and interviews recorded. On *Play Misty for Me* I only met Jessica Walter at the last minute, when I was absolutely certain that it was her that I wanted. That way, you avoid the painful process I know so well, whereby the actor is full of illusions because he has met the director. I suffered from it more than once when I was an unemployed actor. Lisa Gay Hamilton, who portrays the wife, I discovered in the same way. I hadn't seen her in *Beloved* or in her TV series. I immediately liked her audition.

At the heart of the film, you build a parallel between the two families, Everett's and Beechum's.
I wanted a strong contrast. In the script, Everett had a son. I felt a daughter was a must. Why? Not because I have a daughter of that age. Francesca is five and doesn't really need to make a living! No, the reason was that I wanted to reinforce the parallel you are describing. On the one hand, you have a guy condemned to die but who is only worried about the future of his family. On the other, you have a guy who has a family, an interesting job and maybe even some talent, but instead of enjoying what he has, finds nothing better to do than self-destruct.

Transitions from one family to the other account for brutal changes of tone. For instance, after the comedic scene of the speeded-up visit of the zoo, you cut to the solemn arrival of the black woman and her daughter at San Quentin, a world where time seems momentarily suspended.
These changes of tone occur throughout the film. It was very deliberate. I wanted the audience to be constantly jostled around, from beginning to end, since you don't really know how it's going to unfold. The audience has to draw their own conclusion. It's up to you to decide if the final scene is real or imaginary.

What is your next project?
I am going to shoot *Space Cowboys* this summer. Again, the screenplay [by Ken Kaufman and Howard Klausner] was brought to me. It's about a group of test pilots in the mold of Chuck Yeager. In the 1950s they were part of a programme of experimental rockets, but were deprived of their space journey when NASA decided to send monkeys instead. They were deeply frustrated. Corvin, the hero and a guy of my age, goes back into service when a satellite starts malfunctioning. He and his partners are sent into space where they encounter all sorts of obstacles and shenanigans. And this time my character will have an antagonist, a former colleague.

Doesn't that story entail a great number of CGI effects?
It will. I have already started the preparation with Industrial Light & Magic [George Lucas' special effects company]. They have developed a system based on animatronics, which enables you to pre-visualize each shot on the computer. You give them the list of desired shots before the special effects are created. It is very practical and economical because you can judge immediately if the effect is satisfactory and whether or not it deserves to be realized. I didn't have that luxury on *Firefox*! Whatever technologies we use – and we are going to combine several of them, from good old miniatures to computer-generated imagery – the important point is that the story be credible. NASA will help us simulate as exactly as possible the training, the launch of the ship, the state of

weightlessness, etc. There will also be, hopefully, a lot of suspense and many plot twists. But it probably won't be as complex as *True Crime*.

Isn't the complexity you are talking about due essentially to the wide range of emotions that you like to play with? A film like True Crime *overlaps with many different genres. It's neither a comedy, nor a cop show, nor a racial drama, nor a documentary on capital punishment. You circumvent the formulas as soon as they raise their head.*

In the old days, filmmakers didn't hesitate to mix genres. Today, it seems everything has to play on the same note, either all white or all black. Pyrotechnics have taken over. What our young audiences want, we are told, is just to have a good time. I joked on the set, 'The problem with this film is that it has a story. I don't know how we can overcome that.' *True Crime* will probably be better received in Europe, as was the case for *A Perfect World*, which wasn't understood here. I can only say it again, I can't keep doing what I used to do. I'm done with those shoot 'em ups where you stop counting dead bodies – even if they are more lucrative. Been there, done that. I need new challenges.

Above: The comeback of the 'dinosaurs': *Space Cowboys*, with Tommy Lee Jones, James Garner and Donald Sutherland.

Following pages: With age, the hero has gained a new heart, literally. Detective McCaleb in *Blood Work* (2002), with Anjelica Huston.

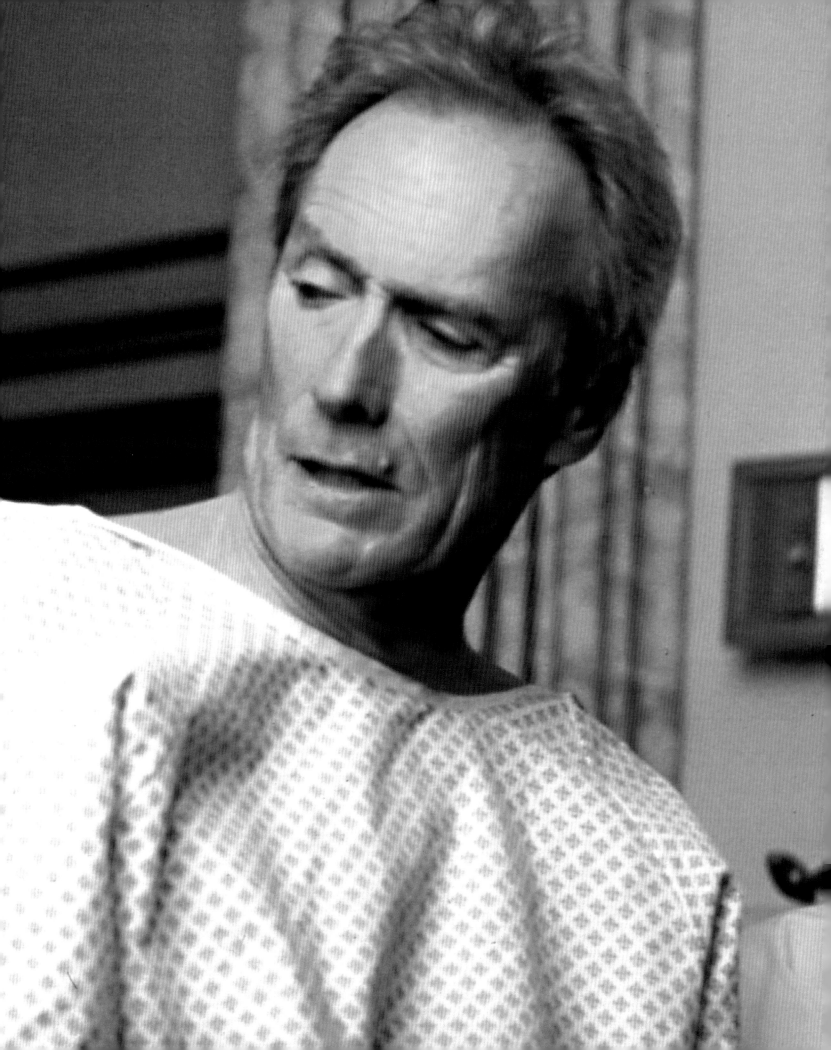

11

'I was always fascinated by victims'
Mystic River

Interview conducted on April 28, 2003

Pride in the new film is running high at Malpaso and, as everyone had hoped, *Mystic River* has just been selected for the Cannes Film Festival. Eastwood greets the news with delight. It is his fourth invitation after *Pale Rider*, *Bird* and *White Hunter, Black Heart*. He also presided over the jury in 1994.

Mystic River is above all a *tour de force*. Dwelling on the darkest recesses of a subject as difficult as pedophilia, it is the most delicate project that Eastwood has ever undertaken. It was no easy pitch. He was urged to water down the screenplay and to give it a less sombre conclusion. Warner Bros. had so many reservations that they even encouraged him to consider another financing partner. The film had to be shot with a Spartan budget, under twenty-five million dollars, and at full tilt in thirty-nine days. We should be grateful to its actors, all of them remarkable in complex parts, for making its production possible by agreeing to the minimum wage set by the Screen Actors Guild's regulations.

The point of departure could have been lifted from one of those Warner Bros. melodramas of the 1930s – with titles like *The Public Enemy* or *Angels with Dirty Faces* – where one followed the divergent destinies of two childhood friends. Dennis Lehane, the author, did acknowledge that genre as a major influence, but the narrative and emotional texture of his novel is fortunately of greater intricacy. It is that depth of feelings that appealed to the filmmaker: the police investigation reveals an abyss of pain before precipitating a tragedy.

One also sees how a crime committed against a child years earlier slowly spreads like gangrene throughout the community. Violence acts like a poison. No regeneration can be expected from it, like at the time of *High Plains Drifter* or *The Outlaw Josey Wales*. In *Mystic River*, as in *Unforgiven* before it, traumatic events corrode the soul and infect the entire social body, starting with those who take the law into their own hands. Once again, vigilantism accelerates this destructive process as the self-appointed judge executes the wrong man. He who would play angel winds up being the beast.

Confounding everyone's expectations at Malpaso, this important film was to return empty-handed from Cannes. It doesn't even muster a best actor's award for Sean Penn or Tim Robbins. One can't help wondering what the jurors had been smoking when they bestowed the Golden Palm on... *Elephant*.

Eastwood would take it all in stride, as he was anxious to get back to the editing of his documentary, *Piano Blues*. Indeed, he had found time to contribute an episode to a TV series on the blues, produced by Martin Scorsese and broadcast by PBS in the autumn of 2003. It was a labor of love, a personal valentine to the indigenous American art form. 'The blues has always been part of my musical environment,' Eastwood remarked. 'And the piano has occupied the place of honor ever since the day my mother brought a whole collection of Fats Waller's records back to the house.'

'All the characters are haunted': Sean Penn in *Mystic River* (2003).

How did you first become acquainted with Mystic River?
I discovered a synopsis of Dennis Lehane's novel on the back page of a newspaper. It was an appealing title and I found the subject matter interesting, especially the focus on child abuse and its devastating consequences. Twenty-five years after the acts of molestation, another tragedy occurs which brings past events into the present. Murder mysteries are usually only about solving the crime, but in this case the story shows how, beyond the murder, all the participants' lives have been screwed up by the crime. One gets to see the impact a violent act has had on the characters' lives many years after the fact. This perspective really fascinated me, so I called up my office and asked for a copy of the book. The author was not a total unknown to me because Dennis Wayne, a friend of mine from up north who liked Lehane's writing, had given me a couple of other titles of his. So when I saw the synopsis in the newspaper, I recognized the author's name and decided to pursue it. Once I began reading the novel, I couldn't put it down.

You have long been interested in the repercussions of violence, as evinced by many of your previous films, from The Outlaw Josey Wales *to* Unforgiven. *This really comes to the foreground in* Mystic River, *where an act of predatory violence not only taints the victim but also spreads out to impact the life of a whole community.*
When someone robs, rapes, murders or creates mayhem, suddenly a very harsh reality can set in. Kids may think they are playing a game, they get caught up in pretending to rob someone, but then their gun goes off accidentally and they shoot a person. Suddenly, they are wrapped up in this deal they can't stop. There is also something interesting about small-time criminality, such as stealing comic books or rare stamps. Movies tend to portray ten-million-dollar heists or the knocking over of a Vegas casino, but crime here is so everyday, so ordinary. That mundane aspect intrigued me. Also, the whole notion of pedophilia has become a very big concern in this country, particularly in the Church. People are wondering, what the hell is going on here? The abuse of children! The older I get, the less tolerance I have for such criminal behavior.

The book predates the major Church scandal in Boston, doesn't it?
No, it was written at the same time as the public scandal, the one involving Cardinal Law. When I first talked to Lehane on the phone after optioning the book, I told him his novel sounded like something right out of the newspapers. It turns out that he is an Irish Catholic and went to the same school that a lot of those people came from who were claiming the abuse. This whole problem within the Church might have influenced his writing.

This is probably the most richly textured canvas you have ever tackled. What were some of the challenges in adapting the story to the screen?
I started thinking about screenwriters and Brian Helgeland immediately came to mind because he is from Boston and knows that area. So I ended up with a whole Massachusetts group! He really liked the book, and after conferring with him briefly, I said, 'Why don't you just dig in?' I gave him a synopsis of how I saw the story, simplifying various elements. He had some ideas as well and ripped right into it, writing the first draft in two weeks. I looked at it and felt it was a terrific interpretation of a complex book, filled with so much discussion and detail. We reworked a couple of things, picking and choosing what was really important. The script was done just before I shot *Blood Work*, which Brian had written as well. Once the *Mystic River* script was fine-tuned, I didn't think too much about it and put it on the shelf. Then as soon as I got into the editing phase of *Blood Work*, I started talking about doing this one.

Were the three lead actors – Sean Penn, Tim Robbins and Kevin Bacon – your first choices?
They were! We didn't have any recalls or turndowns. I sent the script to Sean and he loved it right away. Tim called, and as the word got out, other actors began calling. The only one who wasn't originally part of the group was Laurence Fishburne. I wanted his character to be an ethnic person outside of the Irish neighborhood group, someone who would be an observer from another segment of society. Marcia Gay Harden and Laura Linney were in the right age bracket for their parts and both are terrific actresses with whom I have previously worked. This was a very pleasant experience because the actors all resonated so well together. They learned the accents and hung out a little bit before shooting started. As a matter of fact, I went to see Tim Robbins in a play about 9/11 called *The Guys*; he was playing a fireman and had already begun incorporating the accent into his speech, because we had just signed him. Interestingly, all the male actors – Tim, Sean, Kevin and Laurence – had themselves directed films.

Did the fact that you were not involved as an actor free you to focus on their intricate stories?
And how! It was great! There were so many different layers to the piece that it was less distracting to simply direct. Things can drive you crazy when you are both acting and directing. People keep coming up to you and saying, 'You have to match hair, wardrobe or whatever', and you're constantly being pulled at while you're desperately trying to concentrate on the scene. This time, I could just stand back and look at what was cooking. I had a very interesting new gimmick, a small flat screen with a handle that I could carry around without

Left: He who would play angel ... : Jimmy (Sean Penn) and the Savage brothers (Kevin Chapman and Robert Wahlberg) in *Mystic River*.

having to look through the camera. It is a wireless video monitor. There is no replay to it; it functions as a viewfinder. I used it for the set-ups, or sometimes when people were rehearsing. When we were shooting I could watch the scene unfolding in private, by myself. I hate those video monitors you have to sit in front of, and where everybody can go to look at a replay.

How did you prepare the actors for these challenging roles?
I just talked with them all about it. Sean asked, 'Would you mind if I flew to Boston ahead of you?' and I said, 'Yes, you can sit down with Dennis Lehane and talk with him about the script.' Tim also flew to Boston early, although he didn't meet Dennis. Marcia Gay lives in upstate New York, so she drove in to hang out with us. Ditto with Laura Linney. Kevin Chapman, who plays Val Savage, is from Boston. The actors all went to him to ask him how to pronounce words, so he became the dialogue coach for that distinct Bostonian accent of the Irish blue-collar neighborhood. It was that 'paak the caar' kind of accent. He was a great help. In the evenings, Sean, Tim, Kevin and Laurence would all get together and have meetings on their own. Before they started these readings, they asked me if I minded them getting together. I said, 'Are you kidding? Do it as much as you want! Get as familiar with those characters as you want to be. We're going to do it until it's right, but this will give you more chance to get to know one another.' In the story they are all supposed to have known each other for years, as they were playing husbands and wives. Actually, a lot of the actors already knew one another anyway. Tim and Sean had worked together on a film, Sean and Kevin on a play. The girls were wonderful too and Laurence worked out perfectly. They all were right in sync.

How did they adjust to your famously brisk pace?
Parts of the story required that kind of pace. When doing a rehearsal layout, I would sometimes work on the tempo. Take the two detectives, Kevin and Laurence. I wanted them to keep up a certain pace, like they did in the old Raoul Walsh or Howard Hawks movies. It may be a detective story, but it should be kept going. With the other characters, my approach was different because there was so much dramatic pressure on them. But I did keep everybody at a pretty good pace and didn't let things linger.

Except where things have to stand still like in the scene on the porch between Sean Penn and Tim Robbins, after the murder.
There I did the opposite. I let that one simmer. There weren't any rehearsals for that scene. I brought Tim out, we did the beginning of the scene with him facing Sean, then I came around the other side for the reverse shot and set it up so I could do a master shot favoring Sean. That was done in one take. Sean likes to go right away; good performers want to do that. Then I put the camera on the dolly and took one shot moving on Sean as he is talking. Then I did a reverse shot and moved on Tim. By that time Sean was getting burned out. Tim, whose part is more reserved, understood the necessity of doing it in that order. It flowed very much like *Unforgiven* or *The Bridges of Madison County*: we just did it; we didn't sit there wondering what we were going to do.

There are many echoes between Mystic River *and* Unforgiven. *Were you aware of such resonance when you started the project?*
It was fun to get a piece of material like this. It was a fluke, but that is the way *Unforgiven* came to me too. They were all flukes. The two films resonate in that the interaction of the

characters is kind of similar. They all have a lot of stuff in the back of their minds. When I went to Washington to do a sixtieth anniversary of the arts programme for the American Film Institute, they wanted me to introduce *The Ox-Bow Incident* because they knew I liked that movie. I watched it again when I was there and thought it shared a certain quality with *Unforgiven* and *Mystic River*. Fate is driving the characters and there is nothing you can do to stop it.

There are quite a few striking shots from the point of view of God in this picture. Not necessarily a Catholic God, but more likely some great puppet master pulling the strings of destiny.

It seems that the heavens are called to witness the events or to play a part in it.
The earth is so small, the drama so insignificant in the overall scheme of things, but at the same time, we have to connect very personally with Sean's and Tim's state of agony and with this girl who is lying at the bottom of a bear pit. It seemed like the thing to do. Even though it was an intimate story, I tried not to shoot it in a claustrophobic way, which so many filmmakers seem to favor these days.

In the films you directed, the past is often associated with a trauma, something that has been repressed and needs to be finally dealt with. The past poisons the present for these characters. This is true, for instance, of The Outlaw Josey Wales, Unforgiven, A Perfect World, *even* Pale Rider. *They are all stories about people who strive to overcome devastating experiences.*
You never really know what reasons have shaped these characters and made them the way they are. I have always been fascinated by victims, including the ones in my adventure films and even *Dirty Harry*; how things trigger a certain course of events that lead them to where they are now. In *Mystic River*, one little incident multiplies and spreads outwards over a twenty-five-year period. It is like a cancer, growing and growing, and there is no cure.

The film starts with a baseball discussion and ends with the Columbus Day parade. Two symbols of America frame this very American story.

It is an American tragedy, a story of lost innocence. Tim says, 'I did it because she [Katie, the teenage girl] reminded me of a dream I had. A dream of youth.' Of course his character was robbed of his youth. We know the reason from the beginning. We know how irrevocable fate is. We changed the book's sequential order so that we could cross-cut between the arrest of the kids and the confrontation between Sean and Tim. It worked better for me. The audience already knows the truth. So when Sean demands that Tim confesses, they think, 'You don't have to do it now. Don't!' But it is too late; he is trapped into a false confession.

When you think the story is coming to an end, new dimensions are revealed in the female characters. The story keeps expanding.
Brian's script ended with a final discussion. But I went back to the book because I liked the way Annabeth, Laura Linney's character, takes over everything. She tells her man [Sean Penn] that he is a king and could rule the whole city. She becomes Lady Macbeth, while out on the street there's poor bewildered Celeste [Marcia Gay Harden] wondering what in the hell happened. Kevin Bacon's gesture at the end was inspired by a story Sean Penn told me. He was in a jail once; he happened to look over and saw a notorious mass-murderer across the corridor. The guy recognized him as an actor, made a hand gesture as if to cock the hammer of a gun, and went back to whatever he was doing in his cell!

The film's lighting gets darker and darker, as though dusk is giving way to night.
The piece was lit to look like a day ending. I'm very happy with the picture's look. Cinematographer Tom Stern had been a chief lighting technician for years, working on many of my pictures under Bruce Surtees and Jack Green. He'd been doing such a good job that I thought it was time to give him a shot.

There is also a certain darkness inside the characters, an undercurrent of repressed feelings that are yearning to come out.
It's that tragic circle. The three fellows have unresolved issues in their lives, while at the same time they are trying to solve the crime. Even Kevin Bacon's character, who is now a successful detective, finds his life flawed; everything is dicey now, including his relationship with his wife. They have all been affected by the past, by what happened when one of the kids was abducted. All have been traumatized. They have all become damaged goods.

One feels very strongly your empathy for these haunted characters.
You have to care about them, especially when you have such intriguing material. In its own way, *Mystic River* is a daring piece whose dark subject matter reveals a tragically real aspect of human experience. Sometimes, I wonder how I would have handled the challenge of being a contract director in the old days, when the studio dictated what to make. A filmmaker was exposed to tremendous disappointments. Think about William Wellman with *The Ox-Bow Incident* or Sam Peckinpah with *Ride the High Country*. Wellman tried to make a personal statement, but the studio head looked at *Ox-Bow* and said, 'This is a piece of junk. We'll just let it go out there and die.' It was terribly disappointing because not only did everyone enjoy making it, but also the iconoclastic message was bold and important for that time [1943].

How would you sum up the personal statement you were trying to make with Mystic River?
There have been stories about the criminal act of child molestation. But the question asked less often is, 'How has that tragedy left its mark on the victim and his environment?' This story is about a succession of events spanning decades, an unbreakable chain of dramas that can't be stopped. And all the characters are haunted.

Is your strategy still to make one picture for the studio and one more uniquely personal to you?
There was never any strategy like that per se; it is just the way it happened. I have always been given freedom to make the films I wanted, although this one was a little harder to sell because the subject matter scared them off a little bit. What the film life of *Mystic River* will be I don't know. But I remember thinking, when we were making *Unforgiven*, that this western was not going to make a nickel because the characters had too much baggage. There were bits of humor, but they hardly offset the darkness. It was not a commercial film and I didn't want people to think of it that way. Fortunately, it turned out to be commercial.

What was the studio's initial reaction to the project?
They agreed to do it, either because they liked the material or because of my long-term relationship here [at Warner Bros.], but they also got other companies to buy into the project. They probably thought it had certain limitations. The stipulation was that they would do it for a limited budget. It was fine with me. I said, 'You don't have to pay me now. Pay me later if the picture does something. If it doesn't, I don't care because I just want to make it.' So we agreed on an amount and I built within that framework. It was back almost to the way I started when I did *Play Misty for Me* thirty-three years ago. I was given a limited budget and told I could take a percentage but no salary. At the time, I didn't care; I wanted to make the movie so badly I was willing to pay them! This one was the same thing; I really wanted to make it. So there it is. We worked independently of the studio, from filming it all in Boston right through to the score being done there [Eastwood's compositions were recorded by the Boston Symphony Orchestra]. Nobody saw any dailies or parts of the film; I just made it.

Above: 'Clint, you
are the least
disappointing
cultural icon
I have ever met!'
(Sean Penn,
at the end of the
shoot).

Did your actors share your passion for the material?
When we negotiated with the actors, it was explained that
this is our budget, what we're stuck with. It was fine because
the material attracted them; they were smart enough to
know it's good to work with meaningful material. Real drama
is hard to find nowadays; it seems everything is either
infantile or cartoonish. Every trailer on television is about
someone doing pratfalls, which is fine. I grew up with Harold
Lloyd; he was wonderful. But there should also be a greater
variety with something for everybody. Unfortunately, you
would never know that in this town today.

In that context, Mystic River *stands out because of its
multilayered texture. It can be experienced as a mystery, as it
provides a puzzle to be resolved. But it is also a drama that
looks for the truth on the darker side of human nature.*
The story may satisfy the audience on several different
levels. The 'whodunit' crowd may be happy with just the
mystery and absorb the other content in the periphery.
Others will get into the background of the characters and
the detective story will be meaningful only in relation to
the overall tragedy. The story is layered, and as each layer
gets peeled off, more is revealed. Every time a question is
answered it only raises more questions. Now I'm looking
forward to people's reactions.

You are about to fly again into space…
It's going to be a while. I have only just acquired the rights
to *First Man*, the biography of Neil Armstrong by James
Hansen. The book is not even finished; Hansen will be

working on it for at least another year. I will produce and
direct, but I am not planning to play the part. Why this
interest in Armstrong? Millions of people saw him live as
he made his first steps on the moon, and many more have
watched him do it since that historic day. Yet Armstrong
himself is a very enigmatic character. Hansen's purpose is
to examine the life of this secretive man who has shared a
unique experience with the entire world. It struck me as a
story that could become a good film.

Above: *Piano Blues* (2003): Eastwood makes music with Jay McShann.

Below left: 'Not being afraid to appear different': with Ray Charles in *Piano Blues*.

12

'It was just the angels working for us'
Million Dollar Baby

Interview conducted on February 17, 2005

One film for them, one film for himself: for years, Eastwood has alternated studio commissions with labors of love. This used to be the strategy of Ford and Walsh, of Wellman and Siegel, these masters of storytelling whose tradition Eastwood may be the last to represent. He carries it on with stories of disenchantment that unfold in a twilight world of hard lives and hard times.

Now that he has become a master in his own right, it seems that nothing can stand in his way: 'I have reached the point where I haven't got anything to lose any more!' Having broken free of genres and formulas, he goes right to the heart of his subjects to extract the throbbing truth – a truth ever more complex and rarefied. After the tragedy of *Mystic River*, here is *Million Dollar Baby*, where Maggie's rise and fall is distilled into a modern passion play.

Such simplicity can be deceiving. Courage is as much a mystery as grief. In approaching them, Eastwood remains true to the inspiration he received from the artists of old (including actress and director Ida Lupino, an expert on the subject of afflictions). Clarity and concision, discretion and compassion, are the cardinal virtues of classicism. They've sadly been forgotten, which may be why Eastwood cuts such a solitary figure in today's Hollywood.

What strikes me most during our conversation, which is taking place by the fireplace in a small lounge of Mission Ranch in Carmel, is precisely how much he has come to resemble his predecessors. Like them, he sees himself above all as a storyteller, which has become a vanishing tradition, at least in Hollywood. Will he be 'the last of the Mohicans', as he often quips?

Though he insists that his acting days are over, as a director, Eastwood has no intention of resting on his laurels. He remains on the look-out for 'good stories' that deserve to be passed on to the younger generations. Undoubtedly, the drama of the six soldiers who raised the flag on top of Mount Suribachi on Iwo Jima will be part of that legacy. I can feel that he is already mobilized, at least emotionally, by *Flags of Our Fathers* and is hardly concerned about the Academy Awards campaign, in which *Million Dollar Baby* has kept an exceptionally low profile.

However, just a week later, *Million Dollar Baby* was to reap the four top Oscars: best film, best director, best actress (Hilary Swank) and best supporting actor (Morgan Freeman), an upset for *The Aviator*, which had been favored by most handicappers.

As she did at the time of *Unforgiven*, Mrs Ruth Eastwood, now ninety-six years old, will be sitting in the audience next to her son. On the stage of the Kodak Theater, Clint will acknowledge his triumph with a craftsman's modesty worthy of the old masters: 'I am here because I was lucky; lucky to be able to keep working ... I feel like I'm only a kid. I still have so many things to do.'

Hilary Swank is Maggie, the Christ-like figure in *Million Dollar Baby* .

How did the project of Million Dollar Baby *grow on you?*
I read the collection of short stories by F. X. Toole [*Rope Burns*] about four years ago, when [producer] Al Ruddy submitted it to me. Al recommended in particular the one called *Million Dollar Baby*. Of the six short stories, it was the one that immediately hooked me. As I was busy with another picture – *Space Cowboys*, I think – I told him that I couldn't develop the project, but asked him to come back to me if a screenplay ever came into existence. Well, that's what happened. As soon as I read Paul Haggis' script, I was won over. It struck me as a simple and honest piece about certain human interactions. I particularly liked the fact that Frankie had had a conflicted relationship with his daughter and that at the beginning he harbored strong prejudices against Maggie. I have always liked the dynamic of a character that is biased, thinks he has reasons to reject someone, but ends up overcoming those prejudices. Here, Frankie re-creates with Maggie the family he has lost. Besides, he's a guy of my age. It felt like a good final part for me before retiring as an actor – after fifty-one years!

Did the role of Scrap, played by Morgan Freeman, exist in the story originally?
It originated in another short story. Paul had the excellent idea of lifting the Scrap character so that he could become both our narrator and the lens through which we view the story. Thanks to that device, the screenplay is even better than the short story. This prompted me to tell Al Ruddy, 'Go ahead, mount the production. It will be my next film. I'll do it right away; I am ready'.

Did you rework the screenplay with Paul Haggis?
No, he is the only author. I liked the screenplay as it was. Paul asked me if I wanted him to rewrite certain scenes and I said no. He was surprised. The author of *Bird* [Joel Oliansky] had been just as surprised, and even annoyed, because I wanted to film his first draft! He would say, 'I can make it better'. So I had to insist, 'I don't want you to improve it! I like it as it is! Don't change anything!' Paul is a good writer, and I've hired him for my next project, *Flags of Our Fathers*.

After the happy experience of Mystic River*, you didn't seem to be in a great hurry to go back in front of the camera.*
I had so much fun at just playing the director that I thought my days as an actor were behind me. But this part in *Million Dollar Baby*, I just couldn't resist it. I told myself, 'I'm still going to do that one, and it will be my last'. Who knows?

You are always attracted by subjects where your female partners play substantial roles.
The stronger the female part, the stronger the drama. I learned that from the movies of the 1930s and '40s, which were so rich in strong actresses, from Bette Davis to Ingrid Bergman. That principle got lost in the 1960s, when male camaraderie became the rage. In this regard, Hilary Swank was a good choice. She had already been approached when I committed to the project. She was willing, but I asked to meet her anyway. I liked her straight away. She looked athletic, had good leg movements, but seemed quite skinny to me. I told her, 'We are going to put a little weight on you'. During three or four months she trained seriously: a protein diet, two hours of boxing, two hours of weight-lifting, etc. She gained eighteen or nineteen pounds to reach the appropriate shape. I admired her determination, and knew very quickly that she was the character. She grew into a good boxer. Everything you see Maggie doing on screen is Hilary's work. She never had a double.

As you filmed it, this story could take place in any era. It could be in the 1930s, during the Depression…
… or in the 1940s or '50s. Except for the makes of the cars in the parking lot, the era remains undetermined. That's how I viewed that story. There was no contemporary motif, only an old gym and characters living on the periphery of society. We created our own gym, a funky gym of old, with none of the modern features. When scouting locations, I'd seen two or three of them that were OK, but not very photogenic. So we ended up building a set in a warehouse unearthed by Henry Bumstead. Henry is eighty-nine years old, as you know, and he is a genius. I didn't want to travel all the way to Missouri, where the trailer park was supposed to be, and we spotted one near Pasadena. Thus, we found everything we needed in the vicinity of Los Angeles. That's what they used to do in the golden days. What he couldn't find in Burbank, Raoul Walsh would go and shoot in a Pasadena park, and it's there, in the botanical gardens, that he filmed the war [for *Objective, Burma!*].

You remain true to the ideal of the great storytellers of the classic Hollywood tradition, the ideal of the invisible camera and invisible editing.
I prefer the concise and fluid quality of the films made in that era, particularly the style of films noirs. There are many camera moves in *Million Dollar Baby*, but you don't notice them, probably because I avoided any arbitrary moves. What's important is the story and the characters.

A rare and noticeably expressive camera angle is the vertical crane shot from above the ring before the vicious blow. Is this the point of view of 'God' or one of fate's premonitory signs?
It was a chance, before getting into the third act, to pull back,

to distance ourselves, just as the story is about to take a radically different turn and enter another dimension.

Isn't it, like Mystic River, *a very American story? Maggie achieves her dream, however high the cost might be, while Frankie and Scrap look for a second chance.*
It is a chance for redemption, yes. That's how it felt to me. Their universe is a piece of Americana that no one knows. But it is there, downtown in the heart of Los Angeles, right under our noses – like the *Fat City* community in Stockton. While I was location scouting, I bumped into a seventy-five-year-old trainer named Don Familton. He was the spitting image of Frankie Dunn! He asked me if there was something he could do for us. I told him, 'Go and get a tuxedo. You'll be the ring announcer.' On that day, he did his bit, and it was in the can on the first take. Lucia Rijker, who portrays Billie 'The Blue Bear', is the real deal, a tough gal. She helped us a lot too. Very rigorous and in great physical shape, Lucia was able to help Hilary train and also give her a feminine perspective on this sport.

Where does the Irish background of your character come from?
It all comes from F. X. Toole, a.k.a. Jerry Boyd, who had an Irish Catholic background. He was a 'cutman' [the trainer who cauterizes face wounds], but he had read a lot, notably Yeats and the Irish poets. He taught himself how to write. He passed away a couple of years ago. A well-known actor – Dustin Hoffman, I think – approached him to buy one of his short stories, but he preferred to make a deal with Al Ruddy because somehow they spoke the same language.

Maggie's brief existence is like a passion play. It is the first time that you attack religious questions head-on.

Above: *Million Dollar Baby*: Maggie (Hilary Swank) is Frankie's second chance.

Below right: The mystery of the Trinity: Frankie in *Million Dollar Baby*.

They enrich the drama when they are tied to the development of the characters. Frankie is estranged from both his daughter and the Church, though he goes to mass every day. He has a conflicted attitude towards religion, a love-hate attitude. That dovetails nicely into the final conflict, which is Frankie's inner conflict. Ironically, the priest who has been his antagonist is the sole person he can go to for advice, the only one he can confide in.

An additional irony is that there is more compassion in Frankie than in the priest. The latter is powerless to help him; he seems afflicted by the wooden tongue of ideologues…
He uses the usual rhetoric of the Church: 'Leave it in the hands of God.' Frankie is, of course, frustrated because it doesn't answer his questions. At the end, the priest retreats to a more practical level, where he's probably right, by warning Frankie, 'If you do this, how will you live with yourself?'

The exterminating angel of High Plains Drifter *or of* Pale Rider *has become an angel of mercy. It's a nice evolution. But conservative personalities such as commentator Rush Limbaugh or film critic Michael Medved have accused you of advocating assisted suicide.*
Not to forget euthanasia! I love to listen to extremists of the Right or the Left when they vituperate on the airwaves. In reality, I am playing a part; I am not advocating anything. I wasn't advocating vigilantism in my movies when I was running around with a Magnum 44. Medved is the typical knee-jerk conservative. I don't respect his judgement. He claims that the priest is presented like a bozo, but it's not true. The guy is well intentioned; he does what he can in that situation. What would you tell someone who would ask you such a question? Do you know what you would do in his place, or in Frankie's place? That's a real dilemma, a dilemma few people are confronted with, and that's what makes this story so interesting. I like it when a film raises questions, forces the viewer to consider an issue, but does not supply an answer.

Suffering creates a spiritual community between the three characters, a sort of trinity of pain where Maggie stands as the Christ figure.

To feel that way, one has to go beyond dogmas and what you call the party line. A guy like Medved uses the film to lash out against Hollywood, that dangerous lair of left-wingers! Frank Rich wrote a very amusing reply in *The New York Times*, which he titled: 'When Dirty Harry turns Commie!' To see *Million Dollar Baby* as a political film, from the Left or the Right, is absurd. I'd rather laugh than cry about it. Having said this, everyone is entitled to his or her opinion. It won't prevent me from carrying on.

We find again in the film the counter-society, the small group of misfits and outsiders that you have favored since The Outlaw Josey Wales. *Young Danger, it seems, is also included in it, along with the three protagonists.*
Danger comes right out of *Bronco Billy*. He's obviously retarded and is floating around out there. He's one of those dreamers that you often find in such godforsaken gyms, especially among the underprivileged and ethnic minorities. They may have only one chance in a million to succeed. Scrap tries to help Danger, just like he tries to help Maggie. He feels a deep compassion for them and also for Frankie. Because he's someone who never got his second chance, he finds it through Maggie when he helps her achieve her dream.

At the gas station in Missouri, one can read the numbers 666 and 444 on the meters of the two gas pumps – the number of the beast on the one hand, the number of the angels on the other.
It just came out that way, I can assure you. It was just the angels working for us, one of their little jokes! Someone whom I often quote said, 'Truth is in the eyes of the beholder …' [Kevin Spacey's character in *Midnight in the Garden of Good and Evil*].

Your daughter Morgan certainly looks like a little angel. Her apparition at the gas station has a magical quality. It's the happiest moment in the film.
It's Maggie as a little girl; she sees herself as she was in her youth in the Ozarks. That day, I called Dina [Mrs Eastwood] and asked her to bring Morgan down, without telling her what it was all about. I set her up in the pickup truck with the dog, who happened to belong to Hilary. There was also the father of the child, but in the end you don't see much of him because Frankie is the only father Maggie has at that stage. I never told Morgan that the camera was running. I simply guided her by signalling her to give me a look or a gesture as we moved through the scene. It worked itself out very naturally. And no, Morgan is not an Irish name. And it's

not a tribute to my friend Morgan Freeman either, although at the beginning I managed to convince him it was. In reality, it is the maiden name of Dina's mother!

Music, particularly the 'Blue Morgan' piece, contributes to bind the three characters together, to establish this communion of the afflicted we were talking about.
That was already true in *Mystic River*, where music represented a triad, the three childhood friends growing up together. I wanted the same simplicity here. Music would run under the surface of the story instead of rolling over it. But the process was a little different, more artisan-like. Gennady [Loktionov], the Russian who plays here [at the Mission Ranch piano-bar], is a very gifted jazz pianist. I played the theme of 'Blue Morgan' into his computer, and then he did arrangements with strings, cellos and oboes. We then developed it on his piano. I also called upon a young jazz guitarist named Bruce Forman. He teaches at the school next door, which is equipped with a tiny recording studio. That allowed us to experiment with various styles and to start recording some twenty minutes of music. I could then just give the CD to Joel [Cox], who was editing on his Avid in our conference room. When the editing was completed, we still had only a mock-up of the music. At that stage, Lennie [Niehaus] converted it into a real score by composing for real instruments. But he kept it as simple as possible.

At what stage do you start thinking about the music?
In this case, I started even before we were editing. After the shoot, it took Joel a couple of weeks to catch up and complete the assembly. I used that time to work at home, preparing each piece on my own before Gennady got involved. But on *Unforgiven* I wrote the theme on my way to the location, even before I started the picture. Lennie orchestrated it later. In all cases, it is always the screenplay that determines the nature and placement of the music.

As in Mystic River, *the lighting evolves throughout the film, as the characters' fate gets darker. In the third act, Frankie's face is progressively absorbed by the shadows.*
I approached the film as though it was in black and white. Tom Stern [the cinematographer] was able to get beautiful blacks, real blacks, with a new ultra-fast film. From the third act on, we started desaturating colors and darkening the set. I wanted to avoid a look that would spell 'cinema' – for instance, colors that do not exist in real life. Technicolor – especially three-strip Technicolor – can ruin a lot of pictures. In the past they avoided using it for drama, and there were good reasons for that. Today, we have more latitude, but you still have to work hard on the color scheme.

The shot of Morgan Freeman seeing you leave the hospital is not topographically situated. Scrap is standing in his own space, a kind of mental space, as though he had wanted to accomplish the same gesture as Frankie, but didn't get there first.
That space is deliberately abstract. I could have tied both actions geographically, but I didn't want anything to disturb that moment, to distract from what has just happened between Maggie and Frankie. After Frankie has disappeared, you discover the presence of Scrap, and you assume he has seen everything. You realize that he has lived the whole story from the beginning since he's the one who wrote it in the form of a letter.

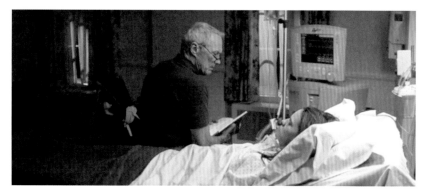

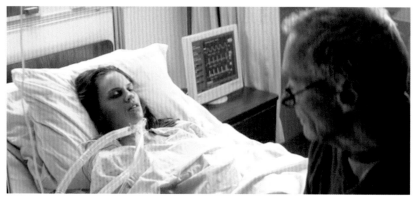

Above:
'A spiritual community': Maggie (Hilary Swank) enacting a modern-day passion in *Million Dollar Baby*. Frankie is reading to her a poem by Yeats.

Like in the endings of The Outlaw Josey Wales *and* Unforgiven, *your character vanishes mysteriously. He becomes a myth.*
I decided to use the little restaurant because it looked like a wooden cabin, similar to the one where Maggie and Frankie had planned to live together. But I had the windowpanes covered with frost so that you couldn't see who was sitting at the counter. Some think they can make out the silhouette of Frankie; others think there's no one there. Did he come back? Did he commit suicide? You remember what he said about the lemon pie, 'Now I can die and go to heaven?' Is that his paradise? I like this ambiguity. I recall, on *Josey Wales*, how Ferris Webster, the editor, kept wanting to superimpose the face of the young girl on the image of the remote ranch at the end. It wasn't necessary. I told him, 'Let the audience will Josey to go back there. That's what they'll imagine, even if he is seen riding alone and in another direction.'

Although Mystic River *was an international success, you met again with strong reticence from Warner Bros. to green-light the picture.*
They really did not want to make this film, but Tom Rosenberg, of Lakeshore Entertainment, liked the script very much; he had financed its development. The brass at Warner's thought a film about boxing wouldn't be commercial. I told them it wasn't about boxing, but about human beings. I even told the boss, 'Instead of giving the screenplay to one of your readers on the lot, why don't you let your wife read it? Ask her what she thinks about it.' He didn't do that. I warned him that I would make the film anyway, with or without the studio. I repeated to him what I had told Bob Daly and Terry Semel [CEOs of Warner Bros.] about *Bird*: 'I can't promise you that it will be a success. However, I will do everything in my power to make a good film, one that Warner Bros. will be proud of.' Rosenberg then approached the other studios, but they turned him down. It was the same refusal as for *Mystic River*. They all want to make a film with me,

but under one condition – it has to be *The Return of Dirty Harry*! Finally, Alan Horn [head of production at Warner Bros.] called me back to tell me they couldn't properly let me go elsewhere. They assumed half of the financing, with Lakeshore raising the rest. In the old days the studio wouldn't have asked so many questions, but I don't detest adversity, especially if I find a way to conquer it!

Don't they know that you are the most economical of today's filmmakers? According to your cinematographer Tom Stern, you shot only 230,000 feet of film. For the sake of comparison, James L. Brooks, on his latest comedy, Spanglish, *printed three million! Stern also says that ninety-nine per cent of the shots in* Million Dollar Baby *are first takes.*
To each his method. I don't like to be scattered; there is a point of view and I stick to it. I have a story to tell and I prefer to tell it well than to tell five different stories at the same time. I preoccupy myself only with the elements composing that story, making sure to get all of them right. There's no room for chaos or confusion if we are all on the same wavelength. You can shoot fairly quickly. It took us thirty-seven days on *Million Dollar Baby*, that is seven five-day weeks, about the same as on *Mystic River*. I think the people at Lakeshore were very pleasantly surprised. They had never experienced such an easy shoot. I do what Don Siegel did: I always try to get what I want on the first take. In most cases, it is the most interesting. I don't believe in rehearsals. There is nothing worse than to rehearse, to shoot, and then discover that the rehearsal was better than the take itself!

You work like Raoul Walsh or William Wellman.
They filmed in a way that protected themselves, making sure that the film couldn't be recut behind their backs. I know that because I worked for Wellman [on *Lafayette Escadrille*] and watched him closely. But there were two schools at the time, that of Ford, Walsh, Hawks, Wellman, and that of Stevens and Wyler, who covered themselves to a maximum, so much so that they could edit the film in several different ways. Others, like Siegel, just couldn't afford that luxury. For my part, I prefer the first school. There's no reason to leave open the option for making another film other than the one you have in your mind. In striving to manifest that vision as concretely as possible, without juggling with the actors, without letting oneself be sidetracked by this or that, you just focus on the essential.

Like the old masters, you don't seem to have any difficulty in cutting the umbilical cord once the picture is completed.
I live with the film when it's being put together, when we shoot it, when we edit it, but once it's out, it doesn't belong to me any more. It belongs to the critics and, more importantly, to the audience. They can interpret it as they like. All points of view are legitimate as long as they are shaped by the movie itself. If there is an ambiguity, and if several interpretations are possible, that's all for the better. You are seeing in it things that I never thought about, like that number 444? Great! What's important to me is that the film does justice to the story it's telling, even if it's a commercial failure, as was the case with *Honkytonk Man*. It might be rediscovered one day. Take *The Ox-Bow Incident*, or some of Walsh's best movies, to quote a few of our favorite references. They were not appreciated properly

upon their release. It's only afterwards that everybody realized that they were masterpieces.

This was also the case, among many others, of the films Ida Lupino directed. She looked grief in the face; she examined it with both minuteness and compassion, as you do in Million Dollar Baby. *What do you think of her work as a director?*
I always found her interesting. I saw her pictures *Not Wanted* and *Outrage* in my youth. When she started directing for television, I tried to get her hired on my *Rawhide* series. All the guys who were working on *Have Gun – Will Travel* were saying how great she was. She was a real dame. But our producer didn't even want to hear about a woman behind the camera. I knew her a little bit personally, and we had a good connection. I regret that we were never able to work together.

It seems to me that you have never been freer than today in your choice of projects and your approach to filmmaking.
It's probably true. I owe it to my venerable age! I have reached a stage where I have nothing to lose any more. What can they do to me at this point? I keep going forwards; I keep looking for good stories to tell. These are stories that can interest adults, not just teenagers. *Unforgiven*, for instance, seemed to me a good way to say farewell to the western genre, but if I was presented a truly original western screenplay, I might get tempted again. Finding a good story, that's the main thing. It's a matter of luck, and I have had quite a lot of it. It is also a question of instinct. In order to seize the opportunity when it presents itself, you've got to trust your inner voice. What I don't want to do is to repeat myself, to become the prisoner of a formula. There's no need for me to do sequels any more; I've done my share at the time of the Leones and the Dirty Harrys. Today, I do what I want to do and the way I want to do it. It took me some time to get there, learning little by little.

You are about to tackle Flags of Our Fathers *by James Bradley, a book that describes with great accuracy the bloodiest battle of the Pacific, the Battle of Iwo Jima.*
It is a moving book. Paul [Haggis]'s screenplay is superb; he has gone deeper into the characters and even given them a new dimension. The high point is the famous photo of the American flag raised on top of Mount Suribachi; it is the most celebrated photo of the Pacific War. Its beauty comes from the fact that these six soldiers were not posing. If the photographer had wanted to stage that moment, he would

have made sure that their faces were perfectly visible. But you practically don't see those faces; you see only their backs and their hands. They are not turning towards the camera lens because they're too busy doing their job.

What happens to the survivors after their victory is heartbreaking. The American dream turns into a nightmare.
It's an important part of the film. Of the six Marines, only three survived: a Pima Indian, a French Canadian and Doc Bradley, the father of the historian who wrote the book. When they were shipped back to the United States, the survivors were treated like heroes and recruited for an extensive bond tour. It enabled the government to raise a fortune; it is on account of that photo that they could finance the end of the war. Only Bradley managed to lead a somewhat normal life, and that was by never talking again about what he had been through at Iwo Jima. The two others were totally screwed up. They couldn't take the adulation that was poured on them. Besides, they were made many promises that were never honored. At that time there were still few psychiatrists or experts capable of identifying post-traumatic stress disorder. People expected these young vets to recover quickly and resume civilian life as if nothing had happened to them.

Each of the six characters represents a facet of the American melting pot. Isn't it an exceedingly ambitious fresco? How do you envisage the scope of the production?
It is a big piece, a real challenge, and I don't know yet how I am going to do it! The process of location hunting will begin in a few weeks and, by the end of March or early April, a visit to Japan and Iwo Jima is scheduled. The island was returned to the Japanese in 1968 but I don't know if we can shoot there. I warned Spielberg [who is co-producing the film through Dreamworks]: 'It will be more complex than *Saving Private Ryan*. Iwo Jima is thirty-four times the Normandy landing!' It took thirty-four days to conquer the island. American casualties were worse than the Japanese, which were already enormous. It was the toughest battle the Marines ever fought; a third of the Marines killed during the entire war died on Iwo Jima! Because of the need for visual effects, I am gearing up for a long post-production phase. But these effects should not overwhelm the story and the characters, which are for me the most essential elements. It won't be a video game; it won't be one of those films where they use computers to generate stupid images from the point of view of the bomb falling! I have an advantage over today's young filmmakers – I was around in that period. I was fifteen years old then. I know where these young Marines came from; they were children of the Great Depression. To convey their story, to capture their spirit, which is very different from today's, I am probably the right person.

13

'I had no mentors other than fate'
Flags of Our Fathers and *Letters from Iwo Jima*

Interviews conducted on September 29-30, and October 3, 2006

The idea of a documentary about Eastwood's creative saga had been pursuing me for a long time. It finally became a reality in the spring of 2006, on a Burbank sound stage where all the actors were speaking... Japanese. Nothing seemed more natural to our subject, who was dividing his time with an impressive serenity between the post-production of *Flags of Our Fathers* and the last shooting days of *Letters from Iwo Jima*.

Didn't this extraordinary film diptych, devoted to a page of history that affected his youth, offer a good opportunity to revisit the past and retrace some of its salient events? Didn't it call for a documentary? He acquiesced with good grace to my proposal, and a rendezvous was planned for the autumn when he would be more available for a thoughtful dialogue before my camera.

One can never stress enough the audacity of these twin films. That boldness digs even deeper because they echo each other. In *Flags*, Eastwood takes on patriotism itself, stripping the war film of its pretences in order to expose the horror of the carnage and the cynicism of government propaganda. A complex narrative sets out to untangle the truth of the combatants from the lies of officials who would use their sacrifices for political gain.

In *Letters*, Eastwood goes even further, since he makes us relive the battle from the point of view of the island's defenders. He provides the audience with the reverse shot of *Flags*: a film where 'the others', the aggressors, are the Marines! Like their antagonists, the Japanese are deceived and exploited by the propaganda machine. And for them, too, the enemy remains faceless for a long time, a distant and mysterious hydra. If their chronicle is more linear, it may be that they have no future; from the outset, their leaders have sacrificed them.

As screenwriter Paul Haggis told us about *Letters*, 'You get to love these characters, and when you see the Americans arrive and they start shooting, you would like to stop them: "No, no, don't kill them. They are not bad guys!" That is what Clint wanted, this unsettling confusion. There's not a good and a bad side. It doesn't mean anything any more on a human level.'

He added that *Letters* contained a couple of scenes that one hadn't seen yet in a war film produced in Hollywood, such as the moment where Marines execute Japanese soldiers who have just surrendered: 'I didn't think Clint would have the guts to film that or, if he did, that it would end up in the final cut. It never presented a problem for him. He is a brave, brave man.'

Only an unrepentant maverick like Eastwood could conceive this double assault against Hollywood clichés. As usual, he embraces the cause of the individual against the institution, of the common man against ideologies. And he focuses on the essential – on what connects these soldiers who couldn't see who they were killing but shared the deepest of human emotions, those that transcend all cultures.

'What were the other people thinking?' Scouting locations on the island of Iwo Jima for *Flags of Our Fathers* (2006).

Below, top: Re-creating Joe Rosenthal's historic photograph in Iceland.

Below, bottom: 'No one would have staged a shot like that.' Bill Genaust (Kirk B. R. Woller) and Joe Rosenthal (Ned Eisenberg) in Flags of Our Fathers.

During our last interview you described Flags of Our Fathers *as a challenge. Can we go back to what attracted you originally to such a complex project?*

What attracted me was the fact that it was not just a war story. The invasion plays a big part in it, because you have to show what the soldiers went through, but it is a character study of three people – people who had complexes about being celebrated when so many of their friends were killed on the island. In fact, half of the group that raised the flag had been killed soon after. So the survivors felt uneasy at being brought back to the States and treated as stars. It's somewhat analogous to a phenomenon of today, where you see celebrity being bestowed on people that haven't really done anything yet. Most celebrities at the time were either singers or motion picture actors, people who had been active for years and became popular little by little. But our three survivors found themselves in that situation all of a sudden. They were young kids, nineteen, twenty years old. It was tough for them to handle, even though a kid at twenty was considerably more mature then than a kid of today.

The film has moments of visceral impact, but at the same time you allow us to reflect on the role played by propaganda, the machinations of the state, the considerable discrepancy between individuals and institutions.

This is a story about propaganda, but I hope the film is devoid of propaganda. As far as the invasion is concerned, we're just trying to tell the fiercest battle in Marine Corps history. An operation that was estimated to be over in three or four days was still going a month later. The estimation was wrong; they had an intelligence failure. Does that sound familiar? The intelligence had estimated the Japanese force to be much smaller and no one knew that General Kuribayashi had figured out a way of tunnelling and connecting pill boxes through the island instead of attempting a beach-head defence which would have probably lasted only three or four days.

All things considered, what cemented your commitment – James Bradley's book or Paul Haggis' screenplay?

It was the book. A friend of mine who owns a small newspaper in Carmel called me up and asked if I had ever read *Flags of Our Fathers*. As I hadn't, he dropped a copy in my mailbox. I started reading it that evening. Unlike so many historical accounts, which unfold in chronological order, this one started

off with the father passing away, and his death inspired his son to investigate the past. I thought it laid itself out naturally that way. I had done fictional stories structured like that – *The Bridges of Madison County*, for instance. But here it was a true story, that of a man who never talked about his war history, not even to his wife. Doc Bradley did talk about it briefly when they were dating one night, but she sensed he didn't want to discuss it. So it was up to his son to dig in the attic, to interview witnesses, to probe the mystery. It is a period in history I have always been curious about. Though I was very young at the time, I do remember the famous photograph, and I do remember the horrendous nature of that battle. When I read the book and learnt about the other characters, Ira Hayes, René Gagnon, I realized it was my kind of material, so I tried to purchase the book, but the rights had already been bought by Dreamworks. Nothing happened with it though. It went on for a year or two, and then Steven [Spielberg] approached me one night. He asked me if I had read the book, and then said, 'Why don't you come over and direct it? You take it over and run with it, and I will produce it.' And I said, 'OK, we'll do that.' So we had a quick handshake and that's the way it came down.

Didn't Spielberg consider directing the film himself at one time?

He had several scripts written, three or four drafts, but he never got one that satisfied him. When he asked me to take it over as the director, I asked him to let me look at the material he got, but he preferred that I start from scratch with a new screenwriter. He was adamant about it. He wanted me in essence to guide it through from a different point of view. When we were in Iceland, he was in Munich. He was so caught up in his own film that he visited us only once on the set, when we were shooting at the Universal Studios.

You chose Paul Haggis to adapt the book on account of his work on Million Dollar Baby?

That's right. I told Steven that I had a very good writer and that we might talk him into taking a shot at it. He agreed, so I gave the book to Paul, who read it and was perplexed by it. There are so many different elements that he couldn't figure out how to adapt it. I told him that it would come to him in due time. So the three of us – Steven, Paul and I – sat down to talk about it. Paul told us, 'The odds for me to find a way to break it down into a script are only one to ten. If I can't find a way, I'll let you know quickly so that it doesn't burden your budget.' At the end of the first week, he hadn't made much progress. We talked on the phone, and then two weeks later, he called me back. He was starting to find his way through the material. I told him, 'Keep going, and just keep flying.' So he did, he flew right through it. His script didn't need any rewrite. We stayed with it pretty much the way it was. I made only a few adjustments when we were shooting. I always change things as I go anyway. Once I have the framework, I'm open to interpretation along the way. And so that's how we went.

At the beginning of the project, you flew to Tokyo to explain what you had in mind.

I wanted to know if we could shoot on Iwo Jima. I met with the governor of Tokyo [Shintaro Ishihara] because the island falls under his jurisdiction. He's an interesting character because he has written screenplays and even directed a film

Left: 'Heroes are something we create': Ira Hayes (Adam Beach), John Bradley (Ryan Phillippe) and René Gagnon (Jesse Bradford) in *Flags of Our Fathers*.

Below: The American Indian Ira Hayes (Adam Beach), the emotional center of *Flags of Our Fathers*.

Following pages: 'I prefer to swing in broad strokes.' Eastwood re-creates the Iwo Jima landing of *Flags of Our Fathers* in Iceland.

or two. He was very sympathetic to the idea of the film once he knew this was not going to be a propagandistic film, but a tribute to all the men who lived and died on that island. However, Iwo Jima is a sacred spot because of the vast amount of Japanese soldiers that died there. And there are still some 12,000 of them whose bodies were never found. I realized that they are never going to really be happy with a full pyrotechnics reinvasion of Iwo Jima. In the end, we filmed there only a day and a half, with a reduced crew. So we started looking elsewhere, and finally we came up with Iceland, which seemed like a long shot, like a far-out thing to do. But it proved to be very practical because Iceland has, like Iwo Jima, a geothermal soil, which excretes a lot of steam and air in various fissures, and all the beaches are black sand. Furthermore, the weather in August is similar to the one in February on Iwo Jima. We found our substitute Mount Suribachi near Keflavík. The ground is even more barren than on Iwo. It is so stark that we had to bring from California the stakes and twigs that existed on the island before it was bombed.

The tragic dimension of that story resides in the fact that the three survivors were manipulated, but for a worthy cause, the financing of the war effort. They were sacrificed on the altar of the common good.
Exactly. The government, in a slightly cynical way, used them as fundraisers. They raised a phenomenal amount of money – $22 billion! You can imagine what that would equate to now. But they did make them do a lot of strange things: they had to get up and speak to crowds; they had to climb papier mâché mountains and simulate what they were doing with fake rifles. Unless you were into the show business part of it, it must have seemed preposterous. You have to remember

that more than a million people came to applaud them in Times Square. This was kind of overwhelming. When you read John Bradley's interviews, it is obvious that he was embarrassed to receive such notoriety when so many of his buddies had given their lives. He wanted to shut it off: 'Let me go back to life, I want to go back to reality.' Even if that reality was a lot less glorious.

What comes up very strongly throughout is your compassion for those kids. They were all victims – whether they died or not.
Most of the survivors were damaged either physically or emotionally or both. But they were told to go home and get over it. Very few were able to receive some psychiatric help. They had to rely on their family or friends to readjust and forget about the experiences of war. Some of them were

Below, top
to bottom: *Sands
of Iwo Jima*
(Allan Dwan),
The Steel Helmet
(Samuel Fuller)
and *Battleground*
(WilliamWellman).

plagued for the rest of their lives and died prematurely. The Bradley character managed to bury it, to raise his family and concentrate on his job. René Gagnon had a disappointing sort of a wind down and Ira Hayes had extremely distressing experiences. These guys who came back all had one thing in common: they didn't talk about what they had endured. If you hear a guy talking about all the heroic things he did, you can pretty well be sure that he was a clerk typist or never got off the ship. Those who were out there and faced that kind of onslaught were shocked for the rest of their lives.

The Indian, Ira Hayes, becomes very quickly the emotional center of the film, maybe because he is the ultimate 'outsider'.
Well, in some ways because he was the one who resisted it. Ira Hayes was a Pima Indian of Arizona. He loved the Marines, their camaraderie and their esprit de corps. They became his family. When the war was over, he had nothing left. When René Gagnon identified him as one of the flag-raisers, Ira was appalled. He asked the others to lie, to pretend he hadn't been there. He wanted to stay with his unit even though this was a dangerous place to be. Most people would have jumped on the opportunity to get off the front lines and come back home to be treated like a hero. Not him. Pretty big for a fellow who had never left his Indian reservation before.

Didn't segregation make it even more difficult for him to handle the stress of the bond tours?
I think so. Even the military was segregated at that time, at least as far as black Americans and white Americans were concerned. Indians were theoretically exempt, but practically it was another story. I am sure it was constantly pointed out to Ira that he was a minority, but in the group he accepted that in good nature, I suppose. However, being denied entrance to a bar was a whole different issue. You have to remember that alcoholism was a scourge to Indians, who had suffered a lot because of it throughout their history. But on the other hand, this hero who was wearing the uniform of the US Marine Corps and served in their biggest battle didn't understand why he couldn't go in and have a drink like everyone else. It is a kind of bitter irony.

His long trek evokes the vagabonds of the Great Depression and the imagery of Dorothea Lange's photographs.
Ira Hayes walked and hitchhiked halfway across the country, down to eastern Texas, just to tell Harlon Block's father that, yes, it was his son who was in the picture, whereas the government had claimed it was Hank Hansen. It was such an unbelievable feat for somebody to do that, to take that kind of interest. Harlon's father was so overwhelmed that he didn't even invite Ira in. And so Ira turned around and walked his way back.

The scenes where we discover the families of those six men, their parents, their farms, are brief, but poignant. It is a forgotten America we don't see on film any more.
Those are the people in Middle America who gave up their sons to go to war and never saw them again. The country was coming out of the Depression, and these kids suddenly found themselves thrown into a war provoked by a foreign nation. They threw themselves into it with the determination to win, not knowing the horrors that awaited them. The

median age of combatants at Iwo Jima was nineteen. I tried to suggest the distress of those families. I remember, when I was a kid, how parents were getting letters from the government notifying them that their sons were killed in battle. *Flags of Our Fathers* is just the story of three of these sons. It's a little medallion of America at that time, not a fresco.

That hard life of people during the Depression and then through World War II – is it something you witnessed in your daily life when you were growing up?
They were tough times, but a kid like myself, who didn't know anything else, didn't think of them as terribly tough. Of course, you watched your parents, you watched them struggling to pay bills, put food on the table and clothes on their kids' backs. You witnessed it and then moved on. I don't think those skinny kids that came out of the Depression and went into World War II thought too much about it. They didn't know what lay ahead, the risks involved. When you're young, you don't think too much about risks anyway.

Didn't your father always say, 'You can't have anything for nothing?'
Yeah, he used to say it very strongly, 'Nothing comes from nothing. You don't get anything unless you work for it.' That was typical of the Depression-era generation. He had had a tough youth. He had to raise himself. His mother died young. His father was a hard-working guy and so was he. In those days there was no such thing as health care, welfare or social protection. You had to work hard just to get work. People were tougher then, they had a tougher attitude. My father would always tell me, 'Nobody is going to give you anything. You go out and earn it. When you look for a job, don't ask what they are going to pay you. Tell them what you want to do, how much you are going to do for their company, how you want to learn everything about the business.'

You were fifteen at the time of Iwo Jima. How did you read or hear about the developments of the war?
The newspapers and also the Movietone News when you'd go to the movies. The war in those days didn't get the coverage it gets now. It wasn't our 'information age', where they even send reporters out to be embedded among the troops. They didn't allow the press to go into battle. Joe Rosenthal, who shot the famous photograph, was quite a few echelons behind the first wave when they took Mount Suribachi.

When you talked with your buddies, did you ever think, 'When will our turn come?'
Oh yeah, all the time. And then when the war ended, everyone thought great, no more war. Of course, they have been saying that after every war for centuries, but peace doesn't seem to be in the book of mankind.

Do you remember the day Pearl Harbor was attacked?
Sure. I was eleven years old. I remember very well the attack because I was delivering magazines, I was working for *Liberty* magazine and it was my first job. The day of Pearl Harbor, I remember my dad coming home with all the newspapers from San Francisco. I remember all the headlines and the wild rumours. Everybody thought that the Japanese were off the California coast. They set up blackouts and block wardens. The windows had to be painted black, so you could turn the lights on inside. It was

Left: Like some
of Dorothea
Lange's
photographs:
Adam Beach
in *Flags of Our
Fathers*.

the first time America was attacked directly. The impact was enormous and public opinion almost unanimous in its reaction. It allowed the country to mobilize in very little time considerable military power.

There was probably a clarity about the nation's goals that has been missing since, especially with the wars in Korea, Vietnam and now Iraq.
The current war is clear – at least, what we call 'the war on terror'. We've been the victims of an attack on our soil and we know that certain powers out there don't want us around. It's clearer now than the Vietnam or Korean wars, but not so different from World War II. The difference is that the enemy of today is essentially motivated by religion, as was the case in more archaic times. My gods are better than yours. And my god is the only god and yours is inferior or not existent.

Have you looked again at Allan Dwan's Sands of Iwo Jima? With good old Duke [John Wayne]! Yes, I did watch it again and realized that only the end takes place on Iwo Jima. I think they shot on Catalina Island [off the coast of Long Beach], but they were filming in black and white and were able to skilfully blend newsreel footage from the battles of Bougainville and Tarawa. Historically speaking, they took considerable liberties. For instance, the flag that was raised was not the right one. They used the first one. The character portrayed by John Wayne met the actual trio of survivors, but he was himself a mythical character, which allowed him to be killed heroically as they reached the summit of Suribachi.

Which were the classic war films of those years that made an impression on you?
Most of the war films then contained some sort of propaganda. I preferred the ones that tried to avoid it, such as *Battleground*,

A Walk in the Sun or *The Steel Helmet*. They were nice little films that hold up well because the emphasis is on what the characters go through. Since then, I have seen lots of war films, ranging from the heroic saga in the style of *The Guns of Navarone* to the outrageous fantasy of *Where Eagles Dare*. As far as *Flags of Our Fathers* is concerned, I hope the audience will become involved because of the characters, their relationships and their veracity.

To honor their memory, says James Bradley, you have to paint the battle 'as it was', as truthfully as possible. Did the archival footage help you achieve this veracity?
I knew the documents by heart. And so did the crew. I had read so many books, I had talked to so many veterans, that I felt capable of suggesting what it felt like to land on that beach. We knew exactly what it should look like. Bummy [Henry Bumstead] and the art department did a terrific job of sculpting the berm that overlooks the Iwo Jima beaches. We were able, naturally, to get angles that you don't see in newsreels, such as shots from the enemy's point of view. Anyone trying to do that would have been immediately killed in reality. But in a movie, of course, you can get more detail, you can get in the center of the battle, and I experimented with a few techniques that I had always wanted to try but had been unable to put into practice.

You're talking about putting small digital cameras in the ammunition boxes, and having yourself and some other members of the crew carry them through the landing?
I carried them myself only on occasions, but most of the time I would assign one to extras, without telling them that they had a high-def camera in their box. I didn't want them to get artistic on me and start wondering where to point it! I just wanted them to run with it, as fast and hard as possible, without thinking about it. These digital cameras enabled us to get shots and points of view that you can't really stage.

Above: Sacrificed on the altar of the common good: Ira Hayes (Adam Beach), John Bradley (Ryan Phillippe) and René Gagnon (Jesse Bradford) in *Flags of Our Fathers*.

turned and looked at the lens, smiling. In reality, they didn't know what they were doing. They didn't even know they were being photographed because it was the second flag. Everybody had already celebrated the first flag, which had been taken down. But Rosenthal's photograph symbolized unity; it signified a great combined effort, the teamwork of ending this war. I don't think any military photograph has had a greater impact. And yet it is not an action picture, nobody is shooting.

The 'heroes' were anonymous. Everyone could identify with them.
They're just working. They are not aware of the camera. Rosenthal himself wasn't aware of what he captured. He realized it only weeks later. The same thing happened to Eddie Adams and his photograph of a Vietcong shot point-blank by a South Vietnamese officer. That was a candid shot, too, and it had a considerable impact because it depicted a certain mentality, a new phase of the war.

You often claim, 'My best films were happy accidents.'
There's no art without accidents. It happens in still photography, it happens in motion pictures. I remember once an actress told me, 'Jesus, you printed all my mistakes!' And I answered, 'They were great mistakes!' Their spontaneity was priceless. I'm often asked, 'Why are you so obsessed by the first take?' Because you never know what's going to happen, what a great surprise you might get. If it doesn't work, you'll do other takes, but they may never be as good as the first one.

Flags of Our Fathers has a non-linear, non-chronological structure, almost as complex as that of Bird. It revolves around a counterpoint between the battle and its aftermath, between the reality and its re-creation by propaganda.
That was the way the screenplay was laid out. The script of *Bird* already had interested me because it had flashbacks within flashbacks. I don't want to say it was difficult because I always think movie-making is fun, but by the same token you have to unravel it the right way or else it becomes totally confusing. Particularly when you have multiple time periods, from 1945 to the 1990s. We were just constantly moving back and forth. And rather than putting dates on the screen every five minutes, you just have to unravel it so the audience stays with it. We tried to make it as clear as possible. But the audience has to come to you a little bit on this picture; they can't just sit there and have the story thrown in their face. It requires your attention. If you enjoy being stimulated, you'll have a pleasant experience. But if you go out for popcorn, you may have a rough time picking up where you left off, so I'd say get the popcorn early and then kind of go along with it.

Did you have to change some of the transitions from the past to the present in the editing?
No, we had to stick to our structure because it had dictated how we framed our shots. You can sometimes make structural changes along the way, but in this kind of format you are married to it. It is not a story that you can take apart and put back in an absolutely linear form. So you have to put your money where your mouth is, you have to have faith in your structure and your ideas, when you are making a film like this. If you changed horses in mid-course, you'd be unravelling a puzzle you could never put back together again.

Now, what was it about Joe Rosenthal's historic photo that struck such a chord? Why that one rather than the photos of the first flag taken by Louis Lowery or the 35mm color film shot by Bill Genaust?
There were thousands of photographs taken throughout World War II, and then all of a sudden a photograph comes out and it is a work of art. It may be because of the way the flag is partly unfurling, because of the angle of the shot or especially because you knew it was a candid shot. No one would have staged a shot like that. The cameraman would have told the six soldiers, 'I can see only your hands and your backs. Turn around, look at me.' They would have all

One of the reasons the experience feels so real is that you chose faces that are mostly unknown. Was there pressure from the financiers to have the three principals played by more famous actors?

No, because it would have been prohibitive financially. Also, most of our famous actors are beyond nineteen years of age. Besides, you brought up an important point. Sometimes in a film, if you don't know the people, you're more apt to buy into them as characters. Otherwise, other images come into your head, and you go, 'Yeah, that's Brad Pitt, and there's … Angelina!' It's better when there are no images to pollute the waters.

When you are casting, you don't request to meet the person face to face. You look at their auditions on videos. Is that because of your past experience, of the discomfort an actor may feel in such a situation?

Sometimes I'll meet the actor if I don't have a good cassette on him but I like his face and I think he has the right look for the character. But if he were an experienced actor, I'd rather watch his cassette and observe what his acting technique is. Otherwise, Phyllis Huffman, my casting director, tapes the actor as he reads sections of the material. Sometimes, another actor will come and read the same material for her, and we'll splice them together just to see how they would sound like if we paired them up. In truth, I just go by instincts, by how I feel when I see and hear an actor. I also try to figure how he'll fit in the ensemble. And I take into consideration how nervous he might be. I have been there before myself. When I'm ready to hire him, I ask him to come and meet me, but in many instances I've hired actors whom I had never met before. You just have to let your gut participate in the whole process.

You don't want a line to sound as though it was written, prepared, rehearsed. It should feel as though that character uttered it for the first time, even if the actor muffles it?

Absolutely. The imperfection of it all is like real life. When you overhear a real conversation – for instance, through a door – you catch only fragments; you don't understand everything. If you shoot a scene ten or twenty times, it's very difficult to recapture the spontaneity of the first take. You have to be a really brilliant actor just to bring that spontaneity back. It doesn't mean that multiple takes are unusable, but simply that the first one is worth trying for. It was the one that filmmakers like Ford and Hawks went for. I like to capture the actor when he is still wondering, asking himself a lot of questions, rather than trying to re-create a previous take.

On the set, I never see you looking at the script. Not even that day's pages!

I keep a copy in my chair, but by the time we are starting a film, it's all here, in my head.

You work without notes?

I make mental notes. The day that I can't remember them, I'll start taking some heavy notes. I used to do that. I used to write my notes on the blank pages of the script, just to remind myself of certain shots that I needed to get. I didn't want to overlook anything. But as the years went by I realized I worked better on an impressionistic mode. You see it and you shoot it. Let the scene unravel, while staying focused and concentrated.

When I start getting analytical or too detailed with a script, it doesn't work for me. It may work for someone else, but I prefer to swing in broader strokes.

How do you prepare for a scene as complex as that of the landing? Do you draw a shot list? Does your art director design a storyboard?

No. I will do it only when there are visual effects or expensive shots that you can't afford to miss. But I didn't need it for the landing. We let it unravel naturally, filming step by step as we went. We sort of laid out a general plan, based on the nature of the location. We just slowly worked our way from the ocean right onto and up the berm, and from there we worked our way towards the field poked with shell holes where the first ambush takes place. From the top of the berm we could do reverse shots on the Marines. As we went, we kept evaluating what could happen here or there. The great thing about Steve Campanelli [the Steadicam operator] and Billy Coe [the focus puller] is that they are ready to improvise at any time. They are not afraid to run and throw themselves in the heart of the action. I can give them a free rein: 'If you see something good, go for it!' We had two great special effects guys too – Steve Riley and Mike Edmonson, our pyrotechnics man. If Mike told you not to go somewhere, you had better listen, all hell was going to break loose. I didn't really rehearse those scenes because I wanted to retain the spontaneity of it, but we'd mark certain areas for the explosive charges and instruct our troops not to step on them.

Above: A film
forcing us to look
war in the face:
*Flags of Our
Fathers*.

You were wearing a uniform through most of the shoot in Iceland.
I wasn't the only one. I had everybody wear the olive drab uniforms, the Marines' wardrobe, so that if one of the cameras picked up one of our crew members inadvertently, you wouldn't see someone standing there in a Hawaiian shirt!

Unlike most directors of today, you don't use a replay monitor. You've always tried to avoid the tribal ritual of the 'video village' where the director sits in front of his TV set, surrounded by a crowd of onlookers?
And how! If I had had one of these video villages on *Flags*, where we had 800 extras, we'd still be in Iceland shooting! I've got something much better, my small wireless monitor, it's a French object actually, which shows me exactly what the camera is seeing. So I can tell the cameraman, 'I'd like to see a two- or three-inch lens instead', and observe the result at once. When setting up the shot, I can determine immediately what works and what doesn't. It gives me great flexibility.

You dedicated Flags of Our Fathers *to your production designer Henry Bumstead and your casting director Phyllis Huffman, who both died after the shoot.*
Bummy wasn't in the greatest of health then. He needed the assistance of a wheelchair, but he was always in good humor. He was a marvellous man, with a million-dollar smile. When he was younger, at the time of *High Plains Drifter*, and we travelled together to scout locations, he was a chick magnet. He was so personable that he held under his sway all the

stewardesses. By the time the flight was ending, he'd have them all hanging around, listening to his stories about Hitchcock, Wyler and so many others. He was a walking film history. Listening to his stories on the good old studio days, it was impossible not to feel a kind of nostalgia. In the end, he made more films with me than with Hitchcock! It was nice having someone older than myself around – a sort of paternal thing.

Flags of Our Fathers *opens with a striking dream sequence.*
That nightmare wasn't in the script. The idea came to me when I was talking to an Iwo Jima vet. He told me that he had a recurring dream for sixty-one years. He hears this voice in the distance yelling, 'Corpsman, corpsman!' And he runs like crazy, but there's nobody in front of him or behind him. He turns and runs back. He does this several times, and finally wakes up in a cold sweat. According to his wife, John Bradley experienced the same kind of nightmare several times a week until his death. But he never described to anybody what the nightmare was.

At the very beginning of the film, when the screen is still totally black, a voice – which could be yours – sings a cappella 'I'll Walk Alone'. How did that magnificent idea come about?
It was in my head from the start, but I didn't have it scripted. I saw this as an experiment. Instead of opening the film with an explosion, something spectacular, we'd come into it little by little and let the picture build up to a crescendo.

Above: 'The sacrifice of youth': Saigo (Kazunari Ninomiya) and Hanako (Nae Yuuki) in *Letters from Iwo Jima.*

Opposite page: 'Language doesn't make any difference.' With Ken Watanabe on *Letters from Iwo Jima* (2006).

Because of the nature of the script, because it keeps straddling several different eras, I felt I had to call on the viewer's imagination; I had to grab his attention so that he would follow us through our meanders. So I asked a musician [Don Runner] to say the lyrics rather than sing them, as though he was thinking those words in his head. But I can assure you that it's not my voice. All I did maybe was to influence his interpretation of the lyrics. I think that song typified that period, when so many people became separated because of the war. It was probably the biggest record of that year, 1944–5. Several singers recorded it. It made Dinah Shore a big star.

In the film, James Bradley, the son, says, 'Heroes are something we create.' Do you think heroism – like truth in Midnight in the Garden of Good and Evil *– lies in the eyes of the beholder? It is as relative a notion?*
I think so. Everything is in the eyes of the beholder. We all interpret things our own way. This is precisely what got me interested in making the Japanese movie [*Letters from Iwo Jima*]. When you start delving into a subject long enough, pretty soon you start wondering, what were the other people thinking? And who was this guy who thought of the idea of hiding inside the volcano, of digging miles of underground galleries rather than fortifying the beaches or staging banzai attacks? I started researching that story. It became my hobby while I was making *Flags*. I had Paul Haggis and Iris Yamashita write a script so that by the time I had finished shooting *Flags*, I actually had a script for *Letters*. Thus I was able to segue from one to the other. I shot the second one during the post-production of the first one. It was fun to go from one to the other.

On both sides, you show young men losing their innocence, discovering a reality that had been concealed from them.
It's the same campaign and the same theme. It boils down to the futility of war and the sacrifice of youth. You look at the real photographs of the fellows on Iwo Jima, like the ones we show in the final credits of *Flags*. They were nineteen years old, but they all looked at least as though they were forty, whether they were American or Japanese.

One of the big breakthroughs in your career was a western remake of Yojimbo. *You started under the auspices of Kurosawa and now you end up making yourself a 100% Japanese film!*
I didn't mean *Letters of Iwo Jima* to be the end of my film career! But it does act as a sort of book end. However, the remake of *Yojimbo* into *A Fistful of Dollars* was in many ways the opposite of *Letters*. It was a remake, but the producers were trying to hide that fact. What is true is that I chose to do *A Fistful of Dollars* because I was a fan of *Yojimbo* and saw an opportunity to make it in the western genre. As you know, Kurosawa had a tremendous admiration for John Ford. We all copy each other. But yes, it was interesting to make a 100% Japanese film!

Originally, weren't you looking for someone else to direct Letters from Iwo Jima?
I wasn't sure. I hadn't searched extensively to get someone else, but a mutual friend of ours [Pierre Rissient] told me, 'Why don't you do it yourself? It will guarantee a consistency between the two films.' So I said OK. I must have thought it somewhat myself because I didn't ponder it too much, I just went ahead.

Tom Stern worked on both films as your cinematographer. Did you ask him for a different visual approach on Letters from Iwo Jima?
The difference was there was a lot more night shooting, and that a good part of the film took place under ground, in the tunnels. So we had a lot of interiors and he had a lot more lighting to set up. Of course, Tom has worked with me for many years. He was a gaffer for Bruce Surtees and Jack Green. He knows the way I work, so we don't need to have long discussions. But we do have conversations on the look of the film. We both make suggestions. On my films, everyone contributes; everyone comes up with ideas. It's not a one-person show by any means.

With your love of chiaroscuro and very dark interiors, you must have been in heaven in the caves of Letters from Iwo Jima!
I was! However, the Japanese had little generators to run a lighting system. We did the same thing when we found a substitute for their tunnels in caves near Barstow. It was in the old silver mine of Calico, which was in use at the end of the nineteenth century. We lived there under ground for several weeks. It was a very inexpensive production. It didn't deter the studio bosses from scratching their heads when I approached them: 'You want to do what?!' They hadn't gotten over *Mystic River* yet!

To express the Japanese's perspective on the battle, didn't you have access to letters from soldiers and officers such as General Kuribayashi and Baron Nishi?

Right: Under the auspices of Kurosawa: General Kuribayashi (Ken Watanabe) in *Letters from Iwo Jima*.

What started me on the project, what led me to want to know more, were the letters that Kuribayashi sent to his family. I discovered them in an anthology that was translated into English. He started writing them to his daughter when he lived in the United States as an envoy. He travelled extensively and illustrated his observations on the American way of life with little drawings. He liked this country. He thought that the Japanese should never go to war with America, that our industrial complex was too powerful.

You portray Kuribayashi and Nishi as elegant, morally outstanding figures, in contrast to the cliché perpetuated by so many Hollywood war films of Japanese officers as cruel monsters.
Kuribayashi's letters reveal a sensitive person, caring deeply for his family. This is true also of many letters from Japanese soldiers, enlisted men. They all had the same concerns that Americans had; they were all dreaming of getting home safely and having a life. Very few of them did. No more than 1,000 prisoners were taken, most of them Koreans who had been forcibly conscripted. As to Baron Nishi, he was a flamboyant character, who had won the gold medal in the equestrian event at the 1932 Olympics in Los Angeles. There, he became good friends with Douglas Fairbanks and Mary Pickford. He spoke several languages. And this worldly traveller who knew the cream of Hollywood ended up on this lost island.

I can't remember a Japanese movie where the protagonist questions so openly what the Army demands of him. Saigo the baker has an unusually critical mind.
Most Japanese movies are about loyalty. In reality, the lot of the besieged was not enviable. It was worse for them than for the Americans, who, by the way, were griping a lot about the conditions. It was tougher because they had been trapped for

months and knew there was no way out. So Saigo is like all the other soldiers, complaining about the heat, the lousy food, the insects. Why defend such a godforsaken place? Why not give the island to the Americans immediately?

It seems they all knew that their fight was hopeless; hence the great sadness of their story.
Kuribayashi's strategy consisted in delaying the inevitable as long as he could, in sparing his homeland, continental Japan, from being bombarded for a few more days. He knew the island would be taken, but wanted the invader to pay a very high price. He also wanted, after the fall of Mount Suribachi, that survivors regroup and join him in the north of the island, rather than commit *seppuku* as demanded by the old-school officers. He was very much a modernist and didn't believe in sacrificing human lives in vain.

Wasn't Kuribayashi inspired by the ideal of the samurais he counted among his ancestors?
Yes, I think so. The Japanese have a very strong spiritual feeling towards the deceased. When I was on Iwo Jima, I visited their memorial. There I saw a bottle of whisky with its cap off, a full bottle of whisky. I marvelled that no one ever picked it up in passing. They told me that it was for the spirits to enjoy a drink. It's very different from our American mentality. We would try and pick up souvenirs, like a bugle or a sword. With them, everything remains untouched, in deference for the spirit of the departed. The day we were shooting on the island, we went down into what used to be General Kuribayashi's cave. You had to crawl through a small claustrophobic tunnel and then you came into a rather large cave with a small memorial and a desk, which still had his personal objects. Ken Watanabe [who plays Kuribayashi] had

brought a bottle of water and he poured it on the memorial. Well, it turned out he had brought this water from Kuribayashi's native province. The Japanese may have forgotten what these men did historically, but they are still very close to them spiritually.

There's never been a Japanese film on Iwo Jima?
For them, the battle is not a subject of discussion. It's not even an historical event. They don't teach it in school. My actors had never read, never seen anything on Iwo Jima. After the war the country was in a state of shock and its history was put into a state of holding pattern for years. With this film we are beginning to resurrect it for a young generation that is curious about what their forefathers did. They want to understand for what reasons, good or bad, they sacrificed their lives.

Didn't Ken Watanabe help you by doing extensive research on his own?
I thought he would be the ideal actor to embody Kuribayashi. When he accepted the role he showed great enthusiasm not only for his character, but also for the film itself. He wasn't an actor just doing a job. He put his heart and soul into it, and worked very hard to ensure that everything would be authentic. He helped a lot with the other Japanese, explaining to them what it was all about. He became, quite naturally, the general of the island, a position that he certainly enjoyed.

Was casting Letters *more difficult given that auditions and recordings were conducted in Japanese?*
Not really. You look at faces you like. You don't understand exactly the words they use, but you know the story and

dialogue. I can tell if the actor has the spark that I want for his role. Language doesn't make any difference. Certainly Sergio Leone didn't speak English, but he did a lot of pictures with English-speaking actors. I found most of our Japanese actors extraordinarily disciplined. Once they were hired, they all did extensive research. And Ken [Watanabe] helped them deal with the language of the time, which was quite different from current Japanese.

What kind of adjustments did that imply in your methods?
Acting is acting, whatever you are speaking. When I did *A Fistful of Dollars*, several languages were spoken on the set, and we were eventually all dubbed into English, French, Italian, etc. I realized then that it forces you to listen to others with more attention. But on *Letters* it had to be entirely in Japanese. Someone suggested, 'Don't you want to shoot two takes, one in English and one in Japanese?' and I said, 'No, it's way too many things to think about.' Plus many of our actors didn't speak any English, so it would have been a struggle for them. But acting or storytelling is something universal. Honesty always comes across. Every culture has its idiosyncrasies, but they are easily transcended.

Have you encountered any surprises in the editing process on either Flags *or* Letters?
Not that I can think of. Editing is the last phase of the process, but not necessarily the most important. I already have it in mind when I am shooting. There are cases where certain changes are made in the editing, but the film is certainly not conceived at that stage. Sometimes, an idea comes to you belatedly, or a scene turned out better than expected, and you give it more importance. When you have worked on as many films as I have and for as long, you know not to become fixated

Right: Going
against
Hollywood
stereotypes:
Baron Nishi
(Tsuyoshi Ihara)
in *Letters from
Iwo Jima*.

Opposite page:
The underground
galleries of
*Letters from Iwo
Jima* were re-
created in an old
silver mine
in California.

on such or such scene. It is possible that a scene is not as well lit as another, but it is the general atmosphere that counts. It is the same for the actors and for all the other departments. What's important is for all the elements to be integrated in a coherent fashion. You must always have in mind the global effect you want to create.

Stanley Kubrick believed that editing is what makes film a specific art form.
Well, it's the final thing. You have gathered all the pieces of your puzzle and you mold it until it comes out the way you want it. But I don't think it's the whole art form. You depend just as much on every other department because it's an ensemble type of painting. People in different departments are helping you obtain the result you are looking for. If one of them fails, it throws everything out of kilter. On the other hand, if everybody works well together, then you can talk about art. I think the editing is just the icing on the cake.

Isn't it like jazz? You have to be thoroughly prepared and yet flexible, totally open to your collaborators' suggestions?
Exactly. A jazz musician has to know the music and if possible the lyrics, but his interpretation may be different each time. It is the same thing here. If I were back shooting this or that shot over again, I would probably light it very differently.

Do you think that jazz helped you retain your spontaneity as a filmmaker?
Yes, I think so, as opposed to classical music where every chord is structured, every note is written out, and you have to be in absolute sync with the orchestra. In jazz, especially as a soloist, you are much freer to interpret within the bars you are playing.

From actor to producer, from director to composer, you have grown to control every aspect of a film's creation.
I got into being the composer because I got into tailoring the music the way I heard it for the film. If I brought in someone else, I'd have to explain what I wanted, and he'd have to interpret what he thought I was talking about. In a couple of instances, I just did it myself and it worked out OK.

You could have had a career as a musician.
I played as a kid, certain things came to me pretty well [see chapter 5 on *Bird*], but then at that stage in my life I didn't have the discipline needed to move to another level. I don't know whether I was more interested in girls or whatever, but for some reason I could never do the practice that is required to become a professional. However, I've been very lucky for a guy who was too lazy to practise. I did play in Carnegie Hall and I've done compositions for my films. So I have no complaints.

On Flags of Our Fathers, *when did you start conceiving the music?*
I had the source music lined up before shooting. Then I started thinking about original themes. It's when we were editing the film that I started writing at home at night. I would take the material to Bruce Forman. I would play it on the piano, he would play it on the guitar and he'd jot down some notes to make sure he had it right. After having run through it, he'd rehearse the piece until he knew it perfectly. At that stage I encouraged him to do his own interpretation. He would use the theme, but play within it. For instance, when we were out on the prairies of Texas, where Ira is hitchhiking his way, the theme took on a Southwestern feel, whereas elsewhere it is more melancholy, particularly in the moments we spend with Bradley Senior at home before he passes away.

Opposite page: Tapping into emotions that are stronger than any ideology: Kazunari Ninomiya in *Letters from Iwo Jima*.

Left: 'He put his heart and soul into it': Ken Watanabe in *Letters from Iwo Jima*.

You called on your son Kyle for the score of Flags of Our Fathers. His group performed two pieces. His piano player was classically trained, so I could say, 'Play it like Chopin' when it was written like Chopin. When it came to the trumpet, several of us played it – I did a bit, Andrew [McCormack] did, and Mike [Stevens] did too. *Flags* is probably the first Marine Corps film that doesn't play 'From the Halls of Montezuma, to the Shores of Tripoli'. I didn't want to get into that kind of expanse. In the final credits, when you see Rosenthal's photograph, I just have that little song … do do do do … which stops in the middle and just dies. That was my tribute to that photograph and to the Marine Corps. The whole picture is a tribute to the people who died on the island and to the people who lived on it and who made it through. It's a tribute to everyone.

It seems to me that you are freer today than you ever were.
Once you get to a certain age, they're afraid to say anything to you, they just figure you're a grouchy old man. Maybe it's just a certain seniority you get after a while. Also if you have turned out a few things that have been successful, people are less inclined to tamper with what you're doing too much.

Do you see yourself as a bridge between the old Hollywood and the new Hollywood?
If I have been a bridge between the old and the new, I think I've reverted more towards the old. I long for the days when the studios would hire a lot of writers and come up with new things all the time. I'd rather entertain new stories and new ideas than repeat or reinterpret ones that have been filmed, as has become the norm today. That's why I've never gotten in on the remake game though I've been asked to on several occasions, particularly classic films. Why remake them if they were great the first time?

When you choose projects, you rely more than ever on your intuition?
Intuition plays a very important part. You have to go with your feelings. It's not an intellectual art form. It can be, I guess, in some ways. You can analyze the material as you would do for a play or a novel, but basically it's your instincts that tell you where to go. My gut has saved me a few times in my life. It saved me, for instance, when I was going to study to be an actor. I remember I called my father to tell him I was going to drop out of school and study acting. He said, 'Oh, don't get caught up in all that dream stuff', and I replied, 'I have no illusions, but it is something I want to fool with. Why not?' Years later, he laughed about it, and it was fun to watch him laugh. I wasn't trying to prove anything. My gut just told me to go in that direction. Whatever you want to call it, a feeling deep inside or a little angel talking into my ear …

Retrospectively, was there any role or any film that you felt was a creative breakthrough?
I would say doing the television series *Rawhide* was a breakthrough for me because it was the first steady job that I had had. I felt very fortunate to work every week on a new episode, to learn a lot about acting and filmmaking, to be able to exercise myself as an actor day after day, even if the material was not always great, even if you had to work hard to make it work, even if you had to force things along. Then, just when the series was winding down and I was searching for something else, I was offered the Sergio Leone films and that kicked me off in another direction. It was the same genre as *Rawhide*, but a very different approach. The films had such an impact that I was able to move out into other genres and try other things. Sometimes, these attempts were great exercises, particularly *The Beguiled*. They were great fun to

try. Not everyone gets such an opportunity. Some thought I was crazy to do them. If you listen to the wrong advisors in life, you may end up thinking, 'I shouldn't do that part because it isn't me; it isn't what I became established in.' I remember that when I was doing *Every Which Way But Loose*, which was an odd little project, all my advisors tried to dissuade me. They said, 'Don't do that picture, it isn't you', and I answered, 'Well, what is me? Am I supposed to just run around and wield a gun for the rest of my life? Am I condemned to redo something that has already worked for me?' You got to keep pushing and reaching out to other audiences and trying different things. That would be the advice I would give to any young person who is trying to get into a career in film or theater. Keep pushing; keep expanding yourself until you run out of ideas. I am here at this stage of life. I still haven't run out of ideas. New ideas come along and I love to embrace them.

A number of your films – probably the most beautiful – are 'Americanas'. You've always paid attention to the heartland. Does that interest come from your roots?

To interest me, a story doesn't have to take place in some large urban area. There are interesting stories going on out there in small towns or in the wide-open spaces that no one is addressing. As you know, I like changes. I'll try any kind of story, whether it's an urban drama like *Mystic River*, or a more intimate story like *Million Dollar Baby*, which feels almost rural because the characters are lost in an urban area. These two broken down guys in their broken down gym, this young girl who wants to become a boxer, they form an odd group on the fringes of society. I must say they were hard pictures to get made because financiers didn't jump on them. They didn't have a wild pitch. It wasn't *Mission Impossible* with all sorts of gadgetry and visual effects. They were just common little stories, but they had an emotional life to them. I don't know why I tell these stories, maybe because no one else does any more.

Do you think the American dream worked for you?

I think so. That dream works for a lot of people, a lot of businesses. I am thinking of these computer wizards who start in their garage, build a company in Silicon Valley and make a fortune … I guess that's one form of the American dream. There are also other forms where you are successful not in monetary terms, but in completing a project you have had a dream about. You can still do that here.

When you look back at your career, what were the most gratifying moments?

The biggest break for me was being able to work in something I liked. I liked being an actor; I enjoyed the Walter Mittyesque aspect of it [in the film *The Secret Life of Walter Mitty*, Danny Kaye dreams of playing many different parts], the opportunity to fantasize your way into a lot of different adventures. To be able to work at something you enjoy doing, and being paid for it, is a great privilege. A lot of jobs I worked on in my life I didn't enjoy at all, but I did them because you had to survive. In my early years as an actor it was a feast or famine deal, and mostly famine. But I was fortunate enough to get into a position where I could be successful and work constantly. Then came filmmaking. I loved directing films and addressing these subjects you and I have talked about, all these dilemmas that mankind is faced with. It's been a great privilege for me to be able to do that, too. Certainly no one in my family ever did that before me and I don't know if any of them will do after. Getting into the arts, either into drama or into music, is something that I wish I had looked at earlier in life. My son became a musician and I see the fun he's having with it now. I am glad he did that at a young age. At least he got an idea of where he was going early. I never knew where I was going to go, I sort of fell into it, I fell into life. Life came along. It made me a fatalist. I believe fate takes a big hand and guides you. I had no mentors other than fate.

14

'Until they send me to pasture ...'
Changeling

Interview conducted on June 20, 2008

The monochromatic set of the County Hospital where I find Eastwood in December (2007) sends shivers down the spine. Limiting his palette to various nuances of muted green, production designer James Murakami has re-created inside a closed-down pavilion the Psychotic Ward where Christine Collins was forcibly locked up. Without make-up and dressed only in their nightshirts (the color of oatmeal, naturally), the female extras have no trouble passing for mental patients.

This general desaturation doesn't seem to affect Clint's good spirits. He takes time to stress for us the authenticity of every detail, from the daily memos where patients were referred to as 'idiots' to draconian regulations making it perfectly clear that 'insolence will not be tolerated'. This bleak purgatory is not some jail in a totalitarian state, but one of the shameful secrets of our fair city of Los Angeles in 1928.

A true story, a judicial file, a film noir riddled with visions of horror, *Changeling* is not constricted by any genre. As with most of the filmmaker's strongest films, it is essentially a long journey into grief and bereavement. But this time the protagonist is a mother and she is confronted with dilemmas that Eastwood commonly allots to fathers: the abuse of power, police misconduct, child molestation, the death penalty ... Furthermore, this is a mother that dares to defy the taboos of her time and rebel against a deeply flawed system.

Injustice wears two masks, that of the serial killer and that of the police. Christine's lost child is victimized, not only by a psychopath, but also by the authorities that stop the investigation after having thrust upon her an impostor, and strive to place her in the position of the accused as soon as she questions their actions. Christine is as cruelly manipulated by Captain Jones as by the murderous Gordon Northcott. The scandal *par excellence* in Eastwood's world, the boundary between justice and injustice has been erased. The protectors have become the persecutors.

Of the City of Angels, we will see only the darker side. First, the heroine discovers her solidarity with an intractable prostitute; then, in a much more traumatic encounter, with the pervert himself. This unwitting communion is conveyed visually at the moment when the psychiatric cell closes in on Christine as an impenetrable barrier. It culminates later in a striking shot, one fraught with a terrible irony, where she finds herself framed behind bars immediately after her confrontation with Northcott has ended: she has taken his place in San Quentin, just as she had taken his in the asylum.

The monster will go to hell, after having done his best to drag his victims down with him. If Christine is able to resist, she owes it both to her personal courage and to a collective movement. Somehow, her struggle against corruption has mobilized outsiders like herself, stirring up a coalition of the righteous: a strange 'family' that is not so dissimilar to the one raised by the Pale Rider or Josey Wales.

'One of our rare actresses who could have thrived in the Hollywood of yesteryear.'
Angelina Jolie in *Changeling* (2008).

Initially, the project was developed by producer Brian Grazer for Ron Howard. How did it land in your lap?
Ron Howard called me one day to recommend this script that he liked very much. I restrained myself from asking him why he didn't want to make it himself. I simply answered, 'Send it to me.' I read it on the plane, flying back from the Berlin Festival where I had presented *Letters from Iwo Jima*. My agent, Lenny [Hirshan], who had already read it, tried to discourage me from reading it. But I had promised an answer to Ron so I did read it, in one stretch. Then I turned to Lenny, 'You know, I like it.' 'You do?' he said, quite surprised. 'Yes, I like it a lot.' So he kept mum. This was not the first time that we have had opposite reactions! When I came back here, Ron had gone to shoot *Frost/Nixon*, but I reached Brian and simply told him, 'I like the project, I'll do it.' I hung up before he could bombard me with questions.

Had Angelina Jolie already committed to the project at this stage?
They asked me whom I saw in the part of Christine Collins. I had several candidates in mind, but first I asked them who had read the script. They answered that Angelina Jolie had read and liked it. We stopped there because Angelina was perfect for me. I like her work and I could see her in a period film. She's so beautiful to look at that we tend to underrate her. She is one of our rare actresses who could have thrived in the Hollywood of yesteryear. She reminds me of the stars of the 1940s – Katharine Hepburn, Bette Davis and Ingrid Bergman, who each had a strong individuality, an original style, and a different type of beauty. Plus, Angelina has a good sense of humor. You heard me kid her on the set: 'How's Angie Dickinson?' or 'Go and get the Tomb Raider!'

What struck your fancy when you first read the script?
It had the particularity of containing, between the pages, lots of press clippings, articles from the *Los Angeles Times*, the *Herald* and other local papers of the time covering the many aspects of the case. Everything Joe [Michael Straczynski] had written was based on actual facts. That fascinated me. Once I became involved, he continued his research in the press of the era. It led me to make the film as honest as possible. Sometimes, we got really lucky. For instance, for the part of Gordon Northcott, the murderer, we got someone who bears an eerie resemblance to him and is also an excellent actor, Jason Butler Harner.

Did you have Straczynski do rewrites on the script?
None whatsoever. When I like a script, as you know, I leave it alone. It was a good job. Joe was very sensitive in the way he assembled all the elements of a complex case and gave the piece a dramatic pulse. As he laid it out, the soul of the story was really the love of a mother for her child.

Isn't it strange that this drama was forgotten for so long?
It was discussed a lot at the end of the 1920s, but it had so much horror that contemporaries erased it from their memory. The case couldn't carry the kind of fascination that gripped people after the war when the Black Dahlia was murdered. Besides, with the Great Depression upon them, they had a lot of other worries. Joe found out about it per chance, when one of his friends at the *Los Angeles Times* invited him to go through stacks of old files that the paper was about to get rid of. That was a lucky break because there are no more witnesses, no more survivors we can talk to.

This dark story contradicts the mythology perpetuated by movies for so long about the Jazz Age, the Roaring Twenties or

California's so-called Golden Age.
This case is a godsend for a screenwriter. Some of those scenes are so strange. They are the kind you would concoct if you were writing fiction. Sometimes, truth really is stranger than fiction. Christine Collins did get locked up in a psychiatric ward because she refused to recognize the impostor and even though she had proved that he couldn't be her son. Reverend Briegleb did exist. He even wrote a book about the case. Joe discovered that this evangelist was constantly at odds with the establishment, whether it be the police or city hall. He had a radio show and may have had a weakness for celebrities, particularly from Hollywood. Was he an opportunist? I don't know what his motives were. What I focused on is that he fought against police corruption in Los Angeles.

It is hard to imagine that the city was once ruled as a police state, one where cops and gangsters happily shared the spoils.
It may have to do with geography. San Francisco was then the cultural and financial center of the West Coast, whereas Los Angeles was more on the fringe, isolated all the way down in the left corner of the country. But the speeches delivered in the film by the chief of police, James Davis, were uttered in reality, textually. Like when he says, 'I don't want criminals in the streets. I want them killed right on the spot. Anybody who doesn't go along with this will suffer the consequences.' Same deal with the tirades of his second-in-command, Captain Jones, or the comments of Doctor Tarr, the one who supported the LAPD against Christine. They all came from their statements to the press or to judges.

Christine Collins was a single mother. What part did this play in the denial of justice?
A considerable part. At that time, a woman raising her child alone had the whole system against her. Her independence certainly made her a target. The police thought they would easily manipulate her and achieve what they wanted. They would have succeeded if she hadn't received support from the Reverend, if he hadn't encouraged her to stand up and fight. About Christine's husband we know practically nothing. He might have been in jail at the time.

The viewer knows from the outset that Christine is a victim because we've seen her at length interacting with her real son, Walter. Did you ever consider a different approach that would have preserved a certain degree of ambiguity, where, for instance, one would not see her with Walter before the abduction?
I didn't want to disorient the audience on that level. Let them wonder, yes, but about the child they substituted for Walter rather than about her. Do you realize the gall of that kid, the length of his journey to Hollywood, and what it took to manipulate all these adults? He wanted to meet Tom Mix, that's authentic! And he did tell the press that it was the police that pressed him to pose as Walter. Rather than cast a doubt on Christine's mental state, I wanted you to share her emotions, to be on her side when she tries to prove that she is not crazy.

The irony of the situation is that an expert in communication, a professional whose job is to connect people, finds herself incommunicado, deprived from any contact with the world.
She is cut off from everything until the moment when she regains access to certain means of communication. Then she is able to resist. Briegleb's campaign on the radio, the newspapers' interest in her case, her own press conference, all that contributed to turn the situation in her favor.

The abuses committed by the judicial system have always made you indignant – ever since Dirty Harry.
The corruption that Harry battled was not worse than that of the 1920s. It is almost a tradition in Los Angeles. I remember that at the time of the *Dirty Harry* sequels I talked at length with a retired cop named Dan Bowser, an eccentric fellow who had lost an eye in a shooting. He was part of a secret group that answered only to the mayor and whose members had been recruited within each police department. The criterion for recruitment was their skill at blending in an underworld milieu. They had to look and behave like street people. Once they fitted in, they were given all sorts of wild missions. We used some of Dan's anecdotes in *The Enforcer*.

The vigilantism of policemen enacting their own brand of justice in Changeling *recalls the premise of* Magnum Force.
That's true, but *Magnum Force* was actually inspired by the example of Brazil and its infamous death squadrons. What you observe, when you take a close look at history, is that such police corruption is a cyclical phenomenon in Los Angeles. It keeps rearing its ugly head. We saw it again recently when the Rampart Division's scandals were in the news.

It rains all the time in Changeling, *though the story takes place in March or April. Does this derive from your research on the spring of 1928?*
No! It is very unlikely that it rained so much that spring. It never rains in LA! However, I couldn't picture Christine being sent off to the psychiatric ward on one of our gorgeously sunny days. You will admit that rain is more in tune with the sadness of this story. But once you're inside the hospital, everything is like it was at the time, including hydrotherapy treatments and electroshocks, which were then called 'electro-convulsive therapy'.

This story contains several archetypal elements of film noir. A sudden twist turns the life of the heroine into a nightmare. Then she starts meeting mirror-characters such as the prostitute (Amy Ryan) or even the criminal who claims that he identifies with her.
It did happen like that. I read the book that Clinton Duffy, the warden of San Quentin, wrote on the penitentiary. It has a whole chapter on Gordon Northcott, whom he couldn't

Below: A sadistic
game: Christine
Collins faces
Gordon Northcott
(Jason Butler
Harner) in
Changeling.

stand and described as a sleazeball. Actually, Northcott had two mothers come up, Christine and another one, under the guise of telling them the truth. In both cases, he reneged and played a sadistic game with them. I don't know if Christine did push him against the wall, but it seemed right to me after everything he had inflicted on her.

The execution is as meticulously realistic as in True Crime.
There too, we stuck to the facts. We don't know Northcott's exact words, but he did lose his cool when he went up the stairs of the gallows. He didn't go quietly. Perhaps the monstrosity of his crimes justified the capital punishment, but what I've always found barbarous is that the families of the victims are invited to witness the execution. How in the world can that help them overcome their grief and regain some kind of serenity? The reality of the execution can only have the opposite effect. It is horrible to look at, and it is that horror that I wanted to focus on as precisely as possible.

If a ray of hope is experienced at the end of the film, it comes from the victory of the heroine over the forces that tried to crush her. The victory of the individual over the system. But what happened to Christine Collins in real life?
We don't know. I wish I could have talked to her, found out what she was thinking. According to Joe, she probably died of a heart failure shortly after the end of our story. At any rate, she didn't have the happy later years that anybody would have hoped for her. In the film, Angelina is so beautiful that you think she must still have some life before her. We also wanted to suggest that she might be able to start again with the boss at her company. But it is up to the audience to draw its own conclusions and write the rest of the story.

Your music score enables us to share the solitude and melancholy of this aggrieved mother. How did it come about?
Very simply. I still like writing music. I compose a little bit every day if I can. I'll sit down and fiddle with something. If I like the melody and I am in the process of shooting or editing, I'll consider incorporating it in the film. I'll play it in the synthesizer and I'll give this mock-up to real musicians so that they can complete the orchestration. My son Kyle, who is an excellent musician, and his partner Michael Stevens give me a hand. That's how we work it out.

What were some of the challenges in re-creating the Los Angeles of the 1920s?
Nothing that we couldn't solve. As you well know, I lived here in the 1930s, but I was a little too young to remember. These were the days when my father was pumping gas at the station on the corner of Sunset Boulevard and the Pacific Coast Highway. Then I came back to LA in the 1950s. The red streetcars were still running. There was only one freeway, the Arroyo Seco Freeway, between LA and Pasadena. Downtown was dominated by the City Hall building. There were no skyscrapers like in New York or Chicago. It was still a mostly horizontal city. I like to find snippets of it, here and there, in the great films noirs of the time: *This Gun for Hire*, *White Heat* … For this film, what I couldn't find locally near Downtown we re-created with computer graphics. We are still working on it. I have to screen later today some of the images of Los Angeles that appear under the end credits. We are adding details to the streets and buildings. On one of the shots, for instance, you'll be able to see a movie theater playing the film Christine liked so much, Capra's *It Happened One Night*.

Apart from special effects, have you ever been tempted to forgo film and go digital?
I haven't shot yet in digital video, except for a few special effects. However, after the shoot, I do work on the digital intermediate to time it. That's what we did when we remastered the *Dirty Harry* series. You can greatly improve the visual aspects of an old film. As for digital cameras, I haven't found one so far that really satisfies me, but I do test them as soon as a new one comes on the market. It is certainly the future,

particularly for 3D, but I'm still attached to film. Except maybe in low-light scenes, I have never had focus problems; I shoot mostly with hard lenses anyway. When film students ask me this kind of question, I always tell them that there are no rules. Good movies come out of what you're feeling in the moment. One day, a cameraman stopped me: 'You can't do that. You're going to cross the line.' What line? What was he talking about? The rule about spatial continuity? It must have been the eighth film I was directing, but I didn't know it existed. You do the right thing automatically, without being conscious of it. So to make a point, I deliberately crossed the line and violated the 180-degree rule!

Without consulting each other, Angelina Jolie and Amy Ryan both told us that Changeling *was the least stressful shoot they had ever experienced. Both were particularly impressed by the silence and the concentration that you maintain on the set.*
It comes from my experiences as an actor. It goes back to my *Rawhide* days. Picture us shooting a scene where you have four horsemen riding towards the camera as they talk. Not a complicated set-up to put together, but as soon as the word 'action' was uttered, the horses would go crazy or fly out, and you had to start again. We were not getting anywhere, so I told the director to stop yelling 'action', to just wave with his hand. I couldn't get through to him. We had to redo the shot the next day and, guess what, it was chaos again. On movie sets who makes the most noise? The assistant director, because he is trying to shush everybody. If he shut up, it would all be quiet. I remember an evening when I was invited to the White House. I don't know who was president. Hoover, maybe? No, it must have been Gerald Ford. The room was perfectly quiet, even though the Secret Service men around us were all talking between one another. They had tiny headsets. You couldn't hear them. When I got back to Hollywood, I told everybody that from now on we were going to use the same technology. No more open mikes, no more walkie-talkies running when we are in the middle of a take. This is how I have been working ever since. I don't even utter the words 'action' and 'cut'. In some instances, notably when I'm dealing with children, whose attention span is limited, I don't say anything. They don't even know that they are being filmed. I'd rather that they don't prepare. It's also true, to a large extent, with professional actors. I prefer that they take the plunge before they have a chance to overthink it. They give their very best when they are not too conscious of what they are doing. I have been spoiled by actors like Gene Hackman or Morgan Freeman who are great on the first take. Some like to do ten or fifteen takes, which allows them to demonstrate their technique, but the last ones are not necessarily the best. Often the best is the one where you are exploring and trying to find your way. I have always appreciated the directors who worked that way with me. Did the filmmakers we revere, guys like Ford, Walsh or Wilder, work like that? I don't know, but their method, whatever it was, certainly seemed to work for them. In any case, it is mine, and will remain so until they send me to pasture.

Thank God, retirement is nowhere on your horizon. You have just celebrated your seventy-eighth birthday, but your projects only seem to multiply.
At that age, Capra and Wilder had been put to pasture. They were still sharp, though. I never understood why we were

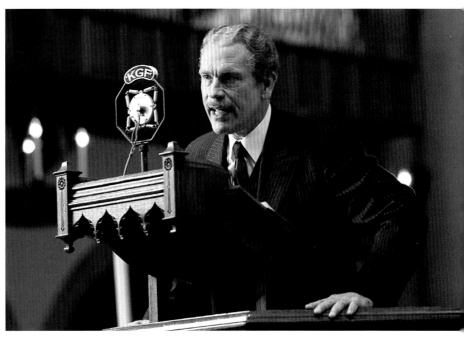

deprived so early of their talent. In my case, there was a time when I had difficulty finding a good script, but now luckily I'm able to move from one project to another. I don't have to do only genre films any more. I can choose whatever I want, and that gives me great pleasure. This is why I'm getting ready to shoot *Gran Torino* this summer in Michigan. Yes, it will be a 'comeback' for me as an actor, still another one! I like the part, that of a Korean War vet who is very incorrect politically but becomes involved with a community of Laotian Hmongs in his neighborhood. I've got the right age for the part, but this crazy guy is everything I'm not. As was Inspector Harry Callahan. Which makes it much more fun to play!

You will embark next on a huge story, the transformation of South Africa at the time of Nelson Mandela's accession to the presidency.
Morgan Freeman called me one day and asked me to read this script [*The Human Factor*] he liked very much. It deals with the transition period, when the country moves from the apartheid regime to a democracy where blacks hold the majority. Everywhere, in all the ministries and administrations, whites are emptying their desks, convinced that they are about to be fired, that the time for revenge has come for the blacks. But Mandela surprises everybody. He retains the good civil servants and dismisses the ones that are not. He even keeps de Klerk's white bodyguards, much to the chagrin of his own bodyguards. Thanks to his pragmatism, the man who was vilified as 'a terrorist renegade' reveals himself a great statesman. And that will serve him well when South Africa hosts the Rugby World Cup [1995]. Except for one player, theirs is an all-white team, the Springboks, and it has been banned from international competitions for nearly twenty years. Now it is invited to play amid the best teams because such is the privilege of the host nation. Mandela sees there an opportunity to unify the whole country. He has to inspire that white team, a bunch of poorly trained, demoralized losers; to see to it that the players surpass themselves and reach the finals against the toughest team ever, New Zealand's All Blacks. It is a great project and I'm going to do my best to realize its potential.

Above: John Malkovich as Reverend Briegleb, who came to the defence of Christine Collins against the police.

15

'You are never too old to learn'
Gran Torino

Interview conducted on December 2, 2008

This dark horse of a movie comes to us from the heart of the Rust Belt in Detroit. Shot very quickly and without any publicity during the lengthy post-production of *Changeling*, *Gran Torino* might have been perceived at the time as a mere interlude between two more ambitious projects. Not only did it become the biggest commercial success Eastwood has ever enjoyed in his career as a director, but it also proved to be much bolder than expected with its depth and complexity of emotional range. Book-ended by a funeral service, the dramatic journey starts on a mode of derision, nearly a parody, but it slowly comes into focus, sharpening, deepening and growing into a tragedy that echoes many of Eastwood's previous works.

The first half-hour seems to play with the notion of a seventy-year-old Dirty Harry, but it is only the beginning of an itinerary across blue-collar America, during which the prejudices of a racist misanthropist all come into question. Walt Kowalski is more dead than alive, but he is granted a second chance and, maybe, in a magnificent finale, a Christ-like redemption. He owes this resurrection to his neighbors, Hmong [ethnic group living on the border of Laos and Vietnam] immigrants who, ironically, are also left-overs from an Asian war. What he receives from them is a lesson in history and cultural relativity. In mixing with these 'barbarians' he used to despise, Walt regains his humanity – and in return sacrifices his life for them.

In the meantime, we see the Dirty Harry persona crack and slowly peel off its acrimony. As the mask starts falling, it reveals several of the roles Eastwood has explored throughout the years: the dissident that begrudgingly inherits a family of have-nots (*Josey Wales*); the blood-coughing uncle who undertakes a teenager's education as a substitute father (*Honkytonk Man*); the tormented Catholic who has no use for a young priest's bland homilies (*Million Dollar Baby*); the Korean war veteran who doesn't recognize any more the country he shed his blood for (*Heartbreak Ridge*); the killer who can't escape his past and the atrocities he perpetrated in the 'heart of darkness' (*Unforgiven*)…

In *Gran Torino*, Eastwood appears to be revisiting some of the key stages of his creative journey with the insight of maturity. We soon realize that the drama also mirrors the evolution of the heartland and maybe that of the American cinema. As Walt is conversing with the Italian barber or the Irish foreman, we are reminded of yesteryear's Americanas, notably John Ford's, but this widower is missing a family, and he is a Catholic without faith, a soldier without a cause, a relic of the 1950s without a community. A sign of the times, he sits alone on his porch when night falls … at least, as long as he remains entrenched in his old ways and ignores the life that blooms around him in new forms and colors.

'This crazy guy is everything I'm not.' Walt Kowalski, the cantankerous veteran of *Gran Torino* (2008).

Right: 'We see in
Gran Torino
the Dirty Harry
persona slowly
peel off
its acrimony.'

How did Nick Schenk's screenplay come to you?
A friend of the writer had called Lenny Hirshan and ran the story by him. As Lenny wasn't too excited by the idea, she went to Bill Gerber [veteran Warner Bros. production executive], who knows me. Bill gave it to Rob Lorenz [producer and Eastwood's right arm at Malpaso] who read it that night and told me the next morning that it was an interesting piece but 'terribly politically incorrect'. I said, 'Well, that doesn't bother me. Political correctness is boring!' He also said the main character was interesting, but he kind of downplayed it. So I said, 'Let me look at it.' I read it and thought, 'I like where it's going, what it's saying.' The next day, I just said, 'Let's do it.' They contacted the writer, bought the script, and we were off and running. It all happened very quickly in a two-day period.

Originally, Nick Schenk had set the story in Minneapolis rather than Detroit. Did you make other changes?
No, we didn't touch the screenplay. I assume he chose Minneapolis because there's a large Hmong population there. We just made it a Detroit neighborhood. Walt Kowalski, the character, really belonged there. He had worked in the Ford factory for fifty years, helped build the Gran Torino, retired not far from the plant. Also, Michigan was offering good tax incentives for filming in the state. I said, 'Lets go look at Michigan.' So Rob [Lorenz] and Tim Moore [executive producer] went over there, looked around, and found everything we needed, including a fairly good population of Hmongs. In the end we cast people from Detroit, Minneapolis, St. Paul and also Fresno, which has a very large Hmong community.

The three automobile giants used to symbolize America's industrial might. So Detroit was an appropriate setting, especially now that that sector has been decimated by the recession. Your character embodies the changes that the country has undergone since the 1950s and '60s.
Walt is very upset about the way his world has gone. He grew up in a neighborhood that was populated by automobile employees, with probably a high percentage of Polish Americans among them. Now, when he looks around, he sees that everything has changed, and for the worst in his opinion. He cherishes his Gran Torino, once a very popular car, but lets it sit in the garage, content with shining it up once in a while. It is the symbol of another time, another America, different values. We picked Highland Park for our location and it served our purpose well. That neighborhood used to be more affluent, it housed a lot of automobile makers, families that were all interconnected. Now it is a depressed area, as depressed as the car industry itself. It all lined up very well.

The character is the last incarnation of a lost America and its blue-collar culture. You capture that beautifully in his interactions at the barbershop. Like in John Ford's Americanas, you get a real sense of the male community, of a vanishing world with its own rules, rituals, even language.
It is a sort of lost America. There are still places like that, men like that, but we don't see them that often any more on the screen. In the John Ford era they used to portray that world because they were doing films about the Depression and the working class. They dealt with the common man out there in the field, whereas today most movies are trying to present the uncommon man.

The barber is Italian, the foreman is Irish, Walt is Polish, yet you feel a solidarity between these old-timers because they have become a threatened white minority. The future belongs to these mysterious Asians that have taken over the neighborhood.
Exactly. I myself didn't know too much about the Hmongs, only that they had helped the Americans in Laos and Thailand during the Vietnam War. Thanks to this project, I got to learn a lot more about their culture and philosophy. They are not a nation, but they have their own language, their own religion. They were brought here as refugees at the end of the conflict. The Lutheran Church worked hard to facilitate their resettlement, but they have been through many hardships. They are a very resilient, determined people.

At first, your cantankerous character sounds like a caricature, but we soon discover what is behind the mask and see him evolve considerably. Isn't that range what made the part so compelling for you as an actor?
Yes, I liked that. I always like to have a character that is full of prejudice, that is totally polarized in one direction. There is plenty of room for him to change. I also believe that you

are never too old to learn things in life. You learn something every day. That's what the film is about, constantly learning, constantly evolving, no matter what your age.

His Asian neighbors are the ones teaching him some of these lessons and offering him a second chance.
The irony of course is that the people next door don't want anything from Walt, they just want to be happy, whereas his own family is fighting over what few items he owns. At first he doesn't want to have anything to do with these Asians. He starts changing when he realizes that they are tough, intelligent and respectful of others. There's a great line in the film that sums it up. 'I have more in common,' he says, 'with these people than I do with my own spoiled, rotten children.' They become his family. And he ends up giving his life for them.

Walt swears like Sergeant Highway in Heartbreak Ridge*, coughs blood like the* Honkytonk Man*, he even spits like Josey Wales … There are so many echoes of your earlier roles that one wonders if the script was actually written for you.*
The writer claims that it wasn't tailored for me, but some people suspect that it was. It does seem like it was written for me, doesn't it? (Laughter.) However, I am sure you could have found another actor of my age to do that part.

Did you see a connection, for instance, between the two Korean vets, Walt Kowalski and Sergeant Highway?
A little bit. Walt is an older version of Sergeant Highway, what he could have become. They don't have the same background, but both are kind of hard-ass guys, guys who find it very hard to accept change.

Like the killer of Unforgiven*, Walt is racked by guilt, haunted by atrocities he committed in the past.*
I do think there is a parallel between this and *Unforgiven*. Like Walt, William Munny was a widower who claimed that his deceased wife kept him on the straight and narrow. In reality, neither of them has overcome the traumas of their violent past. When Walt sees these Asian people next door, he can't help taking offence. He is travelling back in time and fighting the Korean War all over again.

Like Frankie in Million Dollar Baby*, Walt is a Catholic but has a hard time relating to his Church or to his priest.*
Walt has great doubts about religion because of his experiences in the war. He just became cynical. Although Frankie had a contentious relationship with his priest, he expected something from him. Walt Kowalski just doesn't care. 'What the hell, I'll stay home, I'm not interested.' Father Janovich tries very hard to get him to confession, but Walt thinks he's a kid right out of seminary school and calls him … 'a twenty-seven-year-old over-educated virgin'! In the end, Walt does it his way.

Did you want to give the finale a mystical dimension?
Yes, it becomes a tragedy and calls for a sacrifice. I approached it that way.

Below: 'They become his family.' Introducing Ahney Her, who plays Sue in *Gran Torino*.

Your character lies on his back in death, his arms spread out in a Christ-like fashion.
Right, it's like a crucifixion.

Somehow, we are again in Dirty Harry *territory. Harry, too, was identified with Christ when he was beaten up under a huge crucifix. Here, the young priest suspects that Walt will do what Harry would do – take justice into his own hands. But Walt does it in a totally unexpected way, the opposite way. Did you see* Gran Torino *as a response to* Dirty Harry?
I was aware of the connections, but I approached Walt like a totally different guy. Dirty Harry was a disappointed idealist. He had his own ideas about what law enforcement should be and he fought against a bureaucratic system that had bogged everything down. Walt Kowalski couldn't care less about all that. He just thinks, 'I will take it into my own hands.' He's a realist, he doesn't count on the police. He wouldn't expect them to stop a crime in progress. They rarely do. They only show up afterwards to figure out who did what to whom.

There is a low-angle shot on Walt when he is stomping on one of the gangbangers. Is this a deliberate quote from the stadium scene in Dirty Harry?
I don't know. Maybe on a subconscious level, but basically it is a subjective shot from the point of view of the gang member. In *Dirty Harry* there was something else, and it was something I came up with. I felt Harry would have to torture the guy [Scorpio] to find out where the missing girl was.

So you are responsible for the sadism of the scene!
Don Siegel loved it because I was always doing something to make myself unglamorous. Most of the actors he worked with

were trying to protect their image. He said, 'You don't seem to care about your image', and I said, 'I don't. I don't like conscious images, I like raw emotion.'

Gran Torino's *visual look recalls* Mystic River. *It is quite gritty. Was stark realism what you were after?*
Absolutely. There should be no glamour about it. We went for a lot of deep blacks. It is not quite as desaturated as *Mystic River*, but we did go in the same direction. Of course the most desaturated I ever got was *Letters from Iwo Jima*. That was World War II and I almost wanted to go black and white.

Wasn't Gran Torino *one of your fastest shoots ever?*
It was pretty fast – thirty-two days. Some of my early films, like *Play Misty*, were in that range of five weeks. *Breezy* might have been four and a half weeks. Believe me, if I had needed forty or fifty days, I would have taken the time, but I didn't need it for this one. It was present-day, not complicated to shoot. It's just the story of this one crazy character. It seemed to move along. I had fun making it. As you know, I like it when it moves along and we go to some new place every day.

You were working with many non-professional actors, particularly the youngsters from the Hmong family. How did you prepare them?
Ahney Her [who plays Sue] had done some plays in school, and Bee Vang [Thao] might have done something, but they hadn't done a whole lot. They were sixteen. I looked at the videos of their auditions and thought that they would be able to do the parts. I also knew that once they owned the roles, they would study them and become better, which is

true also with professional actors. When I finally met with the kids for the first time, I told them what we were going to do and how. Then, along the way, I just made corrections here and there, but basically they brought a lot of natural talent to it. They were both so bright that they just adapted. Yes, I did give them some room to develop their character, but less than I would with a more experienced actor.

Were there instances where you didn't even tell them the cameras were rolling?
Oh yes, many times. I move along so fast and roll so quietly that they don't have a chance to think too much. I would roll silently whenever possible, especially if I saw actors and extras waiting together and interacting, for instance in the family living-room. I would just wave at Stephen Campanelli [Steadicam operator] and he would turn on the camera and capture scenes where they are not acting, just being natural. I do that all the time. I'm sure I'll do that again in South Africa with my players on the rugby field!

From an actor's perspective, would you say Gran Torino *was one of your most rewarding roles?*
I don't know, they have all been rewarding. I liked Frankie Dunn in *Million Dollar Baby*, too. because he is estranged from his family and finds a daughter in this girl from a poor background. Even though he disapproves of women in boxing, she becomes like family, and he becomes the father she didn't have. I always approached it as a father–daughter love story, and that was difficult in the beginning because people thought it was a girl-boxing movie. To me it was not a girl-boxing movie any more than *The Human Factor* [later retitled *Invictus*] will be a rugby movie. Rugby just happened to be the sport that Nelson Mandela was dealing with at the time of the World Cup.

Are you surprised by the extraordinary reception Gran Torino *is getting?*
Yes, I am. I didn't know if anyone was going to like it. I am always surprised. I just had to make it satisfying for myself. Naturally, you want people to like it, but you can't make it with that in mind. You have to make it with the story you want to tell. If people put an ear to it, fine. If they don't, you are just telling it for yourself, expressing your own personal feelings.

Below: 'A lesson in history and cultural relativity.' Walt Kowalski alone on his porch as night falls.

16

'The world needs leaders like Mandela'
Invictus

Interview conducted on August 24, 2009

Film after film, Eastwood has dwelled on the torments of violence and injustice that have been seared upon the soul of its victims or perpetrators. In Nelson Mandela, Eastwood finds an exemplary hero: a law-abiding individual (and a lawyer to boot) who is transformed into an outlaw when he rebels against an odious system. Viewed as a terrorist by the oppressors and a freedom fighter by the oppressed, he paid dearly for his dissidence: police harassment, multiple arrests and trials, and a total of twenty-seven years of imprisonment…

However, this victim repudiated the primitive response of 'an eye for an eye'. He chose dialogue and forgiveness over hatred and revenge. It was in his Robben Island cell that he understood that the oppressor must be liberated, just as much as the oppressed, as both have been robbed of their humanity. Once released, he made the enemy who had persecuted him a partner in the peace process. Such magnanimity spared South Africa a bloodbath and gave birth to the 'Rainbow Nation'. It is no wonder that it astonished the world and fascinated Eastwood.

At the beginning of *Invictus* the white minority has just ceded power to the black majority after more than three centuries of supremacy. It was an almost miraculous transition for it was accomplished with a minimum of violence in spite of the threats of civil war raised by extremists on all sides. Mandela included in his strategy the 1995 Rugby World Cup where the Springboks – a hated symbol of apartheid – soared from victory to victory. For the first time, a sports triumph united South Africans of all races and creeds in an explosion of joy and pride.

Parallel to *Invictus*, I embark on *Reconciliation*, a documentary tracing the processes of the spirit of reconciliation that Mandela was able to impart to the whole country, from Robben Island's penitentiary to the painful catharsis of the Truth and Reconciliation Commission. It is an opportunity to meet some remarkable survivors and witnesses: Archbishop Desmond Tutu, F. W. de Klerk, Mandela's cellmates, lawyers and advisers, his bodyguards and former warden, and, of course, Morné du Plessis and François Pienaar, the former manager and captain (respectively) of the Springboks.

On my visits to the *Invictus* set in Cape Town, I share with Clint some of these testimonies. But it is only at the end of the summer, when he is finishing mixing *Invictus* in Burbank, that I get a chance to interview him properly. Other journeys are in store for him because he has already started preparing *Hereafter*. The beginning of the shoot – above Chamonix – coincides with his being honored by the Institut Lumière in Lyon with the first Lumière d'Or.

'A million-dollar smile that makes everyone feel happy when they are around him.' Morgan Freeman as Nelson Mandela in *Invictus* (2009).

How did this Mandela project come to you? Was it in the form of John Carlin's book, Playing the Enemy, *or Anthony Peckham's script, which was at the time called* The Human Factor?

I got a call from Morgan Freeman. 'I have a really good script', he said, 'and I'd like you to take a look at it.' I didn't know what it was about. Rather than get into a lengthy discussion, I just said, 'Well, send it over.' I started reading it and liked what it was about, so I went on to read John Carlin's book, which was based on the same material and had been written simultaneously. Then I started reading other material too, researching the 1994–5 period, Nelson Mandela's first year in his presidency. I was particularly focused on the Rugby World Cup as Mandela was instrumental in inspiring the South African team to rise above what were then considered serious limitations.

What was the spark for you? The personality of Nelson Mandela? The rugby tournament of 1995? The political strategies that helped reshape a nation?

I've always viewed Nelson Mandela as a fascinating character. In researching him, I came to learn a lot about him that I didn't know. I had read a book a long time ago that had stayed with me. It was about his experiences in jail. I remember being very interested in his philosophy, the way he handled life in prison and then conceived a unique approach to reuniting his country. This was a much tougher challenge than anyone could imagine because in these last years of apartheid, everyone was up in arms. The whites were suspicious of where the blacks were going, and the blacks, of course, suspicious of what the whites might do when they would lose their privileges. It was a monumental task to bring these communities together. This is when his sense of strategy, his diplomacy, his inspirational abilities came into play.

It is rare to find a statesman who is both a visionary and a pragmatist. Do you think this is why he succeeded in keeping the country together?

Absolutely. Idealism is one thing, but to be able to weave in and out of such a quagmire requires a very pragmatic soul. He is just an amazing guy. This was a man who had spent the best years of his life in prison. Then all of sudden he was released, at age seventy-six, and had to embark on a whole new life. He started out as a president at an age when most people have given up on the idea of running for politics.

Your old friend Morgan Freeman had been wanting to do a film about Mandela for years. Were you ever involved in the script's development?

No. I knew Morgan and his group were working on it, but not the details. I know that the screenplay was well documented, that they were striving for accuracy. And nobody ever doubted that if anyone were to play Mandela it would be Morgan Freeman. They don't look exactly alike, but there are certain similarities in their height and stature, and they both have a certain presence, a certain charisma that makes Morgan the ideal person to play Mandela. Mandela of course has a wonderful presence, sort of a million-dollar smile that makes everyone feel happy when they are around him. That's what it takes to play that kind of character.

Interestingly, Morgan Freeman directed a film over there, Bopha!, *which told the story of a black policeman betrayed by his racist superiors during the apartheid. He made it in 1993 just before Mandela's election.*

Yes, he did. In fact, that was right after we did *Unforgiven*. He wanted to try the director's job, so he went off and did

Bopha! over there. So he was much more familiar with South Africa than I was, that's for sure.

From the Darwinian world of Unforgiven *to the forgiveness of* Invictus, *do you see a natural progression?*
When it comes to violence, these films are at opposite ends of the spectrum. *Unforgiven* was definitely a regression, and I hope people see in this one a break from the old notion of an eye for an eye. Look at how Mandela found ways of using what was a predominantly white sporting event to inspire the whole country to get behind it through the World Cup. Many thought he was crazy because he was embracing the white minority's favorite sport.

He actually confronted his own party, the ANC, when they voted to ban the Springboks, which was then viewed as the symbol of white supremacy.
The whole black population rooted against the Springboks. Mandela himself joked about rooting against them. Every time they lost, they all cheered. After the elections [of 1994], they tried to get rid of the team, to ban their emblems and colors, but Mandela didn't feel that way. His purpose was to reunify the country. He didn't want to alienate the white minority. For the same reason, he kept in place the old regime's civil servants instead of replacing them with his people.

Before you embarked on this project, what was your image of Nelson Mandela? Had you been following closely his political struggles?
Not that closely, but even from an outsider's point of view, he was certainly one of the most charismatic political figures that the world has ever known. What struck me, in particular, was the fact that he was imprisoned for so long in the company of many other intellectuals and educated people that had fought against apartheid. They had nothing to do but read and educate one another. It was such a strong group of people that even their jailers ended up learning from them. They told us great stories about that. And for Mandela to come out of prison after twenty-seven years and forgive the people who imprisoned him and invite his immediate jailer to his own inauguration was something most people can't fathom. Most people could never be so forgiving.

In the film, Mandela states, 'Forgiveness liberates the soul. It removes fear, this is why it is such a powerful weapon.' Do you think forgiveness is the highest form of self-interest? Or, in other words, the most effective way to heal yourself when you have been wronged?
I don't know. It is Mandela's philosophy. He just didn't want to perpetuate the animosity that was raging in the country, the deep animosity between whites and blacks that the apartheid system had fuelled. He wanted to show all his people that they were better than that, that they could overcome their racial divisions and be reunited through forgiveness.

You actually met Mandela when you were in South Africa. Can you tell us about the encounter?
He resides in Johannesburg, but he came down to Cape Town and we all met one Sunday: Morgan Freeman, who knew him well, Matt Damon and his family, my family and me. We all

ONE TEAM ONE COUNTRY

went over and hung out for a little while and it was very, very nice. He is a man in his early nineties, but he still looks fantastic. He is still a great charismatic presence. When you meet him, you feel, oh yeah, this is what it's all about.

How much did he know about the film you were making?
He knew about the project, of course. I am sure he approved it, but there were other people there so we didn't get a chance to be specific. I couldn't run things by him. I just assumed, when he approved the project, that it fit the way he saw it. And so I wasn't going to pester him any more about it. By that time I had a line on the picture, I was about halfway through the film. I knew where I was headed with it, and I hoped that would be the way he would go for it.

What were your impressions of Robben Island's penitentiary where Mandela was incarcerated for years?
Robben Island is a uniquely isolated place. The nearest comparison would probably be Alcatraz, but it's not a rock. It is a little more hospitable. It has got animals and all kinds of bird life. Anyway, a prison is the worst place to be in if you are locked up twenty-four hours a day and have to do hard labor in a quarry for years. But the warders I talked to actually liked the job because they were close to Cape Town and could even kayak around to other local beaches.

Above: Mandela used the Springboks team and the 1995 Rugby World Cup to inspire the whole country.

Left: 'When our players went into the townships and began training the youngsters, the kids got really into the game and forgot they were being filmed.'

Right: Clint
Eastwood on the
set of *Invictus*.

*It is a highly symbolic moment in your story when the Springboks
are taken to the island to visit the prison and Mandela's cell.*
All these young players underwent some kind of experience
on that trip. They come to understand what it must have been
to be a prisoner for some twenty-seven years. With the
exception of Chester Williams, the sole 'colored' team member,
they were all white South Africans, raised in the apartheid
era, whose fathers and grandfathers had all approved of
apartheid. As François Pienaar [the captain of the team] says
in the film, 'Times change. We have to change too.'

*At that point, François Pienaar [Matt Damon] seems to be
undergoing an awakening. Is he tormented by guilt to the point
that he imagines himself as one of the warders?*
Not really. We tried something along those lines at one point,
but decided not to use it in the film. That idea is already
conveyed in more subtle ways. You realize that François
Pienaar becomes aware of what it must have been like to be
jailed in those conditions. He gets a better understanding of
what Mandela went through. And also a better understanding
of 'Invictus', the poem by William Ernest Henley, which was
Mandela's favorite. Mandela had given it to him as an
inspiration for rugby.

*Amazingly, Mandela conceived of the reconciliation process
while incarcerated on Robben Island. This is where he started
learning Afrikaans, the language of apartheid, and strove to
establish a human contact with his warders. He was already
trying to build a bridge between the oppressed and the oppressor,
the victims and the perpetrators.*
He certainly succeeded. I think he looked for that bridge early
in the game while he was a prisoner, and when he got out
and was elected president, he kept building it. Many blacks
refused to learn Afrikaans because it was the enemy's language,
and most whites didn't bother to learn Xhosa or Zulu. But
here is Mandela who learned Afrikaans, and his country's
other languages, so that he could communicate with
everybody in their own languages. He even changed the
national anthem so that it would combine a hymn in Xhosa
and a song in Afrikaans. He knew that some of the measures
he instituted were not going to be popular, but he fought for
them anyway, and he won most of the time.

*Did you meet Morné du Plessis, the remarkable manager of
the team, who was instrumental in shaping the Springboks'
consciousness? It was his idea to take the team to Robben Island.
He also insisted that they do rugby clinics in the black townships.*

I played golf with him and his two sons, six-foot eight-inch
giants, all three of them. We hung out a little bit. We didn't
talk too much about the material, but Morné said he thought
it was accurate. Initially, the idea of doing the clinics and
familiarizing the youth of the country with what the game
was all about was not accepted with great enthusiasm. Most
of the team members I talked to admitted that they really
weren't anxious to do it at the time. They thought it was
beneath them, but once they got into it, they realized it was
great fun. In fact, when our own players got out there in the
townships and started training the kids, they all fell into it.
They forgot we were filming them. They weren't playing to
the cameras at all, they just went with it, and so they were
having a ball.

*Don't you think social inequalities have become the country's
greatest divide?*
The poverty in the townships reminded me of scenes from the
Great Depression in the early 1930s, when people were living
in shacks made out of tin and cigar boxes. The land is certainly
beautiful, but the country is in dire need of development.
There's a tremendous disparity of wealth, a tremendous
amount of crime, a tremendous amount of unemployment.
So they are still struggling, trying to overcome these obstacles.
Zuma was campaigning at the time when we were there and
he was elected president. I understand he is a controversial
figure. So there were mixed feelings – some thought he was
going to be terrible, others that he was going to get things
done. Only time will tell, I suppose.

*The bodyguards play an important part in your story, as a
counterpoint to the high political drama. We see the process
of reconciliation develop at the top with Mandela but also
on a much more mundane, nitty-gritty level, that of the
security teams.*
That was another interesting strategy. Instead of putting on
an all black detail composed of his cohorts, Mandela actually
brought in a lot of the bodyguards who had worked for [former
president] de Klerk. He said they had the right experience
and it was his idea of reconciliation to make the squad colorblind. At first, there was a lot of tension between the two
groups, but they learned to work together and that was the
core of our story – everybody learning to work together.

*Why were the Springboks such underdogs at the beginning of
the 1995 World Cup tournament?*
They weren't such a bad team. Perhaps they needed some
inspiration. Maybe they suffered from having been isolated
and banned from international tournaments for many years.
They hadn't been playing World Cup matches and hadn't
competed with great international teams. They just weren't
used to the kind of power that was out there around the world.
Actually, they didn't earn the right to compete in the 1995
World Cup. The reason they could participate is because they
happened to be the host country that year. And they were
going to face far superior teams, on paper anyway, from
England, Australia, France and especially New Zealand, which
was the most powerful rugby club in the world at that
particular time.

Did you ever play rugby as a youth?
I never did, but I had an uncle who played. My dad played

football and my uncle played rugby. They were always arguing about which was the better sport. Now the University of California has a terrific rugby team that is consistently at the top. There's a fellow there named Jack Clark, a former rugby player, and he's the guy I went to see when I first wanted to learn about the sport. I spent some time with him and he tuned me into what rugby was all about. He also attended the final game between New Zealand and South Africa back in 1995, so he had experienced the feelings of the crowd, the euphoria of victory. I learned a lot from him. I would watch his players and he would analyze for me what was happening on the field.

What was Chester Williams' role on your production?
He was a very important player on the Springbok team, if only because he was the only non-white player. He wasn't a really big guy by the standard of rugby players, but very fast and powerful. He acted as our adviser. The other players of 1995 were around too and I talked to them about the game. They all pretty much came up with the same opinions. François was very helpful, especially to Matt in the beginning, but during the game Chester was our coach. We staged most of the plays based upon his recollections.

The rugby players you hired were all from South Africa?
Most of them. Some had played for European clubs. Very few were actors. First and foremost, they were players and they did a good job.

We all know how much you try to get it right on the first take. Was it more difficult with rugby players that were not professional actors?
Sometimes. You want to get as much as you can on the first take. It is a rough and tumble sport with no helmets, minimal padding and a lot of injuries. Even doing it for a movie, we had injuries. With each take the risk rises that somebody will get hurt or that the moves won't match together. However, we did do a lot of takes because each game needed a proper amount of coverage in order to build up all its aspects, all its moods. In our story, each successive game becomes more difficult. So when we got to the final, Chester told the guys, 'OK, we're going to play proper rugby now, don't hold back!'

How did Matt Damon prepare for his part?
He went to Cape Town early and spent some time with François. They became quite friendly and Matt got an idea of what François' life was about, what his thoughts were at the time, what they are now. He was coached by Chester Williams and everyone was there to make sure he was OK. But at the same time he worked out constantly and stayed in really good shape as rugby players have to if they want to compete on that level. Matt also had to work with the accent. Affecting a South African accent was not easy, but I think he did a great job.

Many of the Springboks' games were very close. The semi-final against France, for instance, was 'a matter of inches' according to most witnesses, including François Pienaar.
It was very close, all of them were close. The Springboks didn't just walk over anybody. They had to hang in by tenacity. What made the semi-final in Durban special was the unusual thunderstorms. It rained so hard that the field became waterlogged. They had to bring out all these Zulu ladies with their brooms to brush it down. Then it would rain again and they would have to start all over again. Finally,

Below: Capturing
the action as
it is happening:
Eastwood with his
cinematographer
Tom Stern on the
set of *Invictus*.

there was a lull and they just decided to play. By then, it was pretty much a mud fest.

Both Morné du Plessis, the team's manager, and Edward Griffiths, the CEO of the rugby federation, started feeling that night that the fates were working on behalf of South Africa.
It was almost like fate was giving Mandela whatever he wanted and that was a victory. It was very important to him. He said that the country needed a great moment and he was determined to do anything in his power to influence it.

Wasn't it a fantastic encouragement for the team to know that Mandela was so passionately interested in their results?
It certainly was. He would make personal appearances at the stadium, talk to the players, encourage them personally. At the same time, he was trying to encourage everybody else, starting with government workers, to participate in making the country as great as it could be. And he was also travelling around the world, tirelessly trying to raise money and attract investments to South Africa. It is pretty impressive for a guy his age, don't you think, to be taking on all of this?

How do you account for South Africa's victory in the final game against the All Blacks?
The game was very close until the end with the All Blacks leading for quite some time. Joel Stransky kicked the winning goal in the game after his counterpart on the New Zealand team missed a couple of shots that would have given the All Blacks a victory. Under the pressure, Stransky managed to score. How? Every one of the Springboks just buckled down. They needed inspiration and probably got it from the

audience, who sensed that their team might have a chance of winning. As a matter of fact, François Pienaar told me that it was a miracle that they won because the New Zealanders were much stronger. They had annihilated England and had run over pretty much everybody. They had Jonah Lomu, considered the best rugby player at the time, who had been running over people like a human tank in the previous games.

Were any of the plays storyboarded beforehand?
No, it is tough to storyboard rugby because it is such a fast game. Chester would tell us what the plays were and we just put them together, designed them on the spot. Everybody just got with the program.

What were your visual references in setting up the choreography of the games? Did you watch videos of the original ones?
Yes, a lot of videos of all the games. And we do include in the film some of the real games – for instance, New Zealand's test match against England where Lomu ran wild. As we progress towards the final, and the Springboks beat all these teams that were on paper considered much stronger, the games take on a more complicated structure. But most important is the fact that the country starts waking up to what's happening. People who normally didn't pay much attention to rugby, and that was probably the case with a vast majority of the black population, started embracing a sport that had been despised as an apartheid sport.

Stephen Campanelli's Steadicam camera played a big part in the filming of the games.
We needed the mobility of the Steadicam or any handheld

camera for that matter. Just as we needed fast carts that could run ahead of the players. We used the Steadicam a lot because we wanted to move in and capture things as they were happening. You have to land on the same spot that the player lands on, so the camera operator has to be ready to constantly adjust his own moves.

Didn't you consider putting the camera inside the ball, like Abel Gance did in Napoléon, *as early as 1927?*
We tried that, but it didn't quite work out. The ball moves too fast, it spins so rapidly that the shots were a little more tricky than they needed to be. It became a bit of a distraction. Instead, we'd sometimes give one of the players a digital camera to capture the action from his point of view. That worked just as well as when we hid cameras in ammunition boxes for the landing of *Flags of Our Fathers*.

You found some interesting positions for Stephen Campanelli. For instance, you had him buried under ground, under a Plexiglas case, filming the scrum from below.
That all worked. The cameras these days are great. They are getting better and better all the time. And smaller. You can move them around any which way you want. You also have cranes that can reach into a scrum, follow any action, shoot every possible angle.

One major challenge was that you were filming your games in mostly empty stadiums. Those would be filled only much later with CGI effects.
It presented a tremendous challenge. It forces you to use your imagination, to visualize a full stadium and to shoot accordingly. Putting 62,000 people on the steps and then having them drum up the enthusiasm they are supposed to feel during a match is not feasible economically. We did have a lot of actors and extras performing in our crowds, but we needed an assist from visual effects. What helped us was having the newsreels from the original games as a reference. It gave us a good idea of how everyone felt. As you know, the day I arrived in Cape Town I was taken to a rugby game by Chester Williams. The stadium was full and I got a good overview of what it must have been like to be there for the final at Ellis Park in Johannesburg. Not all of our CGI shots have come in. We are getting them day by day. So we may have to tweak the sound a bit. Hopefully, we'll be done by the end of September.

The story is at once intimate and spectacular. What kind of musical score are you creating to express both aspects?
It's not going to be the kind of score that you would expect from an African jungle movie starring Clark Gable. It's going to be a little different and suit the sport and the characters involved. It is mostly music that has been popular over the last twenty-five years over there. We actually re-created some of the music played during the event, using the same singers. We have PJ Powers, who sung at the opening ceremony of the tournament. We are using a jazz band that Mandela liked a lot, the Soweto String Quartet. They play at a function he is attending in the film. Another group is a new a cappella band, Overtone, which we discovered in South Africa. We also have Emil Richardson, a drum aficionado who has collected every percussive instrument from around the world. Mike Stevens and Kyle Eastwood wrote some original pieces as well. We all chipped in.

Left: 'The country needed a great moment.' Morgan Freeman and Matt Damon (François Pienaar) in *Invictus*.

Why did you choose the title Invictus *instead of* The Human Factor *or* Playing the Enemy?
The Human Factor didn't say a lot, other than it was the human factor that Mandela inserted into the whole mix of turmoil and reconciliation. It didn't have any punch. *Playing the Enemy* was almost too cute for me. There is an old saying, 'A good title is the title of a hit movie.' So we can't really tell what's a good title. *Invictus* sounds mysterious, but it is a poem that was influential in Mandela's life, and it arouses a certain curiosity. You kind of want to know what it refers to. [This poem by William Ernest Henley inspired Mandela during his incarceration, particularly the verses: 'I am the master of my fate; I am the captain of my soul.']

Many of your films have dealt with the notions of justice and revenge. Taking justice into one's own hands is a temptation your characters have often succumbed to. Mandela is a rare exception who wants to break the cycle of violence and retaliation.
Mandela was thinking on a larger scale. The issue was: how do you get 43 million people to tolerate one another? They don't have to be best friends over night, but they can start respecting one another. The strong points of one group can help the weak points of another. Everybody can gain from it all. It is just very hard to achieve. I am not sure how South Africa is faring now, but Mandela certainly made a great swing at bat, taking chances in alienating some of his own supporters when he wanted to advance the reconciliation process. It didn't appeal to a lot of people, but he saw the overall picture, and that's what made him superior as a politician. He pursued his dream, the dream of putting all this together.

The greatest mystery remains the magnanimity of the man, of a leader who was able to turn his enemy into a partner.
That's a character thing. Not a lot of people could do that, but he did. He went from being a man who was considered a terrorist, an enemy of the state, to being the head of that state.

And he did it not by bringing anybody down, but by being one of the victims. It's a unique story; he is a unique person. Other than fictional characters or figures of biblical stature, it is hard to find anybody that would be in that league, really.

Do you think that his example could inspire other regions of the world, other countries that are deeply divided?
Definitely. I think the world needs leaders like him, and it would behoove a lot of politicians to emulate him. Now, whether they would be as successful, I don't know. It depends on what society they evolve in, and how clever they are. Idealism is one thing, practicality another.

Racial tolerance is something that you have illustrated, and advocated, in all your films for a long time. Do you see this one as a crowning piece in that regard?
We are still fighting for racial tolerance in most societies around the world. Even in this country, which has elected a mixed-race president, you still see people aligning with one side or another. I don't think we have come very far with it. I think we need someone with the cleverness of a Mandela to pull it off.

What can you reveal about your latest project, Hereafter?
Steven Spielberg called me to say he had a good script by Peter Morgan and he wondered if I would consider it. It was well written; it reminded me of some European films where three separate stories converge towards an ironic ending. I liked all the characters, and became interested in what they had to go through. The piece makes fun of pseudo-sciences that claim to know what awaits us at the end of the road. The only supernatural element is that the protagonist [played by Matt Damon] may be clairvoyant, seems to be able to read what is going on in people's lives. Production-wise, we'll be going all over the place. First we shoot in Paris and London, then travel with our two French actors to a tropical setting [Hawaii] for a tsunami sequence. After that, we'll go to San Francisco for scenes with Matt's character and then return to London for scenes with Matt, Cécile [de France] and the twin boys. For me, it is a new kind of story, a new direction, a new challenge.

First Steps

Clinton Eastwood Junior was born on 31 May 1930, in San Francisco. His father, a bond salesman, had a hard time finding stable work in those Great Depression years. He moved his family continually, from Bakersfield to Redding, Spokane to Sacramento. For a while, he pumped gas at a service station in Los Angeles, located at the intersection of Sunset Boulevard and the Pacific Coast Highway. Young Clint is said to have attended eight primary schools. He reflected, 'I was always the new kid on the block.'

The family finally settled near Oakland at Piedmont, where Eastwood Senior worked as a salesman in a jewelery store, then as a pipe fitter in a shipyard during World War II. After the war, he was hired by the California Container Corporation, which produced corrugated cardboard boxes. He would later become one of its executives. Eastwood Junior attended Piedmont Junior High School, then Oakland Technical High School. He held various jobs after school hours and during the holidays. One summer he labored as a lumberjack for the California State Forestry.

Eastwood inherited his passion for jazz from his mother, who collected records by Fats Waller and Art Tatum. In 1946 he discovered Charlie Parker at a 'Jazz at the Philharmonic' concert in Oakland. Abandoning the flugelhorn and the clarinet, he switched to piano. He honed his chops at the Omar Club of Oakland, where he played the blues on an informal basis. He earned pocket money by working as a lifeguard, a swimming-pool digger, an employee in a paper factory, a laborer in a steel mill, a stock taker in an aeronautical company, etc.

His military service was spent at Fort Ord, on the Monterey Peninsula. There, he met Lennie Niehaus, a young sax player who had performed with Stan Kenton. Returning from leave in Seattle, where his parents were living at the time, the Douglas AD-1 plane carrying him crashed in the ocean. He had to swim several miles to shore. While his unit was dispatched to Korea, the accident had to be investigated. Held up at Fort Ord, he was appointed as a swimming instructor and a projectionist for training films.

Freed of his military obligations in February 1953, Eastwood enrolled in a business class at the Los Angeles City College in Hollywood. He also started attending drama classes. Director Arthur Lubin spotted him and set up a screen test at the Universal Studios. Lubin soon became his unofficial agent and mentor. In April 1954, Eastwood signed with the studio a contract renewable every six months, for $75 per week. He joined a stable of young talents including David Janssen, Mamie Van Doren, Barbara Rush and John Saxon. He was also trained by acting professor Jack Kosslyn, whose teaching was centered on visualization exercises.

As a contract player, Eastwood landed small parts in Universal's B films. After a brief stint at RKO, he turned towards television. He was featured in *Allen in Movieland* (1955), *Cochise, Greatest of the Apaches* (1956, *TV Reader's Digest* series), *Motorcycle* (1956, *Highway Patrol* series), *White Fury* (1957, *West Point* series), *The Charles Avery Story* (1957, *Wagon Train* series), *The Lonely Watch* (1958, *Navy Log* series), *The Last Letter* (1958, *Death Valley Days* series) and *Duel at Sundown* (1959, *Maverick* series). In the latter, directed by Arthur Lubin, he landed a substantial part as the antagonist to James Garner's Maverick, in this case a bully named Red Hardigan. Red is the fastest gun in the county, but after having been thrashed by the hero, he cannot find the courage to face him in a duel.

Eastwood got his first lucky break when producer-director Charles Marquis Warren offered him the second lead in the TV western series *Rawhide*, that of cowboy Rowdy Yates. (For his audition, he recited one of Henry Fonda's monologues from *The Ox-Bow Incident*.) The series was to last seven years (1959–66). Eastwood appeared in most of the 217 episodes, shooting an average of thirty a year. Each episode was completed in six days. He learned his craft under the helm of such directors as Tay Garnett, Stuart Heisler, Jack Arnold, Andrew McLaglen and Ted Post. His growing popularity would also spawn the release of a long-playing record, *Rawhide's Clint Eastwood Sings Cowboy Favorites*.

The series was entering its fourth year when Eastwood was offered *The Magnificent Stranger*, a remake of *Yojimbo* as a western, which was going to be shot by an Italian at Almería, in Spain, with German financing and on a shoestring budget ($200,000). Sergio Leone, who had considered Henry Fonda at first, then James Coburn and Rory Calhoun, settled for Eastwood after noticing him in *Rawhide*. In spite of his entourage's warnings, Eastwood accepted a Spartan compensation ($15,000) and crossed the Atlantic for the first time.

It was the nonchalant attitude of the actor in the role of Rowdy Yates that had fascinated Leone. But the Italian director was quick to scrap this wholesome persona in order to fashion the mythical character of a stranger appearing from nowhere. Solitary, laconic, cynical, the Man with No Name was an anti-hero, the opposite of the earnest and naive boy from *Rawhide* whom Eastwood himself had nicknamed 'the idiot of the Prairie'. However, Leone would later acknowledge that 'the character has evolved under the influence of Clint, who is like that in real life: slow, calm, moving like a cat…'

The picture came out in September 1964, under the title *Per un pugno di dollari*, in a small neighborhood theater of Florence, without publicity or reviews, but benefited from word of mouth enthusiasm. After a few days, the miracle started… The film was to gross $7 million in Europe alone. The Man with No Name had one now, at least overseas.

Eastwood returned to the United States to pick up the *Rawhide* harness where he had left it, but Leone called him back for a second adventure, *For a Few Dollars More*, which presented the treacherous West of bounty hunters, '… garbage collectors who rid the country of all the human trash'. The perspective widened again in the last wing of the triptych, *The Good, the Bad and the Ugly*, a large picaresque fresco where the three protagonists witnessed the horrors of the Civil War. The part of Blondie was conceived for Eastwood,

Opposite page: On the set of *Bird* (1988), his most experimental work, with his cinematographer Jack Green.

but as Leone remarked, 'The good is just as much a son of a bitch as the two others.' Endowed with a hefty budget (almost $1.5 million), the picture garnered worldwide success and propelled the actor to international stardom.

Eastwood's career entered a new creative phase when he came back to the United States, where the Leone films opened belatedly (*A Fistful of Dollars* and *For a Few Dollars More* in 1967 and *The Good, the Bad and the Ugly* in 1968). In 1967 he established his production company, Malpaso. The name was a reference to the stream that crosses his property in Carmel. But it also means 'bad move' in Spanish, and some have suspected that it was directed at the producer who tried to discourage him from abandoning his TV series in favor of a spaghetti western! In Eastwood's words, the company was '... a small family enterprise, designed to make films as economically as possible'.

Reacting against the excesses he had observed during the shoot of *Paint Your Wagon*, he turned down *Mackenna's Gold*. He also declined the part of Harmonica (which fell into Charles Bronson's lap) in *Once Upon a Time in the West*, to set his heart on a more modest project, *Hang 'em High*, the subject of which recalled *The Ox-Bow Incident*. Directed by Ted Post, who had helmed many episodes of *Rawhide*, interpreted by several veterans of the series (from Pat Hingle to Bruce Dern) and financed by United Artists, which distributed Leone's films in the United States, this first Malpaso film recouped its production costs in a record ten weeks.

Eastwood was then approached by Universal, the studio where he had served his apprenticeship. He was offered *Coogan's Bluff*, which marked his first collaboration with Don Siegel. Their connection was immediate. The actor admired the director's fearlessness, his scathing irony and his capacity to focus on the essential. Of all the filmmakers he worked with, this was the one from whom he learned the most. Their fruitful association would go on with *Two Mules for Sister Sara* and *The Beguiled*. It reached its acme with *Dirty Harry*, the first instalment of a saga that was soon to become legendary. (The part was originally conceived for Frank Sinatra.) Eastwood also tried his hand at directing when he replaced Siegel, who had fallen sick, and shot a key sequence himself. On the set of *The Beguiled*, he also directed a promotional featurette, *The Storyteller*, where he celebrated Siegel's talents. They were to be reunited one last time, in 1978, for the production of *Escape from Alcatraz*.

In the meantime, Eastwood graduated to director on *Play Misty for Me* (1971). Universal agreed to finance the picture on the condition that he forgo his director's salary. He gave a supporting role to his old friend Siegel, that of the barman. Shot in Carmel and the Monterey Peninsula, the picture was completed two days ahead of schedule, on a tight budget of $1.1 million. In the US alone, it brought in sixteen times that amount.

From then on, Eastwood shared his time between projects he interpreted for others (*Joe Kidd*, *Magnum Force*, *Thunderbolt and Lightfoot*) and those he directed himself (*High Plains Drifter*, *Breezy*, *The Eiger Sanction*). In September 1975, Malpaso left the Universal lot and moved to Burbank's Warner Bros. studios, the entity that would finance or co-finance practically all of Eastwood's films from *The Outlaw Josey Wales* onwards.

Filmography

Small parts

1955

Revenge of the Creature by Jack Arnold. Uncredited part: Jennings, a lab technician. Universal.

Francis in the Navy by Arthur Lubin. Part: Jonesey, a sailor. Universal.

Lady Godiva of Coventry by Arthur Lubin. Uncredited part: first Saxon. Universal.

Tarantula by Jack Arnold. Uncredited part: squadron leader. Universal.

1956

Never Say Goodbye by Jerry Hopper. Uncredited part: Will, a lab assistant. Universal.

Away All Boats by Joseph Pevney. Uncredited part: a sailor. Universal.

The First Traveling Saleslady by Arthur Lubin. Part: Jack Rice. RKO.

Star in the Dust by Charles Haas. Uncredited part: a cowboy. Universal.

1957

Escapade in Japan by Arthur Lubin. Part: Dumbo, a pilot. RKO–Universal.

1958

Lafayette Escadrille by William Wellman. Part: George Moseley, a fighter pilot. Warner Bros.

Ambush at Cimarron Pass by Jodie Copelan. Part: Keith Williams. Fox.

1995

Casper by Brad Silberling. Uncredited cameo.

Starring roles

1964

Per un pugno di dollari (*A Fistful of Dollars*)

Dir.: Sergio Leone (under pseudonym of Bob Robertson). *Prod.*: Arrigo Colombo, Giorgio Papi. *Sc.*: Sergio Leone, Duccio Tessari, from *Yojimbo* by Akira Kurosawa (uncredited). *Ph.*: Massimo Dallamano (Technicolor, Techniscope). *Art Dir.*: Carlo Simi. *Edit.*: Roberto Cinquini. *Mus.*: Ennio Morricone. *Song* int. by Clint Eastwood: 'Sweet Betsy From Pike'.

With: Clint Eastwood (Joe, the Stranger), Gian Maria Volonté (Ramón Rojo), Marianne Koch (Marisol), José Calvo (Silvanito), Wolfgang Lukschy (John Baxter), Mario Brega (Chico), Josef Egger (Piripero), Margherita Lozano (Consuelo Baxter).

Filmed in the province of Almería (Spain) and at Cinecittà.

Dist.: United Artists. 95 mins.

At San Miguel, a border town between Texas and Mexico, two clans are vying for power, the Rojos and the Baxters. Irritated by jesters who find it amusing to frighten his mule, a wandering stranger proves to be an invincible gunman. By selling them his services, he pits the two clans into an escalating war.

1965

Per qualche dollari di più (*For a Few Dollars More*)

Dir.: Sergio Leone. *Prod.*: Alberto Grimaldi. *Sc.*: Luciano Vincenzoni, Sergio Leone, from a story by Sergio Leone and Fulvio Morsella. *Ph.*: Massimo Dallamano (Technicolor, Techniscope). *Art Dir.*: Carlo Simi. *Edit.*: Giorgio Serralonga, Eugenio Alabiso. *Mus.*: Ennio Morricone.

With: Clint Eastwood (Monco, the Stranger), Lee Van Cleef (Colonel Douglas Mortimer), Gian Maria Volonté (El Indio), Klaus Kinski (Juan, the hunchback), Josef Egger (the Prophet), Mario Brega (Nino), Rosemary Dexter (Mortimer's sister), Mara Krup (Mary), Luigi Pistilli (Groggy).

Filmed in the province of Almería (Spain) and at Cinecittà.

Dist.: United Artists. 130 mins.

'Where life had no value, death sometimes had its price.' At El Paso, the Stranger, now a bounty hunter, finds he has a rival in Colonel Mortimer, who is equipped with far more sophisticated firepower. Their target is El Indio, a particularly vicious bandit who long ago raped and killed the colonel's sister.

1966

Il buono, il brutto, il cattivo (*The Good, the Bad and the Ugly*)

Dir.: Sergio Leone. *Prod.*: Alberto Grimaldi. *Sc.*: Age, Scarpelli, Luciano Vincenzoni, Sergio Leone. *Ph.*: Tonino Delli Colli (Technicolor, Techniscope). *Art Dir.*: Carlo Simi. *Edit.*: Nino Baragli, Eugenio Alabiso. *Mus.*: Ennio Morricone.

With: Clint Eastwood (Blondie, the Good), Eli Wallach (Tuco, the Ugly), Lee Van Cleef (Sentenza, the Bad), Rada Rassimov (Maria), Aldo Giuffrè (Union officer), Mario Brega (Corporal Wallace), Luigi Pistilli (Father Ramirez).

Filmed in the provinces of Burgos and Almería (Spain) and at Cinecittà.

Dist.: United Artists. 180 mins.

During the Civil War, three adventurers gallop through the horrors of the conflict while pursuing a treasure hunt with utter disregard for the rules. The stakes are worth $200,000, and the finishing line awaits them at a cemetery. 'Sentenza is all technique, Tuco instinct, and Blondie intelligence, but they are interchangeable' (Sergio Leone).

1967

Le streghe (*The Witches*) – fifth and last sketch: 'Una sera come le altre' ('An Evening Like Any Other')

Dir.: Vittorio De Sica. *Prod.*: Dino De Laurentiis. *Sc.*: Cesare Zavattini, Enzo Muzii, Fabio Carpi. *Ph.*: Giuseppe Rotunno (Technicolor). *Art Dir.*: Piero Poletto. *Edit.*: Adriana Novelli. *Mus.*: Piero Piccioni.

With: Silvana Mangano (Giovanna), Clint Eastwood (Carlo).

Filmed at the De Laurentiis studios in Rome.

Dist.: United Artists. 19 mins.

After ten years of marriage, Giovanna is frustrated by her stay-at-home husband, who is content with his humdrum routine. (Unforgivably, he'd rather doze off than take her to see *A Fistful of Dollars*!) She is reduced to fantasizing, imagining him as a virile seducer or humiliating him by stripping in the middle of a packed stadium.

1968

Hang 'em High

Dir.: Ted Post. *Prod.*: Leonard Freeman, for Malpaso and Leonard Freeman Prod. *Prod. Ass.*: Irving Leonard. *Sc.*: Leonard Freeman, Mel Goldberg. *Ph.*: Richard Kline, Leonard South (color by DeLuxe). *Art Dir.*: John Goodman. *Edit.*: Gene Fowler, Jr. *Mus.*: Dominic Frontiere.

With: Clint Eastwood (Jed Cooper), Inger Stevens (Rachel), Ed Begley (Captain Wilson), Pat Hingle (Judge Adam Fenton), Arlene Golonka (Jennifer), James MacArthur (the Preacher), Ruth White (Madam Peaches Sophie), Bruce Dern (Miller), Alan Hale, Jr (Stone), Dennis Hopper (the Prophet), Ben Johnson (Sheriff Dave Bliss), Bob Steele (Jenkins), L. Q. Jones (Loomis), Bert Freed (Schmidt), Charles McGraw (Red Creek sheriff).

Filmed at Las Cruces, New Mexico, and at the MGM studios.

Dist.: United Artists. 114 mins.

In the Oklahoma Territory (1889), cowboy Jed Cooper, wrongly accused of a double murder, finds himself with a noose around his neck before he can clear himself. Saved and proven innocent, he accepts a sheriff's badge in the hope of taking revenge on the lynching gang, but soon discovers that official justice can be as blind as the 'eye for an eye' of vigilantism.

Coogan's Bluff

Dir. and Prod.: Don Siegel, for Malpaso. *Exec. Prod.*: Richard E. Lyons. *Sc.*: Herman Miller, Dean Riesner, Howard Rodman, from a story by Herman Miller. *Ph.*: Bud Thackery (Technicolor). *Art Dir.*: Alexander Golitzen, Robert MacKichan. *Edit.*: Sam E. Waxman. *Mus.*: Lalo Schifrin.

With: Clint Eastwood (Coogan), Lee J. Cobb (Lieutenant McElroy), Susan Clark (Julie), Tisha Sterling (Linny Raven), Don Stroud (James Ringerman), Betty Field (Mrs. Ringerman), Tom Tully (Sheriff McCrea), Melodie Johnson (Millie), Seymour Cassel (young hood).

Filmed in the Mojave Desert (California), in New York and at the Universal studios.

Dist.: Universal. 94 mins.

The desert holds no secrets for Coogan, an Arizona cop who always gets his man. But the urban jungle is another story. When he travels to New York to bring back a dangerous drug addict, he runs into the local police bureaucracy. And his Wild West methods soon prove inept or out of place.

1969

Where Eagles Dare

Dir.: Brian G. Hutton. *Prod.*: Elliott Kastner. *Sc.*: Alistair MacLean. *Ph.*: Arthur Ibbetson (Metrocolor, Panavision). *Art Dir.*: Peter Mullins. *Edit.*: John Jympson. *Mus.*: Ron Goodwin.

With: Richard Burton (John Smith), Clint Eastwood (Lieutenant Morris Schaffer), Mary Ure (Mary Elison), Ingrid Pitt (Heidi), Michael Hordern (Admiral Rolland), Patrick Wymark (Colonel Wyatt Turner), Anton Diffring (Colonel Kramer).

Filmed in Austria and London.

Dist.: MGM. 155 mins.

In 1943, the MI6 launches a shock commando unit to free a general imprisoned at the Schloss Adler, a Bavarian fortress that can be accessed only by cable car. Lieutenant Schaffer of the US Rangers is the lone American in the group, an expert in explosives and second to none when it comes to annihilating enemies with his machine-gun.

Paint Your Wagon

Dir.: Joshua Logan. *Prod., Sc. and lyrics*: Alan Jay Lerner. *Adapt.*: Paddy Chayefsky. *Ph.*: William Fraker (Technicolor, Panavision). *Art Dir.*: Carl Braunger. *Edit.*: Robert Jones. *Mus.*: Frederick Loewe, André Previn. *Songs* int. by Clint Eastwood: 'I Still See Elisa', 'I Talk to the Trees', 'Best Things', 'Gold Fever'.

With: Lee Marvin (Ben Rumson), Clint Eastwood (Pardner), Jean Seberg (Elizabeth), Harve Presnell (Rotten Luck Willie), Ray Walston (Mad Jack Duncan), Tom Ligon (Horton Fenty), Alan Dexter (parson).

Filmed in Oregon and at the Paramount studios.

Dist.: Paramount. 166 mins.

During the Gold Rush in Northern California, Ben, a seasoned prospector with an addiction to booze and women, joins forces with Sylvester, a.k.a. Pardner, the son of a farmer. The Puritanism of the wholesome country boy is seriously tested when Ben buys a young bride at an auction and offers to share her.

1970

Two Mules for Sister Sara
Dir.: Don Siegel. *Prod.*: Martin Rackin, Carroll Case, for Malpaso. *Sc.*: Albert Maltz, from a story by Budd Boetticher. *Ph.*: Gabriel Figueroa (Technicolor, Panavision). *Cam.*: Bruce Surtees. *Art Dir.*: José Rodriguez Granada. *Edit.*: Robert F. Shugrue, Juan José Marino. *Mus.*: Ennio Morricone. *Song* int. by Clint Eastwood: 'Sam Hal'.
With: Shirley MacLaine (Sara), Clint Eastwood (Hogan), Manolo Fabregas (Colonel Beltran), Alberto Morin (General LeClaire), Armando Silvestre, John Kelly, Enrique Lucero (Americans).
Filmed at Cocoyoc in Mexico and at the Universal studios.
Dist.: Universal. 114 mins.
In Mexico, under the French occupation, a Texan mercenary hired by the Juaristas saves from a rape a nun who is sympathetic to the partisans' cause. Sara proves to be full of resources, helping Hogan first to repel an Indian raid, then to attack the Chihuahua garrison on a 14th of July.

Kelly's Heroes
Dir.: Brian G. Hutton. *Prod.*: Gabriel Katzka, Sidney Beckerman. *Sc.*: Troy Kennedy Martin. *Ph.*: Gabriel Figueroa (Metrocolor, Panavision). *Prod. Des.*: Jonathan Barry. *Edit.*: John Jympson. *Mus.*: Lalo Schifrin.
With: Clint Eastwood (Kelly), Telly Savalas (Big Joe), Don Rickles (Crapgame), Carroll O'Connor (General Colt), Donald Sutherland (Oddball), Gavin MacLeod (Moriarty).
Filmed in Yugoslavia.
Dist.: MGM. 145 mins.
Lorraine, 1944. Upon learning of the existence of a treasure in gold ingots behind the German lines, soldier Kelly recruits a group of misfits to mount their own operation. With their tanks, Kelly and his cronies manage to break through enemy lines, paving the way for a victorious offensive by regular troops.

1971

The Beguiled
Dir. and Prod.: Don Siegel, for Malpaso. *Sc.*: John B. Sherry (Albert Maltz), Grimes Grice (Irene Kamp), Claude Traverse (uncredited) from the novel by Thomas Cullinan. *Ph.*: Bruce Surtees (Technicolor). *Prod. Des.*: Ted Haworth. *Art Dir.*: Alexander Golitzen. *Edit.*: Carl Pingitore. *Mus.*: Lalo Schifrin. *Song* int. by Clint Eastwood: 'The Dove'.
With: Clint Eastwood (John McBurney), Geraldine Page (Martha Farnsworth), Elizabeth Hartman (Edwina Dabney), Jo Ann Harris (Carol), Darleen Carr (Doris), Mae Mercer (Hallie), Pamelyn Ferdin (Amy), Melody Thomas (Abigail), Peggy Drier (Lizzie), Pattye Mattick (Janie).
Filmed near Baton Rouge, Louisiana.
Dist.: Universal. 109 mins.
In the deep woods of Mississippi, during the Civil War, a Union corporal with a wounded leg is sheltered in Miss Farnsworth's boarding house for young girls. He thinks that he can rule the roost, but the presence of a male in this cloistered environment catalyses the desires and rivalries of nine needy females.

Play Misty for Me. See films as a director.

Dirty Harry
Dir. and Prod.: Don Siegel, for Malpaso. *Exec. Prod.*: Robert Daley. *Sc.*: Harry Julian Fink, Rita M. Fink, Dean Riesner. *Ph.*: Bruce Surtees (Technicolor, Panavision). *Aerial Ph.*: Rexford Metz. *Art Dir.*: Dale Hennessey. *Edit. and Ass. Prod.*: Carl Pingitore. *Mus.*: Lalo Schifrin.
With: Clint Eastwood (Police Inspector Harry Callahan), Harry Guardino (Lieutenant Bressler), Reni Santoni (Chico), John Vernon (the mayor), Andy Robinson (Scorpio), John Larch (the chief), John Mitchum (DiGiorgio), Mae Mercer (Mrs. Russell), Lyn Edgington (Norma).
Filmed in San Francisco.
Dist.: Warner Bros. 103 mins.
Convinced that the judicial system favors criminals at the expense of their victims, Inspector Harry Callahan is a one-man army who trusts only his Magnum 44 and transgresses all the rules. Regularly disowned by the San Francisco authorities, he lands the dirtiest jobs, notably the capture of a psychopath who signs his crimes 'Scorpio'.

1972

Joe Kidd
Dir.: John Sturges. *Prod.*: Sidney Beckerman, for Malpaso. *Exec. Prod.*: Robert Daley. *Sc.*: Elmore Leonard. *Ph.*: Bruce Surtees (Technicolor, Panavision). *Art Dir.*: Henry Bumstead, Alexander Golitzen. *Edit.*: Ferris Webster. *Mus.*: Lalo Schifrin.
With: Clint Eastwood (Joe Kidd), Robert Duvall (Frank Harlan), John Saxon (Luis Chama), Don Stroud (Lamarr), Stella Garcia (Helen Sanchez), James Wainwright (Mingo), Paul Koslo (Roy), Gregory Walcott (Mitchell), Dick Van Patten (hotel manager), Lynne Marta (Elma).
Filmed at June Lake, California, and at Old Tucson, Arizona.
Dist.: Universal. 88 mins.

Despoiled of their land by rich speculators, the Mexican peasants of Sinola, New Mexico, rise up. A rehabilitated former bounty hunter who is now a farmer, Joe Kidd is hired as a scout by an American promoter bent on wiping out the rebels by any means necessary.

1973

High Plains Drifter. See films as a director.

Magnum Force
Dir.: Ted Post. *Prod.*: Robert Daley, for Malpaso. *Sc.*: John Milius, Michael Cimino, from a story by John Milius, and from the characters created by Harry Julian Fink and R. M. Fink. *Ph.*: Frank Stanley (Technicolor, Panavision). *Art Dir.*: Jack Collis. *Edit.*: Ferris Webster. *Mus.*: Lalo Schifrin. *2nd unit Dir.*: Buddy Van Horn.
With: Clint Eastwood (Harry Callahan), Hal Holbrook (Lieutenant Briggs), Mitchell Ryan (Charlie McCoy), David Soul (John Davis), Tim Matheson (Sweet), Kip Niven (Astrachan), Robert Urich (Grimes), Felton Perry (Early Smith), John Mitchum (DiGiorgio), Albert Popwell (pimp), Christine White (Carol McCoy), Adele Yoshioka (Sunny).
Filmed in San Francisco.
Dist.: Warner Bros. 124 mins.
After having foiled an attempt to take hostages at the airport, Harry Callahan is reinstated in the Homicide Division, but he must confront a group of young policemen who were trained in Special Forces. Modelled on the Brazilian death squads, they take it upon themselves to execute alleged 'criminals'. Their guru is none other than Harry Callahan!

1974

Thunderbolt and Lightfoot
Dir. and Sc.: Michael Cimino. *Prod.*: Robert Daley, for Malpaso. *Ph.*: Frank Stanley (color by DeLuxe, Panavision). *Art Dir.*: Tambi Larsen. *Edit.*: Ferris Webster. *Mus.*: Dee Barton.
With: Clint Eastwood (John 'Thunderbolt' Doherty), Jeff Bridges (Lightfoot), George Kennedy (Red Leary), Geoffrey Lewis (Goody), Catherine Bach (Melody), Gary Busey (Curly), Jack Dodson (vault manager), Bill McKinney (crazy driver), Vic Tayback (Mario).
Filmed in Montana.
Dist.: United Artists. 115 mins.
A decorated veteran of the Korean War, 'Thunderbolt' owes his notoriety to a bank hold-up he conducted in Montana with an anti-tank gun. He has temporarily recycled himself as a parson when he strikes up a friendship with Lightfoot, a young car thief in search of adventures. The two outlaws will try to repeat the 'historic' heist.

1975

The Eiger Sanction. See films as a director.

1976

The Outlaw Josey Wales. See films as a director.

The Enforcer
Dir.: James Fargo. *Prod.*: Robert Daley, for Malpaso. *Sc.*: Stirling Silliphant, Dean Riesner, from a story by Gail Morgan Hickman, S. W. Schurr, and from the characters created by Harry Julian Fink and R. M. Fink. *Ph.*: Charles W. Short (color by DeLuxe, Panavision). *Art Dir.*: Allen E. Smith. *Edit.*: Ferris Webster, Joel Cox. *Mus.*: Jerry Fielding.
With: Clint Eastwood (Harry Callahan), Tyne Daly (Kate Moore), Harry Guardino (Lieutenant Bressler), Bradford Dillman (Captain McKay), John Mitchum (DiGiorgio), DeVeren Bookwalter (Bobby Maxwell), John Crawford (the mayor), Samantha Doane (Wanda), Robert Hoy (Buchinski), Jocelyn Jones (Miki), M. G. Kelly (Father John), Albert Popwell (Mustapha).
Filmed in San Francisco.
Dist.: Warner Bros. 96 mins.
Having used excessive violence in a hostage rescue mission, Harry Callahan is transferred from Homicide to the Personnel Division. Asked to recruit more female detectives, he rebuffs the proponents of 'political correctness', only to be assigned as his new partner someone who has no experience on the streets ... Officer Kate Moore.

1977

The Gauntlet. See films as a director.

1978

Every Which Way But Loose
Dir.: James Fargo. *Prod.*: Robert Daley, for Malpaso. *Sc. and Ass. Prod.*: Jeremy Joe Kronsberg. *Ph.*: Rexford Metz (color by DeLuxe, Panavision). *Cam.*: Jack Green. *Art Dir.*: Elayne Ceder. *Edit.*: Ferris Webster, Joel Cox. *Mus.*: Snuff Garrett, Steve Dorff.
With: Clint Eastwood (Philo Beddoe), Sondra Locke (Lynn Halsey-Taylor), Geoffrey Lewis (Orville), Beverly D'Angelo (Echo), Ruth Gordon (Ma), Walter Barnes (Tank Murdock), James McEachin (Herb), Bill McKinney (Dallas), William O'Connell (Elmo), Hank Worden (trailer court manager).
Filmed in the San Fernando Valley (Los Angeles area) and in Denver, Colorado.
Dist.: Warner Bros. 114 mins.
Trucker Philo Beddoe lives with his buddy Orville, an eccentric old woman and orangutan Clyde. This diehard individualist loves a fight, and he's got a full plate, fending off both the cops and the bikers of the Black Widows gang. He's also a bit of a romantic, falling heads over heels for a honky-tonk harlot.

1979

Escape From Alcatraz

Dir. and Prod.: Don Siegel, pour Malpaso. *Exec. Prod.*: Robert Daley. *Ass. Prod.*: Fritz Manes. *Sc.*: Richard Tuggle, from the novel by J. Campbell Bruce. *Ph.*: Bruce Surtees (color by DeLuxe). *Prod. Des.*: Allen E. Smith. *Edit.*: Ferris Webster. *Mus.*: Jerry Fielding. *With*: Clint Eastwood (Frank Morris), Patrick McGoohan (the warden), Roberts Blossom (Doc), Jack Thibeau (Clarence Anglin), Fred Ward (John Anglin), Paul Benjamin (English), Larry Hankin (Charley Butts), Bruce M. Fischer (Wolf), Frank Ronzio (Litmus), Candace Bowen (English's daughter), Danny Glover (inmate).
Filmed on the island of Alcatraz (San Francisco Bay).
Dist.: Paramount. 112 mins.
In January 1960, Frank Morris, an expert in prison breaks, is transferred to the Alcatraz penitentiary. 'Nobody has ever escaped from this place. No one ever will', the warden warns him. Stripped of all rights, under constant surveillance, the inmates are cut off from the outside world, but Morris has an exceptional IQ.

1980

Bronco Billy. See films as a director.

Any Which Way You Can

Dir.: Buddy Van Horn. *Prod.*: Fritz Manes, for Malpaso. *Exec. Prod.*: Robert Daley. *Sc.*: Stanford Sherman, from the characters created by Jeremy Joe Kronsberg. *Ph.*: David Worth (color by DeLuxe). *Cam.*: Jack Green. *Prod. Des.*: William J. Creber. *Edit.*: Ferris Webster, Ron Spang. *Mus.*: Snuff Garrett, Steve Dorff. *Songs*: 'Beers to You' by S. Dorff, John Durrill, S. Pinkard, S. Garrett, int. by Ray Charles, Clint Eastwood.
With: Clint Eastwood (Philo Beddoe), Sondra Locke (Lynn Halsey-Taylor), Geoffrey Lewis (Orville), William Smith (Jack Wilson), Harry Guardino (James Beekman), Ruth Gordon (Ma), Michael Cavanaugh (Patrick Scarfe), Barry Corbin (Fat Zack), Roy Jenson (Moody), Bill McKinney (Dallas), William O'Connell (Elmo).
Filmed in the San Fernando Valley (Los Angeles area) and in Jackson Hole, Wyoming.
Dist.: Warner Bros. 115 mins.
The adventures of Philo Beddoe continue in the redneck hinterland. Like the Roadrunner of Chuck Jones' cartoons, the roving trucker gets out of every scrape. On top of cops and bikers, he battles mafiosi, finally wins his sweetheart and even finds a fiancée for his orangutan Clyde.

1982

Firefox. See films as a director.

Honkytonk Man. See films as a director.

1983

Sudden Impact. See films as a director.

1984

Tightrope. *Dir.*: Richard Tuggle, Clint Eastwood (uncredited). See films as a director.

City Heat

Dir.: Richard Benjamin. *Prod.*: Fritz Manes, for Malpaso and Deliverance. *Ass. Dir.*: David Valdes. *Sc.*: Sam O. Brown (Blake Edwards), Joseph C. Stinson. *Ph.*: Nick McLean (Technicolor). *Prod. Des.*: Edward Carfagno. *Edit.*: Jacqueline Cambas. *Mus.*: Lennie Niehaus. 'Montage Blues' by Lennie Niehaus, int. on the piano by Clint Eastwood, Mike Lang, Pete Jolly.
With: Clint Eastwood (Lieutenant Speer), Burt Reynolds (Mike Murphy), Jane Alexander (Addy), Madeline Kahn (Caroline Howley), Rip Torn (Primo Pitt), Irene Cara (Ginny Lee), Richard Roundtree (Dehl Swift), Tony Lo Bianco (Leon Coll), Jack Nance (Aram Strossell).
Filmed at the Warner Bros. studios in Burbank and at the Universal studios.
Dist.: Warner Bros. 94 mins.
The heat is on in the Kansas City of the 1930s. Lieutenant Speer, a hard-nosed champion of law and order, and Mike Murphy, an irresponsible charmer, used to work as a team in the police. But Murphy, who is now on his own as a 'private', plays fast and loose with the rules. Time and again, Speer has to get him out of trouble.

1985

Pale Rider. See films as a director.

1986

Heartbreak Ridge. See films as a director.

1988

The Dead Pool

Dir.: Buddy Van Horn. *Prod.*: David Valdes, for Malpaso. *Sc.*: Steve Sharon, from a story by Steve Sharon, Durk Pearson, Sandy Shaw, and from characters created by Harry Julian Fink, R. M. Fink. *Ph.*: Jack N. Green (Technicolor). *Prod. Des.*: Edward Carfagno. *Edit.*: Joel Cox, Ron Spang. *Mus.*: Lalo Schifrin.
With: Clint Eastwood (Harry Callahan), Patricia Clarkson (Samantha Walker), Liam Neeson (Peter Swan), Evan C. Kim (Al Quan), David Hunt (Harlan Rook), Michael Currie (Captain Donnelly), Michael Goodwin (Lieutenant Ackerman), Darwin Gillett (Patrick Snow), Anthony Charnota (Lou Janero), Jim Carrey (Johnny Squares).

Filmed in San Francisco.
Dist.: Warner Bros. 91 mins.
After having successfully pursued the indictment of a powerful mafioso, Harry Callahan has become so popular that he is reassigned to the police's public relations. He is partnered with a Chinese-American detective. But his notoriety makes him a perfect target for a schizophrenic who is creating havoc on the set of a horror flick, *Hotel Satan*.

1989

Pink Cadillac

Dir.: Buddy Van Horn. *Prod.*: David Valdes, for Malpaso. *Exec. Prod.*: Michael Gruskoff. *Sc.*: John Eskow. *Ph.*: Jack N. Green (Technicolor). *Prod. Des.*: Edward Carfagno. *Edit.*: Joel Cox. *Mus.*: Steve Dorff.
With: Clint Eastwood (Tommy Nowak), Bernadette Peters (Lou Ann McGuinn), Timothy Carhart (Roy McGuinn), John Dennis Johnston (Waycross), Michael Des Barres (Alex), Jimmie F. Skaggs (Billy Dunston), Bill Moseley (Darrell), William Hicky (Mr. Barton), Geoffrey Lewis (Ricky Z), Frances Fisher (Dinah), Jim Carrey (Post-Nuclear Elvis Lounge Act), Bill McKinney (barman).
Filmed near Sacramento and in the Reno area (Nevada).
Dist.: Warner Bros. 122 mins.
Tom Nowak is a 'skip tracer'. He goes after felons who have abused their parole. One of these fugitives is a mother with a newborn baby. She also happens to be hunted by a gang of white supremacists and survivalists after having swiped a pink Cadillac loaded with counterfeit bank notes.

1990

White Hunter, Black Heart. See films as a director.

The Rookie. See films as a director.

1992

Unforgiven. See films as a director.

1993

A Perfect World. See films as a director.

In the Line of Fire

Dir.: Wolfgang Petersen. *Prod.*: Jeff Apple, for Castle Rock. *Exec. Prod.*: Wolfgang Petersen, Gail Katz, David Valdes. *Co-Prod.*: Bob Rosenthal. *Sc.*: Jeff Maguire. *Ph.*: John Bailey (Technicolor, Panavision). *Prod. Des.*: Lilly Kilvert. *Edit.*: Anne V. Coates. *Mus.*: Ennio Morricone. 'I Didn't Know What Time It Was' by Richard Rodgers, Lorenz Hart, int. by Clint Eastwood.
With: Clint Eastwood (Frank Horrigan), John Malkovich (Mitch Leary), Rene Russo (Lilly Raines), Dylan McDermott (Al D'Andrea), Gary Cole (Bill Watts), Fred Dalton Thompson (Harry Sargent), John Mahoney (Sam Campagna), Jim Curley (President Traveller), Sally Hughes (Mrs. Traveller), John Heard (Professor Riger).
Filmed in Washington DC, Los Angeles and at the Sony studios in Culver City.
Dist.: Columbia. 126 mins.
Washington DC. A former Secret Service agent, Frank Horrigan is haunted by a past failure: in Dallas, the day President Kennedy was assassinated, he was unable to stop the second and fatal bullet. In spite of his age, he goes back into service when he suspects a psychopath and ex-CIA man to be plotting an assassination against the current president.

1995

The Bridges of Madison County. See films as a director.

1997

Absolute Power. See films as a director.

1999

True Crime. See films as a director.

2000

Space Cowboys. See films as a director.

2002

Blood Work. See films as a director.

2004

Million Dollar Baby. See films as a director.

2008

Gran Torino. See films as a director.

Films as a director

1971

Play Misty for Me

Dir.: Clint Eastwood. *Prod.*: Robert Daley, for Malpaso. *Exec. Prod.*: Jennings Lang. *Ass. Prod. and Ass. Dir.*: Bob Larson. *Sc.*: Jo Heims, Dean Riesner, from a story by Jo Heims. *Ph.*: Bruce Surtees (Technicolor). *Aerial Ph.*: Jack Green. *Art Dir.*: Alexander Golitzen. *Cost.*: Helen Colvig, Brad Whitney. *Edit.*: Carl Pingitore. *Paintings*: Don Heitkotter. *Mus.*: Dee Barton. 'Misty' by and int. by Erroll Garner. 'The First Time I Saw Your Face' by Ewan MacColl, int. by Roberta Flack. 'Squeeze Me' by and int. by Duke Ellington.
With: Clint Eastwood (Dave Garber), Jessica Walter (Evelyn Draper), Donna Mills (Tobie Williams), John Larch (Sergeant McCallum), Jack Ging (Frank), Irene Harvey (Madge Brenner), James McEachin (Al Monte), Clarice Taylor (Birdie), Donald Siegel (Murphy), Duke Everts (Jay Jay), George Fargo, Paul E. Lippman (men), Mervin W. Frates (locksmith), Tim Frawley (deputy sheriff), Otis Kadani (policeman), Brit Lind (Anjelica), Jack Kosslyn (cab driver), Ginna Paterson (Madalyn), Malcolm Moran (man in window), Johnny Otis, Cannonball Adderley and His Quartet.
Filmed in Carmel and Monterey (California).
Dist.: Universal. 102 mins.
Night after night, Dave Garber, a disc-jockey at a small radio station in Carmel, receives a call from a female listener asking him to play Erroll Garner's 'Misty'. They eventually meet and spend the night together. To him the tryst is only a one-night stand, but it fuels the flames of her obsession. Evelyn begins to stalk him, jeopardizing his relationship with girlfriend Tobie and soon threatening to destroy everything he holds dear.

1973

High Plains Drifter

Dir.: Clint Eastwood. *Prod.*: Robert Daley, for Malpaso. *Exec. Prod.*: Jennings Lang. *Sc.*: Ernest Tidyman. *Ph.*: Bruce Surtees (Technicolor). *Art Dir.*: Henry Bumstead. *Cost.*: Glenn Wright, Jim Gilmore, Joanne Haas. *Edit.*: Ferris Webster. *Ass. Dir.*: James Fargo. *Stunts*: Buddy Van Horn. *Mus.*: Dee Barton.
With: Clint Eastwood (The Stranger), Verna Bloom (Sarah Belding), Mariana Hill (Callie Travers), Mitchell Ryan (Dave Drake), Jack Ging (Morgan Allen), Stefan Gierasch (Mayor Jason Hobart), Ted Hartley (Lewis Belding), Billy Curtis (Mordecai), Geoffrey Lewis (Stacey Bridges), Scott Walker (Bill Borders), Walter Barnes (Sheriff Sam Shaw), Paul Brinegar (Luthe Naylor), Richard Bull (Aba Goodwin), Robert Donner (preacher), John Hillerman (bootmaker), Anthony James (Cole Carlin), William O'Connell (barber), John Quade (Jake Ross), Jane Aull (townswoman), Dan Vadis (Dan Carlin), Reid Cruickshanks (gunsmith), James Goss (Tommy Morris), Jack Kosslyn (saddlemaker), Russ McCubbin (Fred Short), Belle Mitchell (Mrs. Lake), John Mitchum (warden), Carl C. Pitti (teamster), Chuck Waters (stableman), Buddy Van Horn (Marshal Jim Duncan).
Filmed at Mono Lake, California.
Dist.: Universal. 105 mins.
The Stranger arrives at Lago, a small town in the California desert, whose sheriff was sadistically tortured. His expeditious methods impress the populace, who ask him to ensure their security against the hired guns of a mining company. The Stranger demands absolute power and unlimited credit in their shops. He replaces the mayor with a dwarf, trains a band of militiamen for combat and has the whole town repainted in red so that he can rename it 'Hell'. Villagers discover too late that there is no stopping an exterminating angel.

Breezy

Dir.: Clint Eastwood. *Prod.*: Robert Daley, for Malpaso. *Exec. Prod.*: Jennings Lang. *Sc. and Ass. Prod.*: Jo Heims. *Ph.*: Frank Stanley (Technicolor). *Art Dir.*: Alexander Golitzen. *Cost.*: Glenn Wright. *Edit.*: Ferris Webster. *Ass. Dir.*: James Fargo. *Mus.*: Michel Legrand. 'Breezy's Song', lyrics by Marilyn and Alan Bergman, mus. by Michel Legrand.
With: William Holden (Frank Harmon), Kay Lenz (Breezy), Roger C. Carmel (Bob Henderson), Marj Dusay (Betty), Joan Hotchkis (Paula), Jamie Smith Jackson (Marcy), Norman Bartold (man in car), Lynn Borden (overnight date), Shelley Morrison (Nancy), Dennis Olivieri (Bruno), Eugene Peterson (Charlie), Lew Brown (police officer), Richard Bull (doctor), Johnnie Collins III (Norman), Don Diamond (maitre d'), Scott Holden (veterinarian), Sandy Kenyon (real estate agent), Jack Kosslyn (driver), Mary Munday (waitress), Frances Stevenson (saleswoman), Buck Young (Paula's escort), Priscilla Morrill (dress customer), Clint Eastwood (a stroller).
Filmed in Los Angeles.
Dist.: Universal. 108 mins.
Frank Harmon, in his late fifties, leads the humdrum existence of a successful real estate promoter in Los Angeles. Divorced, he lives alone in a posh mansion of Laurel Canyon and contents himself with short-term affairs, until the day he picks up Breezy, a fifteen-year-old hitchhiker. She is a homeless drifter on the fringes of the hippie scene. Upsetting his material and intellectual comfort, she will at once exasperate and fulfil him, force him to question his lifestyle and prompt him to follow his heart.

1975

The Eiger Sanction

Dir.: Clint Eastwood. *Prod.*: Robert Daley, for Malpaso. *Exec. Prod.*: Richard D. Zanuck, David Brown. *Sc.*: Hal Dresner, Warren B. Murphy, Rod Whitaker, from the novel by Trevanian. *Ph.*: Frank Stanley (Technicolor). *Art Dir.*: George Webb (USA), Aurelio Crugnola (Switzerland). *Cost.*: Charles Waldo, Sheila Mason. *Edit.*: Ferris Webster. *Ass. Dir.*: James Fargo. *Expedition leader*: Norman Dyhrenfurth. *Climbing advisor*: Mike Hoover.

Ph. of climbing scenes: John Cleare, Jeff Schoolfield, Peter Pilafian, Pete White. *Aerial Ph.*: Rexford Metz. *Mus.*: John Williams.
With: Clint Eastwood (Jonathan Hemlock), George Kennedy (Ben Bowman), Vonetta McGee (Jemima Brown), Jack Cassidy (Miles Mellough), Heidi Brühl (Anna Montaigne), Thayer David (Dragon), Reiner Schoene (Freytag), Michael Grimm (Anderl Meyer), Jean-Pierre Bernard (Jean-Paul Montaigne), Brenda Venus (George), Gregory Walcott (Pope), Candice Rialson (art student), Elaine Shore (Miss Cerberus), Dan Howard (Dewayne), Jack Kosslyn (reporter), Walter Kraus (Kruger), Frank Redmond (Wormwood), Siegfried Wallach (hotel manager), Susan Morgan (Buns), Jack Frey (cab driver), and the participation of Dougal Haston, David Knowles, Bev Clark, Martin Boysen, Guy Neithardt, Hamish McInnes (alpine climbers).
Filmed at Monument Valley (Arizona), Zion National Park (Utah), Carmel-Monterey (California), Zürich and Grindelwald in the Swiss Alps.
Dist.: Universal. 128 mins.
A former secret agent, Jonathan Hemlock teaches art history. To legitimize a collection of paintings acquired fraudulently, he must yield to the blackmail of his former boss, an albino named Dragon, and agree to execute a 'sanction' against two enemy spies. He throws the first one, a Cuban, out of a window in Zürich. The second one is part of an international group of climbers that is about to attack the north face of the Eiger. An experienced alpinist, Jonathan has never completed that ascent successfully. He asks his old friend Ben to train him on the peaks of Monument Valley.

1976

The Outlaw Josey Wales

Dir.: Clint Eastwood. *Prod.*: Robert Daley, for Malpaso. *Ass. Prod. and Ass. Dir.*: James Fargo. *Sc.*: Phil Kaufman, Sonia Chernus, from the novel *Gone to Texas* by Forrest Carter. *Ph.*: Bruce Surtees (color by DeLuxe). *Prod. Des.*: Tambi Larsen. *Cost.*: Glenn Wright, Susan Irene. *Edit.*: Ferris Webster. *Ass. Edit.*: Joel Cox. *Stunts*: Walter Scott. *Mus.*: Jerry Fielding.
With: Clint Eastwood (Josey Wales), Chief Dan George (Lone Watie), Sondra Locke (Laura Lee), Bill McKinney (Terrill), John Vernon (Fletcher), Paula Trueman (Grandma Sarah), Sam Bottoms (Jamie), Geraldine Keams (Little Moonlight), Woodrow Parfrey (carpetbagger), Joyce Jameson (Rose), Sheb Wooley (Travis Cobb), Royal Dano (Ten Spot), Matt Clark (Kelly), John Verros (Chato), Will Sampson (Ten Bears), William O'Connell (Sim Carstairs), John Quade (Comanchero leader), Frank Schofield (Senator Lane), Buck Kartalian (shopkeeper), Len Lesser (Abe), Doug McGrath (Lige), John Russell (Bloody Bill Anderson), Charles Tyner (Zukie Limmer), Bruce M. Fischer (Yoke), John Mitchum (Al), John Chandler, Tom Roy Lowe (bounty hunters), Clay Tanner, Bob Hoy (Texas Rangers), Madeline T. Holmes (Grannie Hawkins), Erik Holland (Union Army Sergeant), Cissy Wellman (Josey's wife), Faye Hamblin (Grandpa Samuel), Danny Green (Tempel), Richard Farnsworth (a Comanchero), Kyle Eastwood (Josey's son).
Filmed in Tucson (Arizona), Kanab (Utah) and Orville (California).
Dist.: Warner Bros. 134 mins.
At the end of the Civil War, Josey Wales, a peaceful Missouri farmer, loses his wife and son in a massacre by a band of Union soldiers, the Red Legs. Subsequently, he joins a group of Confederate rebels, but they walk into a trap and are exterminated because their leader Fletcher has betrayed them. For Wales, who manages to escape, the war is just starting. Driven by his obsession for revenge, he becomes a legendary outlaw. Although a loner, he ends up gathering around him a community of victims and outcasts encountered on his trail of tears.

1977

The Gauntlet

Dir.: Clint Eastwood. *Prod.*: Robert Daley, for Malpaso. *Ass. Prod.*: Fritz Manes. *Sc.*: Michael Butler, Dennis Shryack. *Ph.*: Rexford Metz (color by DeLuxe). *Aerial Ph.*: Jack Green. *Art Dir.*: Allen E. Smith. *Cost.*: Glenn Wright. *Edit.*: Ferris Webster, Joel Cox. *Stunts*: Wayne Van Horn. *Mus.*: Jerry Fielding. *Soloists*: Art Pepper, Jon Faddis.
With: Clint Eastwood (Ben Shockley), Sondra Locke (Gus Mally), Pat Hingle (Josephson), William Prince (Blakelock), Bill McKinney (constable), Michael Cavanaugh (Feyderspiel), Carole Cook (waitress), Mara Corday (jail matron), Douglas McGrath (bookie), Jeff Morris (desk sergeant), Samantha Doane, Roy Jenson, Dan Vadis (bikers), Carver Barnes (bus driver), Robert Barrett (paramedic), Teddy Bear (lieutenant), Mildren J. Brion (old lady on the bus), Ron Chapman (veteran cop), Don Circle (bus clerk), James W. Gavin, Tom Friedkin (helicopter pilots), Darwin Lamb (police captain), Roger Lowe (paramedic driver), Fritz Manes (helicopter gunman), John Quiroga (cab driver), Joe Rainer (rookie cop), Art Rimdzius (judge), Al Silvani (police sergeant).
Filmed in Nevada and Arizona.
Dist.: Warner Bros. 109 mins.
Ben Shockley, an Arizona cop with an undistinguished record, is assigned the mission of escorting, from Las Vegas to Phoenix, 'a nothing witness for a nothing trial'. Ben, who joined the police because he saw it as the last bastion of righteousness, has never been one to ask questions; he has always obeyed orders. However, the witness for the prosecution is a prostitute, and she refuses to leave her cell. Ben carts her away forcibly, but quickly realizes that her paranoia is amply justified. The mafia and the police will stop at nothing to prevent them from reaching their destination.

1980

Bronco Billy

Dir.: Clint Eastwood. *Prod.*: Dennis Hackin, Neal Dobrofsky, for Malpaso. *Exec. Prod.*: Robert Daley. *Ass. Prod.*: Fritz Manes. *Sc.*: Dennis Hackin. *Ph.*: David Worth (color by

DeLuxe). *Cam.*: Jack Green. *Art Dir.*: Gene Lourie. *Cost.*: Glenn Wright, Aida Swinson. *Edit.*: Ferris Webster, Joel Cox.
Mus.: Snuff Garrett, Steve Dorff. 'Misery and Gin' by John Durrill, Snuff Garrett, int. by Merle Haggard. 'Cowboys and Clowns' by Steve Dorff, G. Harju, Larry Herbstritt, Snuff Garrett, int. by Ronnie Milsap. 'Bronco Billy' by M. Brown, Steve Dorff, Snuff Garrett, int. by Ronnie Milsap. 'Bar-room Buddies' by M. Brow, Cliff Crofford, Steve Dorff, Snuff Garrett, int. by Merle Haggard, Clint Eastwood. 'Bayou Lullaby' by Cliff Crofford, Snuff Garrett, int. by Penny DeHaven. 'Stardust Cowboy' by Cliff Crofford, Snuff Garrett, int. by The Reinsmen. 'Stars and Stripes Forever' by John Philip Sousa.
With: Clint Eastwood (Bronco Billy), Sondra Locke (Antoinette Lily), Geoffrey Lewis (John Arlington), Scatman Crothers (Doc Lynch), Bill McKinney (Lefty LeBow), Sam Bottoms (Leonard James), Dan Vadis (Chief Big Eagle), Sierra Pecheur (Lorraine Running Water), Walter Barnes (Sheriff Dix), Woodrow Parfrey (Dr. Canterbury), Beverlee McKinsey (Irene Lily), Douglas McGrath (Lieutenant Wiecker), Hank Worden (station mechanic), William Prince (Edgar Lipton), Pam Abbas (mother superior), Edye Byrde (Eloise, the maid), Douglas Copsey, Roger Dale Simmons (reporters at the bank), John Wesley Elliott, Jr (sanatorium attendant), Chuck Hicks, Bobby Hoy (cowboys at the bar), Jefferson Jewell (boy at the bank), Dawneen Lee (bank teller), Don Mummert (chauffeur), Lloyd Nelson (sanatorium policeman), George Orrison (cowboy at the bar), Michael Reinbold (King), Tessa Richards (Mitzi Fritts), Tanya Russell (Doris Duke), Valerie Shanks (Sister Maria), Sharon Sherlock (license clerk), James Simmerhan (bank manager), Jenny Sternling (reporter at the sanatorium), Chuck Waters, Jerry Wills (bank robbers), Merle Haggard (himself), Alison Eastwood, Kyle Eastwood (orphans).
Filmed in the Boise area (Idaho).
Dist.: Warner Bros. 119 mins.
At age thirty-one, Billy left his shoemaker's shop in New Jersey to live out his dream in a travelling Wild West show. His troupe consists of outsiders who have chosen, like him, a beautiful illusion over a grim reality. Billy holds a special fascination for kids who look upon him as a legendary figure. Needing an assistant for his sharpshooting routine, he hires a spoiled New York heiress who has just been ditched by her swindler husband. But she quickly makes life impossible for the circus. With dwindling resources, Billy devises a plan to hold up a train in the style of old West bandits.

1982
Firefox
Dir. and Prod.: Clint Eastwood. *Exec. Prod.*: Fritz Manes. *Sc.*: Alex Lasker, Wendell Wellman, from the novel by Craig Thomas. *Ph.*: Bruce Surtees (color by DeLuxe, Panavision). *Cam.*: Jack Green. *Art Dir.*: John Graysmark, Elayne Ceder. *Cost.*: Glenn Wright. *Edit.*: Ferris Webster, Ron Spang. *Visual sp. effects*: John Dykstra, Robert Shepherd. *Optical sp. effects*: Roger Dorney. *Sp. effects technology*: Apogee. *Mus.*: Maurice Jarre.
With: Clint Eastwood (Mitchell Gant), Freddie Jones (Kenneth Aubrey), David Huffman (Buckholz), Warren Clarke (Pavel Upenskoy), Ronald Lacey (Semelovsky), Kenneth Colley (Colonel Kontarsky), Klaus Löwitsch (General Vladimirov), Nigel Hawthorne (Pyotr Baranovich), Stefan Schnabel (First Secretary), Thomas Hill (General Brown), Clive Merrison (Major Lanyev), Kai Wulff (Lieutenant Colonel Voskov), Dimitra Arliss (Natalia), Austin Willis (Walters), Michael Currie (Captain Seerbacker), James Staley (Lieutenant Commander Fleischer), Ward Costello (General Rogers), Alan Tilvern (Air Marshal Kutuzov), Oliver Cotton (Dmitri Priabin), Bernard Behrens (William Saltonstall), Richard Derr (Admiral Curtin), Woody Eney (Major Dietz), Bernard Erhard (KGB guard), Hugh Fraser (Police Inspector Tortyev), David Gant (KGB official), John Grillo (customs officer), Czeslaw Grocholski (old man), Barrie Houghton (Boris Glazunov), Neil Hunt (Richard Cunningham), Vincent J. Isaac (sub radio operator), Alexei Jawdokimow, Phillip Littell (code operators), Wolf Kahler (KGB Chairman Andropov), Eugene Lipinski (KGB agent), Curt Lowens (Dr. Schuller), Lev Mailer (guard at showers), Fritz Manes (captain), David Meyers (Grosch), Alfredo Michelson (interrogator), Zenno Nahayevsky (officer at plane), George Orrison (Leon Sprague), Tony Papenfuss, Grisha Plotkin (GRU officers), Olivier Pierre (Borkh), George Pravda (General Borov), John Ratzenberger (Chief Peck), Alex Rodine (captain of the Riga), Lance Rosen (agent), Eugene Scherer (Russian captain), Warwick Sims (Shelley), Mike Spero (Russian guard), Malcolm Storry (KGB agent), Chris Winfield (RAF operator), John Yates (Admiral Pearson), Alexander Zale (Riga fire control chief), Igor Zatsepin (flight engineer), Konstantin Zlatev (Riga technician).
Filmed in Vienna, the Austrian Alps, Greenland (aerial base of Thule), Montana, Los Angeles and San Diego.
Dist.: Warner Bros. 137 mins.
A former bomber pilot during the Vietnam War, Mitchell Gant is asked to serve again when the Pentagon entrusts him with a mission that only an ace like him is capable of carrying through successfully: to infiltrate the Soviet Union and steal the Firefox prototype, the MIG 31. It can fly at Mach 5 undetected by radar and is equipped with missiles operated by pilot thoughtwaves. His local contacts are dissidents ready to sacrifice their life. Mitchell speaks Russian, can 'think' in Russian, but is afflicted with blackouts during which he relives the atrocities of Vietnam.

Honkytonk Man
Dir. and Prod.: Clint Eastwood. *Exec. Prod.*: Fritz Manes. *Sc.*: Clancy Carlile, from his novel. *Ph.*: Bruce Surtees (Technicolor). *Cam.*: Jack Green. *Prod. Des.*: Edward Carfagno. *Cost.*: Glenn Wright. *Edit.*: Ferris Webster, Michael Kelly, Joel Cox.
Mus.: Snuff Garrett, Steve Dorff. 'When I Sing About You' by De Wayne Blackwell, int. by Clint Eastwood. 'Ricochet Rag' by Herb Remington, int. by Johnny Gimble and The Texas Swing Band. 'In the Jailhouse Now' by J. Rodgers, int. by Marty Robbins, John Anderson, David Frizell, Clint Eastwood. 'One Fiddle, Two Fiddle' by Cliff Crofford, John Durrill, Snuff Garrett, int. by Ray Price and The Texas Swing Band. 'San Antonio Rose' by Bob Wills, int. by Ray Price and The Texas Swing Band. 'When the Blues Comes Around' by Cliff Crofford, John Durrill, int. by Linda Hopkins. 'These Cotton Patch Blues' by Cliff Crofford, int. by John Anderson. 'Texas Moonbeam Waltz' by Cliff Crofford, John Durrill, Snuff Garrett, int. by Johnny Gimble and The Texas Swing Band. 'Turn the Pencil Over' by DeWayne Blackwell, int. by Porter Wagoner. 'Please Surrender' by Cliff Crofford, John Durrill, Snuff Garrett, int. by David Frizzell and West. 'No Sweeter Cheater Than You' by M. Torok, R. Reed, int. by Clint Eastwood. 'Honkytonk Man' by DeWayne Blackwell, int. by Marty Robbins, Clint Eastwood.
With: Clint Eastwood (Red Stovall), Kyle Eastwood (Whit), John McIntire (Grandpa), Alexa Kenin (Marlene), Verna Bloom (Emmy), Matt Clark (Virgil), Barry Corbin (Arnspringer), Jerry Hardin (Snuffy), Tim Thomerson (highway patrolman), Macon McCalman (Dr. Hines), Joe Regalbuto (Henry Axle), Gary Grubbs (Jim Bob), Rebecca Clemons (Belle), Johnny Gimble (Bob Wills), Linda Hopkins (Flossie), Bette Ford (Lulu), Jim Boelson (Junior), Tracey Walter (Pooch), Susan Peretz (Miss Maud), John Russell (Jack Wade), Charles Cyphers (Stubbs), Marty Robbins (Smoky), Ray Price (Bob Wills band singer), Shelley West, David Frizzell (Grand Ole Opry singers), Porter Wagoner (Dusty), Bob Ferrera (oldest son), Tracy Shults (daughter), R. J. Ganzert (rancher), Hugh Warden (grocer), Kelsie Blades (veteran), Jim Ahart (waiter), Steve Autry (mechanic), Peter Griggs (Mr. Vogel), Julie Hoopman (whore), Rozelle Gayle (club manager), Robert V. Barron (undertaker), DeForest Covan (gravedigger), Lloyd Nelson (radio announcer), George Orrison, Glenn Wright (jailbirds), Frank Reinhardt (stand-in), Roy Jenson (Dub), Sherry Allurd (Dub's wife), Gordon Terry, Tommy Alsup, Merle Travis (Texas playboys), Robert D. Carver, Thomas Powels (bus drivers).
Filmed in Central California, Nevada, Oklahoma and Tennessee.
Dist.: Warner Bros. 122 mins.
In the Oklahoma of the Dust Bowl, down and out guitarist Red Stovall is reunited with his family after having wandered across the country from one honky-tonk to another. He didn't find his promised land in California; that's where he lost it all, sweetheart included. Befriending his nephew Whit, he initiates him into various 'guilty pleasures'. He then takes the boy with him to Nashville, where he is hoping to get an audition at the Grand Ole Opry, the temple of country music. For Red, drained by tuberculosis and booze, this represents his last chance. It will also be his final journey, at once picaresque and pathetic.

1983
Sudden Impact
Dir. and Prod.: Clint Eastwood. *Exec. Prod.*: Fritz Manes. *Ass. Prod.*: Steve Perry. *Sc.*: Joseph C. Stinson, from a story by Earl E. Smith, Charles B. Pierce, and from the characters created by Harry Julian Fink, R. M. Fink. *Ph.*: Bruce Surtees (Technicolor). *Cam.*: Jack Green. *Prod. Des.*: Edward Carfagno. *Cost.*: Glenn Wright, Sue Moore. *Edit.*: Joel Cox. *Ass. Dir.*: David Valdes. *Stunts*: Wayne Van Horn. *Mus.*: Lalo Schifrin. 'This Side of Forever' by Dewayne Blackwell, int. by Roberta Flack.
With: Clint Eastwood (Harry Callahan), Sondra Locke (Jennifer Spencer), Pat Hingle (Chief Jannings), Bradford Dillman (Captain Briggs), Paul Drake (Mick), Audrie J. Neenan (Ray Parkins), Jack Thibeau (Kruger), Michael Currie (Lieutenant Donnelly), Albert Popwell (Horace King), Mark Keyloun (Officer Bennett), Kevin Major Howard (Hawkins), Bette Ford (Leah), Nancy Parsons (Mrs. Kruger), Joe Bellan (burly detective), Wendell Wellman (Tyrone), Mara Corday (coffee shop waitress), Russ McCubbin (Eddie), Robert Sutton (Carl), Nancy Fish (Historical Society woman), Carmen Argenziano (D'Ambrosia), Lisa Britt (Elizabeth), Bill Reddick (police commissioner), Lois de Banzie (judge), Matthew Child (Alby), Michael Johnson, Nick Dimitri (assassins), Michael Maurer (George Wilburn), Pat DuVal (bailiff), Christian Phillips, Steven Kravitz (Hawkins' cronies), Dennis Royston, Melvin Thompson, Jophery Brown, Bill Upton (young guys), Lloyd Nelson (desk sergeant), Christopher Pray (Detective Jacobs), James McEachin (Detective Barnes), Maria Lynch (hostess), Ken Lee (Loomis), Morgan Upton (bartender), John X. Heart (uniformed policeman), David Gonzalez, Albert Martinez, David Rivers, Robert Rivers (gang members), Harry Demopoulos (Dr. Barton), Lisa London (young hooker), Tom Spratley (senior man), Eileen Wiggins (hysterical female customer), John Nowak (bank robber).
Filmed in Santa Cruz and in the San Francisco area.
Dist.: Warner Bros. 117 mins.
Disgusted by the laxity of the judicial system, Inspector Harry Callahan is still raising hell, seeking confrontations with all the hoods and mafiosi that cross his path. To get rid of this 'dinosaur', his superiors send him to San Paulo, a coastal resort that happens to be plagued by a serial killer. Far from enjoying his vacation, Harry continues attracting violence wherever he goes. He also becomes acquainted with an artist, Jennifer, who shares his philosophy of self-reliance. Haunted by the memory of a gang rape, she has taken the law into her own hands.

1984
Tightrope
Dir.: Richard Tuggle, Clint Eastwood (uncredited). *Prod.*: Clint Eastwood, Fritz Manes. *Sc.*: Richard Tuggle. *Ph.*: Bruce Surtees (Technicolor). *Cam.*: Jack Green. *Prod. Des.*: Edward Carfagno. *Cost.*: Glenn Wright. *Edit.*: Joel Cox. *Ass. Dir.*: David Valdes. *Stunts*: Buddy Van Horn. *Mus.*: Lennie Niehaus. 'Amanda's Theme' comp. by Clint Eastwood.
With: Clint Eastwood (Wes Block), Geneviève Bujold (Beryl Thibodeaux), Dan Hedaya (Detective Molinari), Alison Eastwood (Amanda Block), Jennifer Beck (Penny Block), Marco St. John (Leander Rolfe), Rebecca Perle (Becky Jacklin), Regina Richardson (Sarita),

Randi Brooks (Jamie Cory), Jamie Rose (Melanie Silber), Margaret Howell (Judy Harper), Rebecca Clemons (girl with whip), Janet MacLachlan (Dr. Yarlofsky), Graham Paul (Luther), Bill Holliday (police chief), John Wilmot (medical examiner), Margie O'Dair (Mrs. Holstein), Joy N. Houk, Jr (swap meet owner), Stewart Baker-Bergen (blond surfer), Donald Barber (Shorty), Robert Harvey (Lonesome Alice), Ron Gural (Coroner Dudley), Layton Martens (Sergeant Surtees), Richard Charles Boyle (Dr. Fitzpatrick), Becki Davis (nurse), Jonathan Sacher (gay boy), Valerie Thibodeaux (black hooker), Lionel Ferbos (Plainclothes Gus), Eliott Keener (Sandoval), Gary Wilmot Alden (secretary), David Valdes (Manes), James Borders (Carfagno), Fritz Manes (Valdes), Jonathan Shaw (Quono), George Wood (conventioneer), Kimberly Georgoulis (Sam), Glenda Byars (Lucy Davis), John Schluter, Jr (piazza cop), Nick Krieger (Rannigan), Lloyd Nelson (Patrolman Restic), Rod Masterson (Patrolman Gallo), David Dahlgren (Patrolman Julio), Glenn Wright (Patrolman Redfish), Angela Hill (woman reporter), Ted Saari (TV news technician). Filmed in New Orleans.
Dist.: Warner Bros. 117 mins.

Divorced, Inspector Wes Block of the New Orleans Vice Squad does his best to raise his two charming daughters. Although he is the type to rescue lost pets, he has a weakness for the clubs and bordellos of the French Quarter, where he seems to be in his element. When several young women fall prey to a serial killer, Wes finds himself 'on a tightrope' because he has known them all. Does he share the peculiar tastes of the strangler? Is he suffering from a double personality? Who is Jekyll, and who is Hyde, in this mysterious machination?

1985
Pale Rider
Dir. and Prod.: Clint Eastwood, for Malpaso. *Exec. Prod.*: Fritz Manes. *Ass. Prod. and Ass. Dir.*: David Valdes. *Sc.*: Michael Butler, Dennis Shryack. *Ph.*: Bruce Surtees (Technicolor, Panavision). *Cam.*: Jack Green. *Prod. Des.*: Edward Carfagno. *Cost.*: Glenn Wright. *Edit.*: Joel Cox. *Stunts*: Wayne Van Horn. *Mus.*: Lennie Niehaus. 'Megan's Theme' comp. by Clint Eastwood.
With: Clint Eastwood (Preacher), Michael Moriarty (Hull Barret), Carrie Snodgress (Sarah Wheeler), Christopher Penn (Josh LaHood), Richard Dysart (Coy LaHood), Sydney Penny (Megan Wheeler), Richard Kiel (Club), Doug McGrath (Spider Conway), John Russell (Sheriff Stockburn), Charles Hallahan (McGill), Marvin J. McIntyre (Jagou), Fran Ryan (Ma Blankenship), Richard Hamilton (Jed Blankenship), Graham Paul (Ev Gossage), Chuck LaFont (Eddie Conway), Jeffrey Weissman (Teddy Conway), Allen Keller (Tyson), Tom Oglesby (Elam), Herman Poppe (Ulrik Lindquist), Kathleen Wygle (Bess Gossage), Terrence Evans (Jake Henderson), Jim Hitson (Biggs), Loren Adkins (Bossy), Tom Friedkin (miner Tom), S. A. Griffin (Deputy Folke), Jack Radosta (Deputy Grissom), Robert Winley (Deputy Kobold), Billy Drago (Deputy Mather), Jeffrey Josephson (Deputy Sedge), John Dennis Johnston (Deputy Tucker), Mike Adams, Clay Lilley, Gene Hartline, R. L. Tolbert, Cliff Happy, Ross Loney, Larry Randles, Mike McGaughy, Gerry Gatlin (horsemen), Lloyd Nelson (bank teller), Jay K. Fishburn (telegrapher), George Orrison (stationmaster Whitey), Milton Murrill (porter), Mike Munsey (dentist-barber), Keith Dillin (blacksmith), Wayne Van Horn, Fritz Manes, Glenn Wright (stage riders). Filmed at Sun Valley (Idaho) and Sonora (California).
Dist.: Warner Bros. 113 mins.

In Carbon Canyon, California, a community of independent prospectors is attacked by the militia of an all-powerful trust. After the devastating raid, young Megan asks God to grant her a miracle. She has the vision of a lonely rider appearing on a pale horse amid the snowcapped mountains. When the stranger comes to the rescue of the prospectors' leader, he seems endowed with almost supernatural powers. He wears a pastor's collar, but his back is branded with the mark of Cain, a pentacle formed by the scars of five bullets.

'Vanessa in the Garden'
Dir.: Clint Eastwood. *Prod.* for Amblin Entertainment: David E. Vogel. *Exec. Prod. and Sc.*: Steven Spielberg. *Prod. Superv.*: Joshua Brand, John Falsey. *Ph.*: Robert Stevens (Technicolor). *Prod. Des.*: Rick Carter. *Cost.*: Jane Ruhm, Joseph Roveto. *Edit.*: Jo Ann Foggle. *Mus.*: Lennie Niehaus. *Theme*: John Williams. *Sp. effects*: Dream Quest Images. *Paintings*: Jaroslav Gebr, Yvonne Nagel.
With: Harvey Keitel (Byron Sullivan), Sondra Locke (Vanessa), Beau Bridges (Teddy), Margaret Howell (Eve), Thomas Randall Oglesby (Dr. Northrup), Jamie Rose (Mrs. Northrup), Milton Murrill (waiter).
Broadcast: NBC. 25 mins. An episode from the *Amazing Stories* TV series.

At the end of the nineteenth century, artist Byron Sullivan is about to be honored with a prestigious exhibition when his wife and model is killed in a carriage accident. Drowning in the darkest of melancholy, he starts burning some of his canvases and announces that he is giving up painting. But one night, he discovers that he can give Vanessa a new existence through his art.

1986
Heartbreak Ridge
Dir. and Prod.: Clint Eastwood, for Malpaso. *Exec. Prod.*: Fritz Manes. *Sc.*: James Carabatsos (and Joseph C. Stinson, uncredited). *Ph.*: Jack N. Green (Technicolor). *Prod. Des.*: Edward Carfagno. *Cost.*: Glenn Wright. *Edit.*: Joel Cox. *Stunts*: Wayne Van Horn.
Mus.: Lennie Niehaus. 'Sea of Heartbreak' by Hal David, Paul Hampton, int. by Don Gibson. 'Secret Love' and 'A Very Precious Love' by Sammy Fain, Paul Francis Webster, int. by Jill Hollier. 'How Much I Care' by Clint Eastwood, Sammy Cahn, int. by Jill Hollier. 'I Love You, But I Ain't Stupid' by Mario Van Peebles, Desmond Nakano, int. by Mario

Van Peebles. 'Bionic Marine' and 'Recon Rap' by and int. by Mario Van Peebles.
With: Clint Eastwood (Sergeant Tom Highway), Marsha Mason (Aggie), Everett McGill (Major Powers), Moses Gunn (Sergeant Webster), Eileen Heckart (Little Mary), Bo Svenson (Roy Jennings), Boyd Gaines (Lieutenant Ring), Mario Van Peebles (Stitch Jones), Arlen Dean Snyder (Master Sergeant Choozoo), Vincent Irizarry (Fragetti), Ramon Franco (Aponte), Tom Villard (Profile), Mike Gomez (Quinones), Rodney Hill (Collins), Peter Koch ('Swede' Johnson), Richard Venture (Colonel Meyers), Peter Jason (Major Devin), J. C. Quinn (quartermaster), Begonia Plaza (Mrs. Aponte), John Eames (Judge Zane), Thom Sharp, Jack Gallagher (emcees), John Hostetter (Reese), Holly Shelton-Foy (Sarita Dwayne), Nicholas Worth (jail binger), Timothy Fall (kid in jail), John Pennell (jail crier), Trish Garland (woman marine officer), Dutch Mann, Darwyn Swalve (bar tough guys), Christopher Lee Michael, Alex M. Bello (Marines), Steve Halsey, John Sasse (bus drivers), Rebecca Perle (student in shower), Annie O'Donnell (telephone operator), Elizabeth Ruscio (waitress), Lloyd Nelson (deputy), Sergeant Major John H. Brewer (sergeant major in court), Michael Maurer (bouncer), Tom Ellison (Marine corporal). Filmed at Camp Pendleton (California) and Vieques Island (Puerto Rico).
Dist.: Warner Bros. 128 mins.

After twenty-four years in the Army, Sergeant Highway is still a rebel. This old warhorse, one of the rare survivors of the battle of Heartbreak Ridge in Korea, is not cut out for peace. He has the knack of antagonizing his superiors, who dismiss him as a 'relic'. When he is assigned a platoon of young Marines with low morale, he puts them through an intensive training that turns them into top-notch combatants: 'I won't lose the next war because my men are not thoroughly prepared.' They get a chance to prove themselves during the invasion of Grenada.

1988
Bird
Dir. and Prod.: Clint Eastwood, for Malpaso. *Exec. Prod.*: David Valdes. *Sc.*: Joel Oliansky. *Ph.*: Jack N. Green (Technicolor). *Prod. Des.*: Edward Carfagno. *Cost.*: Glenn Wright, Deborah Hopper. *Sound*: Dick Alexander, Willie D. Burton, Les Fresholtz, Vern Poore. *Edit.*: Joel Cox.
Mus.: Lennie Niehaus. 'Maryland, My Maryland' by Lennie Niehaus. 'Lester Leaps In' int. by Charlie Parker, Monty Alexander, Ray Brown, John Guerin. 'Reno Jam Session' int. by Lennie Niehaus, James Rivers, Red Rodney, Pete Jolly, Chuck Berghofer, John Guerin. 'Young Bird' int. by James Rivers, Pete Jolly, Chuck Berghofer, John Guerin. 'I Can't Believe That You're in Love with Me' int. by Charlie Parker, Monty Alexander, Ray Brown, John Guerin. 'Why Do I Love You?' int. by James Rivers, Lennie Niehaus. 'Moonlight Becomes You' int. by Ronny Lang, Gary Foster, Bob Cooper, Pete Christlieb, Chuck Findley, Conte Candoli, Rick Baptist, Dick Nash, Bill Watrous, Barry Harris, Chuck Berghofer, John Guerin. 'Moose the Mooche' int. by Charles McPherson, Jon Faddis, Walter Davis, Jr, Ron Carter, John Guerin. 'Ornithology' int. by Charlie Parker, Charles McPherson, Jon Faddis, Mike Lang, Chuck Domanico, John Guerin, Charlie Shoemaker. *The Firebird* by Igor Stravinsky int. by Wolfgang Swallisch and the Symphonic Orchestra of Vienna. 'Lover Man' int. by Charlie Parker, Charles McPherson, Jon Faddis, Walter Davis, Jr, Ron Carter, John Guerin. 'April in Paris' int. by Charlie Parker, Barry Harris, Chuck Berghofer, John Guerin plus strings. 'All of Me' int. by Charlie Parker, Monty Alexander, Ray Brown, John Guerin. 'Jewish Wedding' int. by Charles McPherson, Red Rodney, Walter Davis, Jr, John Guerin. 'One for Red' int. by Red Rodney, Mike Lang, Chuck Domanico, John Guerin. 'Now's the Time' int. by Charlie Parker, Charles McPherson, Red Rodney, Walter Davis, Jr, Ron Carter, John Guerin. 'Albino Red Blues' int. by Red Rodney, Walter Davis, Jr, Ron Carter, John Guerin. 'Cool Blues' int. by Charlie Parker, Walter Davis, Jr, Ron Carter, John Guerin. 'Laura' int. by Charlie Parker, Barry Harris, Chuck Berghofer, John Guerin plus strings. 'Be My Love' int. by Mario Lanza. 'Parker's Mood' int. by King Pleasure, John Lewis, Percy Heath, Kenny Clarke. 'This Time the Dream's on Me' int. by Charlie Parker, Monty Alexander, Ray Brown, John Guerin. 'Ko Ko' int. by Charlie Parker, Walter Davis, Jr, Ron Carter, John Guerin. 'Buster's Last Stand' with Ronny Lang on the sax. 'Parker's Mood' int. by Charlie Parker, Barry Harris, Chuck Berghofer, John Guerin plus strings.
With: Forest Whitaker (Charlie 'Bird' Parker), Diane Venora (Chan Parker), Michael Zelniker (Red Rodney), Samuel E. Wright (Dizzy Gillespie), Keith David (Buster Franklin), Michael McGuire (Brewster), James Handy (Esteves), Damon Whitaker (young Bird), Morgan Nagler (Kim), Arlen Dean Snyder (Dr. Heath), Sam Robards (Moscowitz), Penelope Windust (Bellevue nurse), Glenn T. Wright (alcoholic patient), George Orrison (patient with checkers), Bill Cobbs (Dr. Caulfield), Hamilton Camp (Mayor of 52nd Street), Chris Bosley, George T. Bruce (doormen), Joey Green (Gene), John Witherspoon (Sid), Tony Todd (Frog), Jo De Winter (Mildred Berg), Richard Zavaglia (Ralph the Narc), Anna Levine (Audrey), Al Pugliese (Three Deuces owner), Hubert Kelly (Wilson), Billy Mitchell (Prince), Karl Vincent (Stratton), Lou Cutell (bride's father), Roger Etienne (Parisian MC), Jason Bernard (Benny Tate), Gretchen Oehler (Southern nurse), Richard McKenzie (Southern doctor), Tony Cox (Pee Wee Marquette), Diane Salinger (Baroness Nica), Johnny Adams (bartender), Natalia Silverwood (Red's girlfriend), Duane Matthews (engineer), Slim Jim Phantom (Grainger), Matthew Faison (judge), Peter Crook (Bird's lawyer), Alec Paul Rubinstein (recording producer), Patricia Herd (nun), Steve Zettler (Oasis Club owner), Ann Weldon (Violet Welles), Charley Lang (DJ at the Paramount), Tim Russ (Harris), Richard Jeni (Morello), Don Starr (doctor at Nica's), Richard Mawe (medical examiner).
Filmed in the Los Angeles area, the Sacramento Valley and at the Warner Bros. studios, Burbank.
Dist.: Warner Bros. 163 mins.

The tragic destiny of Charlie Parker, jazzman and junkie, virtuoso and visionary, revolved around a saxophone that plumbed the depths of human grief. Sapped by a stomach ulcer, constantly flirting with the danger of a heroin overdose, this tortured soul had few survival skills. Instead of preserving his gifts, he destroyed himself while simultaneously creating breakthrough music. At his death, the coroner estimated he was sixty-five years old; in reality he was thirty-four. This multifaceted portrait is also a saga of jazz in its golden age, from the birth of bebop to the emergence of rock 'n' roll.

1990
White Hunter, Black Heart
Dir. and Prod.: Clint Eastwood, for Malpaso and Rastar. *Exec. Prod.*: David Valdes. *Co-Prod.*: Stanley Rubin. *Sc.*: Peter Viertel, James Bridges, Burt Kennedy, from the novel by Peter Viertel. *Ph.*: Jack N. Green (Technicolor). *Prod. Des.*: John Graysmark. *Cost.*: John Mollo. *Edit.*: Joel Cox. *2nd unit Dir.*: Simon Trevor.
Mus.: Lennie Niehaus. 'Satin Doll' by Duke Ellington, Johnny Mercer, Billy Strayhorn.
With: Clint Eastwood (John Wilson), Jeff Fahey (Pete Verrill), Charlotte Cornwell (Miss Wilding), Norman Lumsden (butler George), George Dzundza (Paul Landers), Edward Tudor-Pole (Reissar), Roddy Maude-Roxby (Thompson), Richard Warwick (Basil Fields), John Rapley (gun shop salesman), Catherine Neilson (Irene Saunders), Marisa Berenson (Kay Gibson), Richard Vanstone (Phil Duncan), Jamie Koss (Mrs. Duncan), Anne Dunkley (scarf girl), David Danns (bongo man), Myles Freeman (ape-man), Geoffrey Hutchings (Alec Laing), Christopher Fairbank (Tom Harrison), Alun Armstrong (Ralph Lockhart), Clive Mantle (Harry), Mel Martin (Mrs. MacGregor), Martin Jacobs (Dickie Marlowe), Norman Malunga (desk clerk), Timothy Spall (Hodkins), Alex Norton (Zibelinsky), Eleanor David (Dorshka), Boy Mathias Chuma (Kivu), Andrew Whaley (photographer), Conrad Asquith (Ogilvy), George Orrison (stunts), Bill Weston (riding double), David Mabukane (Kivu's stunt double).
Filmed in London, Pinewood Studios and Zimbabwe.
Dist.: Warner Bros. 112 mins.
John Wilson is preparing a film entitled *The African Trader* in London. The maverick director is a high-stakes gambler, a self-serving daredevil with 'the magical gift of always landing on his feet'. Treating his collaborators with an infuriating offhandedness, he insists on shooting on location in colonial Uganda. Once in Entebbe, he discovers an affinity with the Africans and seems much more interested in a safari than his movie. One obsession drives him: to kill an elephant. That would be more than a crime; it would be 'a sin'.

The Rookie
Dir.: Clint Eastwood. *Prod.*: Howard Kazanjian, Steven Siebert, David Valdes, for Malpaso. *Sc.*: Boaz Yakin, Scott Spiegel. *Ph.*: Jack N. Green (Technicolor). *Prod. Des.*: Judy Cammer. *Cost.*: Glenn Wright, Deborah Hopper. *Edit.*: Joel Cox. *2nd unit Dir.*: Buddy Van Horn.
Mus.: Lennie Niehaus. 'All the Things You Are' by Jerome Kern, Oscar Hammerstein II. 'Red Zone' by Kyle Eastwood, Michael Stevens.
With: Clint Eastwood (Nick Pulovski), Charlie Sheen (David Ackerman), Raul Julia (Strom), Sonia Braga (Liesl), Tom Skerritt (Eugene Ackerman), Lara Flynn Boyle (Sarah), Pepe Serna (Lieutenant Ray Garcia), Marco Rodriguez (Loco), Pete Randall (Cruz), Donna Mitchell (Laura Ackerman), Xander Berkeley (Blackwell), Tony Plana (Morales), David Sherrill (Max), Hal Williams (Powell), Lloyd Nelson (freeway motorist), Pat DuVal, Mara Corday, Jerry Schumacher (interrogators), Matt McKenzie (Wang), Joel Polis (Lance), Rodger LaRue (maitre d'), Robert Dubac (waiter), Anthony Charnota (Romano), Jordan Lund (bartender), Paul Ben-Victor (Little Felix), Jeanne Mori (Connie Ling), Anthony Alexander (Alphonse), Paul Butler (Captain Hargate), Seth Allen (David as a child), Coleby Lombardo (David's brother), Roberta Vasquez (Heather Torres), Joe Farago (anchorman), Robert Harvey (Whalen), Nick Ballo (Vito), Jay Boryea (Sal), Marylou Kenworthy (receptionist), George Orrison (Detective Orrison), James Gavin, Thomas Friedkin, Craig Hosking (pilots), Terry Leonard (stunt coordinator).
Filmed in Los Angeles, San Jose and Mojave (California).
Dist.: Warner Bros. 121 mins.
Since his partner has been killed during an undercover operation, cop Nick Pulovski lives with only one obsession: to capture the mastermind of a gang of car thieves. He is paired with a naive and idealistic young man of privilege, whom he must thoroughly educate. As the investigation leads them into the barrio of East Los Angeles, the veteran initiates the novice into his unorthodox methods. If Pulovski is too old to play the part of a Dirty Harry, his protégé is soon experienced enough to take over.

1992
Unforgiven
Dir. and Prod.: Clint Eastwood, for Malpaso. *Exec. Prod.*: David Valdes. *Ass. Prod.*: Julian Ludwig. *Sc.*: David Webb Peoples. *Ph.*: Jack N. Green (Technicolor, Panavision). *Prod. Des.*: Henry Bumstead. *Cost.*: Glenn Wright. *Edit.*: Joel Cox. *Mus.*: Lennie Niehaus. 'Claudia's Theme' comp. by Clint Eastwood (guitar solo: Laurindo Almeida).
With: Clint Eastwood (William 'Bill' Munny), Gene Hackman (Little Bill Daggett), Morgan Freeman (Ned Logan), Richard Harris (English Bob), Jaimz Woolvett (The Schofield Kid), Saul Rubinek (W. W. Beauchamp), Frances Fisher (Strawberry Alice), Anna Thomson (Delilah Fitzgerald), David Mucci (Quick Mike), Rob Campbell (Davey Bunting), Anthony James (Skinny Dubois), Tara Dawn Frederick (Little Sue), Beverley Elliott (Silky), Liisa Repo-Martell (Faith), Josie Smith (Crow Creek Kate), Shane Meier (Will Munny, Jr), Aline Levasseur (Penny Munny), Cherrilene Cardinal (Sally Two Trees), Robert Koons (Crocker), Ron White (Clyde Ledbetter), Mina E. Mina (Muddy Chandler), Henry Kope (German Joe Schultz), Jeremy Ratchford (Deputy Andy Russell), John Pyper-Ferguson (Charley

Hecker), Jefferson Mappin (Fatty Rossiter), Walter Marsh (barber), Garner Butler (Eggs Anderson), Larry Reese (Tom Luckinbill), Blair Haynes (Paddy McGee), Frank C. Turner (Fuzzy), Sam Karas (Thirsty Thurston), Lochlyn Munro (Texas Slim), Ben Cardinal (Johnny Foley), Philip Hayes (Lippy MacGregor), Michael Charrois (Wiggens), Bill Davidson (Buck Barthol), Paul McLean, James Herman, Michael Maurer (train passengers), Larry Joshua (Bucky), George Orrison (The Shadow), Greg Goossen (fighter).
Filmed in the Calgary region (Alberta) and at Sonora (California).
Dedicated to Sergio (Leone) and Don (Siegel).
Dist.: Warner Bros. 130 mins.
Wyoming, 1880. After a cowboy disfigures a prostitute with a knife, the sheriff merely slaps him with a fine. Incensed, the bordello's girls pool their resources, offering a reward of $1,000 to whoever will kill the culprit. The Schofield Kid needs the assistance of a sharpshooter to execute the contract, so he approaches William Munny, a rehabilitated killer haunted by his abominable past. Munny has a pig farm, but has lost his wife and can barely feed his children. Even though he has a hard time mounting a horse, he picks up his gun and sets off to find his former partner whom he will enroll for one last dark ride.

1993
A Perfect World
Dir. and Prod.: Clint Eastwood. *Prod.*: Mark Johnson, David Valdes, for Malpaso. *Sc.*: John Lee Hancock. *Ph.*: Jack N. Green (Technicolor, Panavision). *Prod. Des.*: Henry Bumstead. *Cost.*: Erica Edell Phillips. *Edit.*: Joel Cox, Ron Spang.
Mus.: Lennie Niehaus. 'Ida Red' by Bob Wills, int. by Bob Willis and his Texas Playboys. 'Abilene' by John D. Loudermilk, Lester Brown, Bob Gibson, int. by George Hamilton IV. 'South' by Bennie Moten, Thamon Hayes, int. by Bob Willis and his Texas Playboys. 'Please Help Me, I'm Falling (in Love with You)' by Don Robertson, Hal Blair, int. by Hank Locklin. 'Blue Blue Day' by and int. by Don Gibson. 'Catch a Falling Star' by Paul Vance, Lee Pockriss, int. by Perry Como. 'Guess Things Happen That Way' by Jack Clement, int. by Johnny Cash. 'Sea of Heartbreak' by Hal David, Paul Hampton, int. by Don Gibson. 'Night Life' by Willie Nelson, Walt Breeland, Paul Buskirk, int. by Rusty Draper. 'Dark Moon' by Ned Miller, int. by Chris Isaak. 'The Little White Cloud That Cried' by Johnnie Ray, int. by Chris Isaak. 'Funny How Time Slips Away' by and int. by Willie Nelson. 'Don't Worry' by and int. by Marty Robbins. 'Big Fran's Baby' by Clint Eastwood.
With: Kevin Costner (Robert 'Butch' Haynes), Clint Eastwood (Red Garnett), Laura Dern (Sally Gerber), T. J. Lowther (Phillip 'Buzz' Perry), Keith Szarabajka (Terry Pugh), Leo Burmester (Tom Adler), Paul Hewitt (Dick Suttle), Bradley Whitford (Bobby Lee), Ray McKinnon (Bradley), Jennifer Griffin (Gladys Perry), Leslie Flowers (Naomi Perry), Belinda Flowers (Ruth Perry), Darryl Cox (Mr. Hughes), Jay Whiteaker (Superman), Taylor Suzanna McBride (Tinkerbell), Christopher Reagan Ammons (Dancing Skeleton), Mark Voges (Larry Billings), Vernon Grote (prison guard), James Jeter (old-timer), Ed Geldart (Fred Cummings), Bruce McGill (Paul Saunders), Nik Hagler (general store manager), Gary Moody (local sheriff), George Haynes (farmer), Marietta Marich (farmer's wife), Rodger Boyce (Mr. Willits), Lucy Lee Flippin (Lucy), Elizabeth Ruscio (Paula), David Kroll (newscaster), Gabriel Folse (Officer Terrance), Gil Glasgow (Officer Pete), Dennis Letts (governor), John Hussey (governor's aide), Margaret Bowman (Trick 'r Treat Lady), John M. Jackson (Bob Fielder), Connie Cooper (Bob's wife), Cameron Finley (Bob Fielder, Jr), Katy Wottrich (Patsy Fielder), Marco Perella (road block officer), Linda Hart (Eileen), Brandon Smith (Officer Jones), George Orrison (Officer Orrison), Wayne Dehart (Mack), Mary Alice (Lottie, Mack's wife), Kevin Woods (Cleveland, Mack's grandson), Tony Frank (Arch Andrews), Woody Watson (Lieutenant Hendricks), James W. Gavin, Craig Hosking (helicopter pilots).
Filmed in Austin and central Texas.
Dist.: Warner Bros. 138 mins.
In November 1963, as Dallas, Texas, is preparing to receive President Kennedy, Butch and his accomplice escape from the penitentiary and take eight-year-old Phil hostage. Having spent his youth in a reformatory, Butch recognizes himself in the boy, who was raised in a repressive environment after being abandoned by his father. At the same age, Butch had killed a customer who abused his mother, a New Orleans prostitute. After eliminating his accomplice, Butch sets off on back roads with the child. A Texas Ranger who has had a hand in shaping the fugitive's tragic fate tracks him down.

1995
The Bridges of Madison County
Dir.: Clint Eastwood. *Prod.*: Clint Eastwood, Kathleen Kennedy, for Amblin and Malpaso. *Ass. Prod.*: Tom Rooker, Michael Maurer. *Sc.*: Richard LaGravenese, from the novel by Robert James Waller. *Ph.*: Jack N. Green (Technicolor, Panavision). *Prod. Des.*: Jeannine Claudia Oppewall. *Cost.*: Colleen Kelsall. *Edit.*: Joel Cox.
Mus.: Lennie Niehaus. 'Doe Eyes' by Lennie Niehaus, Clint Eastwood, int. by Lennie Niehaus and Michael Lang (piano solo). 'Music! Music! Music!' by Bernie Baum, Stephan Weiss, int. by Ahmad Jamal. 'Casta diva' by Vincenzo Bellini from the opera *Norma*, int. by Maria Callas and the Milan Teatro Alla Scala Orchestra. 'Blue Gardenia' by Bob Russell, Lester Lee, int. by Dinah Washington. 'Leader of the Pack' by George Morton, Jeff Barry, Ellie Greenwich, int. by The Shangri-Las. 'Easy Living' by Leo Robin, Ralph Rainger, int. by Johnny Hartman. 'I'll Close My Eyes' by Buddy Kaye, Billy Reid, int. by Dinah Washington. 'Baby, I'm Yours' by Van McCo, int. by Barbara Lewis. 'Poinciana' by Buddy Bernier, Nat Simon, int. by Ahmad Jamal. 'Mon coeur s'ouvre à ta voix' by Camille Saint-Saëns, from the opera *Samson and Delilah*, int. by Maria Callas and the Orchestre National de la Radiodiffusion Française. 'Soft Winds' by Fletcher Henderson, Fred Royal, int. by Dinah Washington. 'I See Your Face Before Me' by Howard Dietz, Arthur Schwartz, int. by Johnny

Hartman. 'It Was Almost Like A Song' by Hal David, Archie Jordan, int. by Johnny Hartman. 'Jammin' with J. R.' by and int. by James Rivers. 'For All We Know' by Hal David, Archie Jordan, int. by Johnny Hartman. 'This Is Always' by Harry Warren, Mack Gordon, int. by Irene Kral and the Junior Mance Trio. 'It's A Wonderful World' by Johnny Watson, Harold Adamson, Jan Savitt, int. by Irene Kral and the Junior Mance Trio.

With: Clint Eastwood (Robert Kincaid), Meryl Streep (Francesca Johnson), Annie Corley (Carolyn Johnson), Victor Slezak (Michael Johnson), Jim Haynie (Richard Johnson), Sarah Kathryn Schmitt (young Carolyn), Christopher Kroon (young Michael), Phyllis Lyons (Betty), Debra Monk (Madge), Richard Lage (Peterson, the lawyer), Michelle Benes (Lucy Redfield), Alison Wiegert, Brandon Bobst (children), Pearl Faessler (wife), R. E. 'Stick' Faessler (husband), Tania Mishler, Billie McNabb (waitresses), Art Breese (cashier), Lana Schwab (saleswoman), Larry Loury (UPS driver), James Rivers, Mark A. Brooks, Peter Cho, Eddie Dejean, Sr, Jason C. Brewer, Kyle Eastwood (James Rivers Band), George Orrison, Ken Billeter, Judy Trask, David Trask, Edna Dolson, Dennis McCool, Michael C. Pommier, Jana Corkrean, M. Jane Seymour, Karla Jo Soper (café patrons), James W. Gavin (helicopter pilot).

Filmed in Madison County (Iowa).

Dist.: Warner Bros. 135 mins.

At the death of their mother Francesca, her children discover that she had an affair many years earlier with Robert Kincaid, a photojournalist working for *National Geographic*. Although it took place in 1965, neither lover ever recovered from the brief encounter. Robert was researching a story on the covered bridges of Iowa. Francesca, who had stayed alone on her farm while her husband and children attended a fair, helped the globetrotter find his way. They quickly found that they had a lot in common, starting with a taste for the blues. She soon began revealing her intimate frustrations: she was the prisoner of a sedentary life, 'a life of details … '.

1997

Absolute Power

Dir.: Clint Eastwood. *Prod.*: Clint Eastwood, Karen Spiegel, for Castle Rock Entertainment and Malpaso. *Exec. Prod.*: Tom Rooker. *Ass. Prod.*: Michael Maurer. *Sc.*: William Goldman, from the novel by David Baldacci. *Ph.*: Jack N. Green (Technicolor, Panavision). *Prod. Des.*: Henry Bumstead. *Cost.*: Deborah Hopper. *Edit.*: Joel Cox. *Stunts*: Buddy Van Horn. *Mus.*: Lennie Niehaus. 'Power Waltz' and 'Kate's Theme' comp. by Clint Eastwood.

With: Clint Eastwood (Luther Whitney), Gene Hackman (President Allen Richmond), Ed Harris (Seth Frank), Laura Linney (Kate Whitney), Scott Glenn (Bill Burton), Dennis Haysbert (Tim Collin), Judy Davis (Gloria Russell), E. G. Marshall (Walter Sullivan), Melora Hardin (Christy Sullivan), Ken Welsh (Sandy Lord), Penny Johnson (Laura Simon), Richard Jenkins (Michael McCarty), Mark Margolis (Red Brandsford), Elaine Kagan (Valerie), Alison Eastwood (art student), Yau-Gene Chan (waiter), George Orrison (airport bartender), Charles McDaniel (medical examiner), John Lyle Campbell (repairman), Kimber Eastwood (White House tour guide), Eric Dahlquist, Jr (Oval Office agent), Jack Stewart Taylor (Watergate doorman), Joy Ehrlich (reporter), Robert Harvey (cop).

Filmed in Washington, Baltimore, and in a studio in Los Angeles.

Dist.: Sony–Columbia. 121 mins.

A former hero of the Korean War, Luther Whitney is a gentleman burglar, an ace at his profession. He has meticulously prepared what is meant to be his last job. As he is emptying the safe of a rich philanthropist, a two-way mirror allows him to catch the homeowner's wife and the president engaged in a tryst. The erotic game degenerates into violence. In a cover up, the FBI cleans up the scene of the crime, but Luther, who managed to retrieve the weapon, is now in a position to blackmail the White House. With all the president's men on his heels, he is taking a big chance.

Midnight in the Garden of Good and Evil

Dir.: Clint Eastwood. *Prod.*: Clint Eastwood, Arnold Stiefel, for Malpaso and Silver Pictures. *Co-Prod.*: Tom Rooker. *Exec. Prod.*: Anita Zuckerman. *Sc.*: John Lee Hancock, from the book by John Berendt. *Ph.*: Jack N. Green (Technicolor, Panavision). *Prod. Des.*: Henry Bumstead. *Cost.*: Deborah Hopper. *Edit.*: Joel Cox. *Stunts*: George Orrison. *Mus.* Lennie Niehaus. 'That Old Black Magic' by Johnny Mercer, int. by Kevin Spacey. 'Skylark' by Johnny Mercer, Hoagy Carmichael, int. by k.d. lang. 'Fools Rush In (Where Angels Fear To Tread)' by Johnny Mercer, Rube Bloom, int. by Rosemary Clooney. 'Autumn Leaves' by Johnny Mercer, Jacques Prévert, Joseph Kosma, int. by Paula Cole. 'Come Rain or Come Shine' by Johnny Mercer, Harold Arlen, int. by Alison Eastwood. 'Too Marvelous for Words' by Johnny Mercer, Richard A. Whiting, int. by Joe Williams. 'Days of Wine and Roses' by Johnny Mercer, Henry Mancini. 'Tangerine' by Johnny Mercer, Victor Schertzinger. 'This Time the Dream's on Me' by Johnny Mercer, Harold Arlen, int. by Alison Krauss and the Charlie Haden Quartet West. 'And the Angels Sing' by Johnny Mercer, Ziggy Elman. 'Dream' by Johnny Mercer, int. by Brad Mehldau. 'Laura' by Johnny Mercer, David Raksin, int. by Kevin Mahogany. 'In the Cool Cool Cool of the Evening' by Johnny Mercer, Hoagy Carmichael. 'I'm an Old Cowhand' by Johnny Mercer, int. by Joshua Redman. 'Early Autumn' by Ralph Burns, Woody Herman. 'I Wanna Be Around' by Johnny Mercer, Sadie Vimmerstedt, int. by Tony Bennett. 'Jeepers Creepers' by Johnny Mercer, Harry Warren. 'P.S. I Love You' by Johnny Mercer, Gordon Jenkins.

With: John Cusack (John Kelso), Kevin Spacey (James 'Jim' Williams), Jack Thompson (Sonny Seiler), Irma P. Hall (Minerva), Jude Law (Billy Carl Hanson), Alison Eastwood (Mandy Nicholls), Paul Hipp (Joe Odom), The Lady Chablis (Chablis Deveau), Dorothy Loudon (Serena Dawes), Anne Haney (Margaret Williams), Kim Hunter (Betty Harty), Geoffrey Lewis (Luther Driggers), Richard Herd (Henry Skerridge), Leon Rippy (Detective Boone), Bob Gunton (Finley Largent), Michael O'Hagan (Geza Von Habsburg), Gary

Anthony Williams (bus driver), Tim Black (Jeff Braswell), Muriel Moore (Mrs. Baxter), Sonny Seiler (Judge White), Terry Rhoads (Assistant DA), Victor Brandt (bailiff), Patricia Herd (juror #1), Nick Gillie (juror #20), Patricia Darbo (Sara Warren), J. Patrick McCormack (doctor), Emma Kelly (herself), Tyrone Lee Weaver (Ellis), Greg Goossen (cell mate), Shannon Eubanks (Mrs. Hamilton), Virginia Duncan, Rhoda Griffis, Judith Robinson (Card Club women), Joann Pflug (Cynthia Vaughn), James Moody (Mr. Glover), John Duncan (gentleman in park), Bess S. Thompson (pretty girl), Jin Hi Soucy (receptionist), Michael Rosenbaum (George Tucker), Dan Biggers (Harry Cram), Georgia Allen (Lucille Wright), Collin Wilcox Paxton (woman at party), Charles Black (Alpha), Aleta Mitchell (Alphabette), Michael 'Kevin' Harry (Phillip), Dorothy Kingery (Jim Williams' sister) Amanda and Susan Kingery (Jim Williams' nieces), Ted Manson (passer-by), Margaret R. Davis (Ruth), Danny Nelson (senator), Bree Luck (woman at the club), Ann Cusack (delivery woman), Jerry Spence (hair dresser).

Filmed in Savannah (Georgia) and at the Warner Bros. studios, Burbank.

Dist.: Warner Bros. 155 mins.

Writer John Kelso arrives in Savannah, Georgia, to research an article on collector Jim Williams, a local celebrity who resides in the Johnny Mercer House. He discovers a nonchalant melting pot of merry widows, voodoo priestesses, transsexuals and other eccentric types. He also witnesses an altercation between Williams and his live-in lover, a young drug dealer. Later that night, the lover is gunned down. The case fascinates Kelso because of its seemingly impenetrable mysteries, so much so that he decides to stay in Savannah to write a book about it: 'It will be like *Gone with the Wind* on mescaline!'

1999

True Crime

Dir.: Clint Eastwood. *Prod.*: Clint Eastwood, Lili Fini Zanuck, Richard Zanuck, for Zanuck Company and Malpaso. *Exec. Prod.*: Tom Rooker. *Sc.*: Larry Gross, Paul Brickman, Stephen Schiff, from the novel by Andrew Klavan. *Ph.*: Jack N. Green (Technicolor). *Prod. Des.*: Henry Bumstead. *Cost.*: Deborah Hopper. *Edit.*: Joel Cox. *Mus.*: Lennie Niehaus. 'Little Drummer Boy' by Katherine Davis, Henry Onorati, Harry Simeone, int. by Kenny Burrell. 'Why Should I Care' by Clint Eastwood, Carole Bayer Sager, Linda Thompson, int. by Diana Krall.

With: Clint Eastwood (Steve Everett), Isaiah Washington (Frank Louis Beechum), Lisa Gay Hamilton (Bonnie Beechum), James Woods (Alan Mann), Denis Leary (Bob Findley), Bernard Hill (Warden Luther Plunkitt), Diane Venora (Barbara Everett), Michael McKean (Reverend Shillerman), Michael Jeter (Dale Porterhouse), Mary McCormack (Michelle Ziegler), Hattie Winston (Angela Russel), Penny Bae Bridges (Gail Beechum), Francesca Fisher-Eastwood (Kate Everett), John Finn (Reedy), Laila Robins (Patricia Findley), Sydney Tamiia Poitier (Jane March), Erik King (Pussy Man/Santa Claus), Graham Beckel (Arnold McCardle), Frances Fisher (DA Cecilia Nussbaum), Marissa Ribisi (Amy Wilson), Christine Ebersole (Bridget Rossiter), Anthony Zerbe (Henry Lowenstein), Nancy Giles (Leesha Mitchell), Tom McGowan (Tom Donaldson), William Windom (Neil, the bartender), Don West (Dr. Roger Waters), Lucy Alexis Liu (toy store girl), Dina Eastwood (Wilma Francis), Leslie Griffith, Dennis Richmond (TV anchors), Frank Sommerville (afternoon news anchor), Dan Green (field producer), Nicholas Bearde (Reuben Skycock), Frances Lee McCain (Mrs. Lowenstein), Rev. Cecil Williams (Reverend Williams), Casey Lee (Warren Russel), Jack Kehler (Mr. Ziegler), Colman Domingo (Wally Cartwright), Linda Hoy (counter woman), Danny Kovacs (Atkins), Kelvin Han Yee (Zachary Platt), Kathryn Howell (nurse), Beulah Stanley (female guard), George Maguire (Frederick Robertson), Bill Wattenburg (radio reporter), Roland Abasolo (guard, first night), Michael Halton (guard, execution day), Jade Marx-Berti (waitress), Velica Marie Davis (purse whacker), John B. Scott (Colonel Drummond), Edward Silva (Colonel Hernandez), Jordan Sax (Colonel Badger), Rob Reece (executioner), Walter Brown (Beechum family member).

Filmed in Oakland, San Leandro, Petaluma and at the Naval Air Station of Alameda (Northern California).

Dist.: Warner Bros. 127 mins.

A reporter for the *Oakland Tribune*, Steve Everett used to be a top-drawer journalist, but his alcoholism, lack of discipline and quixotic temperament have jeopardized his career. He has stopped taking anything seriously, especially justice. But when a young female colleague is killed in a car accident, he feels compelled to follow up on the story of Frank Beechum, an African–American who is about to be executed for the murder of a pregnant woman during a heist at a convenience store. To Steve, the case turns into an opportunity to redeem himself. He starts his own investigation and sets off to interview the condemned man at San Quentin.

2000

Space Cowboys

Dir.: Clint Eastwood. *Prod.*: Clint Eastwood, Andrew Lazar for Malpaso and Mad Chance. *Exec. Prod.*: Tom Rooker. *Sc.*: Ken Kaufman, Howard Klausner. *Ph.*: Jack N. Green (Technicolor). *Prod. Des.*: Henry Bumstead. *Cost.*: Deborah Hopper. *Edit.*: Joel Cox. *Superv. visual effects*: Michael Owens. *Sp. effects and animation*: Industrial Light & Magic. *Mus.*: Lennie Niehaus. 'Espacio' by Clint Eastwood, int. by Mitch Holder. 'Patricia' by and int. by Perez Prado. 'The Best is Yet to Come' by Cy Coleman, Carolyn Leigh, int. by Joshua Redman. 'Grazin' in the Grass' by Harry Elston, Philemon Hou, int. by Boney James and Rick Braun. 'Hit the Road, Jack' by Percy Mayfield, int. by Joshua Redman. 'Take It to the Limit' by Glenn Frey, Don Henley, Randy Meisner, int. by Chad Brock. 'Space Cowboy (Yippie-Yi-Yay)' by J. C. Chasez, Alex Greggs, Bradley Daymond, int. by NSYNC. 'Last Night' by Charles Axton, Chips Moman, Floyd Newman, Gilbert Caple, Jerry Smith, int. by Larry Goldings. 'Old Man' by Neil Young, int. by Brad Mehldau. 'Still Crazy After All

These Years' by Paul Simon, int. by Willie Nelson, then by Brad Mehldau Trio. 'The Chain of Love' by Jonnie Barnett, Rory Lee, int. by Clay Walker. 'I Only Have Eyes for You' by Al Dubin and Harry Warren, int. by Alison Eastwood. 'Fly Me to the Moon (in Other Words)' by Bart Howard, int. by Frank Sinatra and the Count Basie Orchestra.

With: Clint Eastwood (Frank Corvin), Tommy Lee Jones (Hawk Hawkins), Donald Sutherland (Jerry O'Neill), James Garner (Tank Sullivan), James Cromwell (Bob Gerson), Marcia Gay Harden (Sara Holland), William Devane (Eugene Davis), Loren Dean (Ethan Grace), Courtney B. Vance (Roger Hines), Barbara Babcock (Barbara Corvin), Rade Serbedzija (General Vostov), Blair Brown (Dr. Anne Caruthers), Jay Leno (himself), Nils Allen Stewart (Tiny), Deborah Jolly (cocktail waitress), Toby Stephens (young Frank), Eli Craig (young Hawk), John Asher (young Jerry), Matt McColm (young Tank), Billie Worley (young Gerson), Chris Wylde (Jason), Anne Stedman (Jason's girlfriend), James MacDonald (Capcom), Kate McNeil, Karen Mistal (female astronauts), John K. Linto (male astronaut #1), Mark Thomason (technician in control room), Georgia Emelin (Jerry's girlfriend), Rick Scarry (State Department official), Paul Pender (JBC security guard), Tim Halligan (Qualls), Manning Mpinduzi-Mott (press reporter in 1958), Steve Monroe (waiter), J. M. Henry (centrifuge tech), Steven West (construction tech), Cooper Huckabee (trajectory engineer), Hayden Tank (Andrew), Jock MacDonald (press reporter), Gerald Emerick (T-38 pilot), Renee Olstead (little girl), Don Michaelson (NASA doctor), Artur Cybulski (second reporter), Gordy Owens (Simsupe), Steve Stapenhorst (vice-president), Lauren Cohn (teacher), Michael Louden, Jon Hamm (young pilots), Deborah Hope (female engineer), Lamont Lofton (KSC guard), Alexander Kuznetsov (Russian engineer), Erica Grant (female engineer), and uncredited: Chip Chinery (Tom), Craig Hosking (pilot), Lisa Malone (herself), Denise Marek-Plumb (administrator of data bank), Kristin Quick (young employee at museum).

Filmed in the Los Angeles region, at the Johnson Space Center of Houston (Texas), at the Kennedy Space Center of Cape Canaveral (Florida) and at the Warner Bros. studios, Burbank.

Dist.: Warner Bros. 129 mins.

At the end of the 1950s, NASA technocrats deprived astronaut Frank Corvin of a flight in space. The agency calls on him again when a dysfunctional Russian telecommunications satellite, a relic of the Cold War, threatens to crash into the earth: 'Your country needs you!' Though retired, Frank eventually accepts the mission, but under one condition: that NASA rehires his 1958 team of space pioneers. The aces of yesteryear are now gruff old gents: one a Baptist preacher, the other a designer of roller-coasters, the last one a stunt pilot. A sceptical NASA demands that they add to the crew two young astronauts, even though they have not yet proved themselves.

2002
Blood Work

Dir. and Prod.: Clint Eastwood for Malpaso. *Exec. Prod.*: Robert Lorenz. *Co-Prod.*: Judie G. Hoyt. *Sc.*: Brian Helgeland, from the novel by Michael Connelly. *Ph.*: Tom Stern (Technicolor). *Prod. Des.*: Henry Bumstead. *Cost.*: Deborah Hopper. *Edit.*: Joel Cox. *Stunts*: Buddy Van Horn. *Mus.*: Lennie Niehaus.

With: Clint Eastwood (Terry McCaleb), Jeff Daniels (James 'Buddy' Noone), Anjelica Huston (Dr. Bonnie Fox), Wanda De Jesus (Graciella Rivers), Tina Lifford (Jaye Winston), Paul Rodriguez (Detective Ronaldo Arrango), Dylan Walsh (Detective John Waller), Mason Lucero (Raymond), Gerry Becker (Mr. Toliver), Rick Hoffman (James Lockridge), Alix Koromzay (Mrs. Cordell), Igor Jijikine (Bolotov), Dina Eastwood, Beverly Leech (reporters), June Kyoko Lu (Mrs. Kang), Chao Li Chi (Mr. Kang), Glenn Morshower (captain), Robert Harvey (restaurant manager), Matt Huffman (young detective), Mark Thomason (James Cordell), Maria Quiban (Gloria Torres), Brent Hinkley (cab driver), Natalia Ongaro (receptionist), Amanda Carlin (office manager), Ted Rooney, P. J. Byrne (forensics experts), Sam Jaeger (deputy), Derric Nugent (LAPD officer), Craig Hosking, James W. Gavin (helicopter pilots).

Filmed in Los Angeles, Long Beach, San Pedro and at the Warner Bros. studios, Burbank.

Dist.: Warner Bros. 108 mins.

Terry McCaleb, who used to be the top FBI detective in Los Angeles, survives a heart attack after receiving a heart transplant from a young Mexican woman killed during a robbery. To help her sister track down the criminal, McCaleb takes it upon himself to reopen the investigation, which puts him at odds with police brass. He discovers that a serial killer is playing a coded game with him. All the victims shared the same blood type. It is a truly perverse game as it enables the psycho to share in the lawman's celebrity: 'We are Abel and Cain, Kennedy and Oswald.'

2003
Mystic River

Dir.: Clint Eastwood. *Prod.* Robert Lorenz, Judie G. Hoyt, Clint Eastwood for Malpaso and Lakeshore Entertainment. *Exec. Prod.*: Bruce Berman. *Sc.*: Brian Helgeland, from the novel by Dennis Lehane. *Ph.*: Tom Stern (Technicolor). *Prod. Des.*: Henry Bumstead. *Cost.*: Deborah Hopper. *Edit.*: Joel Cox. *Stunts*: Buddy Van Horn.

Mus.: Clint Eastwood, orch. by Pat Hollenbeck. Boston Symphony Orchestra and Tanglewood Festival Chorus dir. by Lennie Niehaus. *Spec. arr.*: Gennady Loktionov. 'Mystic River' by Clint Eastwood. 'Cosmo' and 'Black Emerald Blues' by Kyle Eastwood, Michael Stevens.

With: Sean Penn (Jimmy Markum), Tim Robbins (Dave Boyle), Kevin Bacon (Sean Devine), Laurence Fishburne (Sergeant Whitey Powers), Marcia Gay Harden (Celeste Boyle), Laura Linney (Annabeth Markum), Kevin Chapman (Val Savage), Thomas Guiry (Brendan Harris), Emmy Rossum (Katie Markum), Spencer Treat Clark (Silent Ray Harris), Andrew Mackin (John O'Shea), Adam Nelson (Nick Savage), Robert Wahlberg (Kevin Savage), Jenny O'Hara (Esther Harris), John Doman (driver), Cameron Bowen

(young Dave), Jason Kelly (young Jimmy), Connor Paolo (young Sean), Bruce Page (Jimmy's father), Miles Herter (Sean's father), Cayden Boyd (Michael Boyle), Tori Davis (Lauren Devine), Jonathan Togo (Pete), Shawn Fitzgibbon (funeral director), Will Lyman (FBI agent Birden), Celine du Tertre (Nadine Markum), Ari Graynor (Eve Pigeon), Zabeth Russell (Diane Cestra), Joe Stapleton (Drew Pigeon), Susan Willis (Mrs. Prior), José Ramón Rosario (Lieutenant Friel), Tom Kemp (CCS tech), Charles Broderick (medical examiner), Lonnie Farmer (lab technician), Celeste Oliva (Trooper Jenny Coughlin), Bates Wilder (loudmouthed cop), Douglass Bowen Flynn (cop at barricade), Bill Thorpe (neighbor at barricade), Matty Blake (cop in park), Ken Cheeseman (Dave's friend in bar), Scott Winters (detective), Thomas Derrah (headstone salesman), Jim Smith (reporter), Patrick Shea (handcuffed man), Duncan Putney (solicitor in car), Ed O'Keefe (communion priest), Dave Zee Garison (1975 police officer), Michael McGovern (1975 reporter), Bill Richards, Michael Peavey (helicopter pilots), and uncredited: Eli Wallach (Mr. Loonie, wine and spirits merchant).

Clips: *John Carpenter's Vampires* by John Carpenter.

Filmed in Boston.

Dist.: Warner Bros. 137 mins.

In Boston, three boys are practising hockey in the street. One of them is kidnapped by two pedophiles posing as undercover cops. Twenty-five years later, Dave, the victim, remains haunted by the abuse he suffered, while Jimmy runs a small grocery business and Sean has become a police detective. One night, Dave comes back home covered in blood; he tells his wife that he was attacked in the street. The next day, the police find the body of Katie, Jimmy's daughter, in a public park. Blinded by grief, Jimmy pledges to avenge her. Nothing and no one can break the subsequent chain of violence.

'Piano Blues'

Dir.: Clint Eastwood. *Prod.*: Clint Eastwood, Bruce Ricker, for Vulcan Prods. and Road Movies. *Exec. Prod.*: Martin Scorsese. *Ph.*: Vic Losick (color). *Add. Ph.*: Ron Kienhuis, Stephen S. Campanelli. *Mix.*: Steve Reynolds. *Edit.*: Joel Cox, Gary Roach.

With Marcia Ball, Dave Brubeck, Ray Charles, Dr. John, Henry Gray, Pete Jolly, Jay McShann, Pinetop Perkins.

Mus.: 'You Can't Lose What You Ain't Never Had' by McKinley Morganfield, int. by Muddy Waters. 'Doe Eyes' by Clint Eastwood, Leonard Niehaus, int. by Clint Eastwood. 'What'd I Say' by and int. by Ray Charles. 'Boogie Woogie Dream' int. by Pete Johnson, Albert Ammons. 'Martha's Boogie' int. by Martha Davis. 'The Hungarian Rhapsody' by Franz Liszt, int. by Dorothy Donegan. 'Duke's Place' by Edward Ellington, William Katz, Ruth Rob, int. by Duke Ellington and Ray Charles. 'Piney Brown Blues' by Pete Johnson, Joe Turner, int. by Big Joe Turner and Jay McShann. 'When The Blues Come Round This Evening' by Clifton Crofford, John Durrill, int. by Linda Hopkins. 'Driftin' Blues' by Charles Brown, Johnny Moore, Edward W., int. by Charles Brown. 'Humoresque' by Anton Dvorak, int. by Art Tatum. 'You Are My Heart's Delight' by Harry Graham, Herzer Ludwig, Franz Lehar, int. by Oscar Peterson. 'It's Better To Be Yourself' by Nat King Cole, Robert Wells, Howard Lee, int. by Nat King Cole. 'Baby Let Me Hold Your Hand' by and int. by Ray Charles. 'Tipitina' by Roy Byrd, int. by Professor Longhair. 'Red Beans' by McKinley Morganfield, int. by Marcia Ball. 'The Fat Man' by Dave Bartholomew, Antoine Domino, int. by Fats Domino. 'Swanee River Hop' by Dave Bartholomew, Antoine Domino, int. by Fats Domino. 'Swanee River Boogie' by Albert Ammons, int. by Professor Longhair. 'Big Chief' by Earl King Johnson, int. by Dr. John. 'So Long Baby' int. by Muddy Waters. 'Ain't Nobody's Business (If I Do)' by Porter Grainger, Everett Robbins, int. by Otis Spann. 'Red Rooster' by Willie Dixon, int. by Henry Gray. 'Blues Don't Like Nobody' by and int. by Otis Spann. 'Hootie's Blues' by Jay McShann, Charlie Parker, Walter Brown, int. by Jay McShann. 'Little Bird' by Richard Grove, Pete Jolly, Thomas Wolf, int. by Pete Jolly. 'Lush Life' by Billy Strayhorn, int. by Phineas Newborn, Jr. 'Evidence' by and int. by Thelonious Monk. 'Blue Monk' by Thelonious Monk, int. by Dr. John. 'Travelin' Blues' by Dave Brubeck, Iola Brubeck, int. by Dave Brubeck. 'Three Fingered Boogie' by Willie Joe Perkins, int. by Pinetop Perkins. 'Joyce's Blues' by and int. by Charles Brown. 'Mission Ranch Blues' by Jay McShann, Dave Brubeck, int. by Dave Brubeck and Jay McShann. 'Boogie Woogie' by Clarence Smith a.k.a. Pinetop Smith, int. by Professor Longhair. 'America The Beautiful' by Ray Charles. 'How Long Blues' by LeRoy Carr, int. by Jimmy Yancey.

Clips: *Honkytonk Man* by Clint Eastwood.

Filmed in Carmel (California).

Broadcast: PBS. 92 mins.

This is one of the seven episodes of *The Blues* series executive-produced by Martin Scorsese. Sitting at the piano, Eastwood celebrates the instrument that he calls 'the fountain of American music'. Gathered by his side are some of the key figures of the blues, from Ray Charles to Jay McShann. They talk extemporaneously about their career and that of such departed giants as Duke Ellington and Fats Domino. As Eastwood is fond of saying: 'Jazz taught me to remain true to what I first admired.'

2004
Million Dollar Baby

Dir.: Clint Eastwood. *Prod.*: Clint Eastwood, Albert S. Ruddy, Tom Rosenberg, Paul Haggis, for Malpaso and Lakeshore Entertainment. *Exec. Prod.*: Gary Lucchesi, Robert Lorenz. *Co-Prod.*: Bobby Moresco. *Sc.*: Paul Haggis, from three short stories by F.X. Toole in the volume *Rope Burns* ('The Monkey Look', 'Million Dollar Baby' and 'Frozen Water'). *Ph.*: Tom Stern (Technicolor). *Prod. Des.*: Henry Bumstead. *Cost.*: Deborah Hopper. *Edit.*: Joel Cox.

Mus.: Clint Eastwood, orch. and dir. by Lennie Niehaus. spec. arr.: Gennady Loktionov. 'Blue Morgan' by Clint Eastwood. 'Boxing Baby' and 'Blue Diner' by Kyle Eastwood, Michael Stevens. 'Solferino' by Kyle Eastwood, Michael Stevens, David Potaux-Razel.

With: Clint Eastwood (Frankie Dunn), Hilary Swank (Maggie Fitzgerald), Morgan Freeman (Eddie Scrap-Iron Dupris), Jay Baruchel (Danger Barch), Mike Colter (Big Willie Little), Lucia Rijker (Billie 'The Blue Bear'), Brian O'Byrne (Father Horvak), Anthony Mackie (Shawrelle Berry), Margo Martindale (Earline Fitzgerald), Riki Lindhome (Mardell Fitzgerald), Michael Peña (Omar), Benito Martinez (Billie's manager), Bruce MacVittie (Mickey Mack), David Powledge (counterman at diner), Joe D'Angerio (cutman), Marcus Chait (J. D. Fitzgerald), Tom McCleister (lawyer), Erica Grant (nurse), Naveen (Pakistani), Morgan Eastwood (little girl in pickup truck), Jamison Yang (paramedic), Dean Familton, Dr. Louis Moret, V. J. Foster, Jon D. Schorle II, Marty Sammon, Steven M. Porter, Ray Corona (referees), Ming Lo (rehab doctor), Miguel Pérez (restaurant owner), Jim Cantafio, Ted Grossman (ring doctors), Ned Eisenberg (Sally Mendoza), Marco Rodriguez (second at Vegas fight), Roy Nugent (fan in Vegas), Don Familton (ring announcer), Mark Thomason (radio commentator), Brian T. Finney, Spice Williams-Crosby, Kim Strauss, Rob Maron, Kirsten Berman (Irish fans), Susan Krebs, Sunshine Chantal Parkman, Kim Dannenberg (rehab nurses), Eddie Bates (rehab resident).
Filmed in the Los Angeles region.
Dist.: Warner Bros. 132 mins.
A boxing manager in his twilight years, Frankie runs an old gym in a dilapidated area of LA. Alienated from his daughter for many years, he leads a solitary life. He is assisted by Scrap, a former champ who lost an eye in a fight that Frankie was powerless to stop. When he is approached by a penniless young woman who is barely surviving as a waitress but has grand plans to become a boxer, Frankie begins by turning her down: 'I don't train girls. Girlie tough ain't enough.' But Maggie has courage to spare. She is prepared to sacrifice everything to achieve her dream. Scrap, who is the first to realize it, takes her under his wing.

2006
Flags of Our Fathers
Dir.: Clint Eastwood. *Prod.*: Clint Eastwood, Steven Spielberg, for Malpaso and Amblin Entertainment. *Exec. Prod.*: Robert Lorenz. *Sc.*: William Broyles, Jr, Paul Haggis, from the book by James Bradley and Ron Powers. *Ph.*: Tom Stern (Technicolor). *Steadicam*: Stephen Campanelli. *Prod. Des.*: Henry Bumstead. *Art Dir.*: Jack G. Taylor. *Cost.*: Deborah Hopper. *Edit.*: Joel Cox. *Stunts*: Buddy Van Horn. *Sp. effects*: Michael Owens, Mathew Butler, Bryan Grill, Steven Riley, Digital Domain.
Mus.: Clint Eastwood, orch. by Lennie Niehaus. 'Knock Knock' by and int. by Kyle Eastwood, Michael Stevens, Andrew McCormack, Graeme Flowers. 'Summit Ridge Drive' by Artie Shaw, int. by Artie Shaw and His Gramercy Five. 'I'll Walk Alone' by Sammy Cahn, Jule Styne, int. by Dinah Shore and Don Runner. 'Victory Polka' by Sammy Cahn, Jule Styne. 'Any Bonds Today' by Irving Berlin. 'Flags of Our Fathers' by Clint Eastwood, int. by Bruce Forman, Kyle Eastwood, Michael Stevens, Andrew McCormack, Graeme Flowers.
With: Ryan Phillippe (John Bradley), Jesse Bradford (René Gagnon), Adam Beach (Ira Hayes), John Benjamin Hickley (Keyes Beech), John Slattery (Bud Gerber), Barry Pepper (Sergeant Mike Strank), Jamie Bell (Ralph 'Iggy' Ignatowski), Paul Walker (Hank Hansen), Robert Patrick (Colonel Chandler Johnson), Neal McDonough (Captain Severance), Melanie Lynskey (Pauline Harnois), Tom McCarthy (James Bradley), Chris Bauer (Commandant Vandegrift), Judith Ivey (Belle Block), Myra Turley (Madeline Evelley), Joseph Cross (Franklin Sousley), Benjamin Walker (Harlon Block), Alessandro Mastrobuono (Lindberg), Scott Reeves (Lundsford), Stark Sands (Gust), George Grizzard (John Bradley), Harve Presnell (Dave Severance), George Hearn (Walter Gust), Len Cariou (Mr. Beech), Christopher Curry (Ed Block), Bubba Lewis (Belle's young son), Beth Grant (Mrs. Gagnon), Connie Ray (Mrs. Sousley), Ann Dowd (Mrs. Strank), Mary Beth Peil (Mrs. Bradley), David Patrick Kelly (President Truman), Jon Polito (borough president), Ned Eisenberg (Joe Rosenthal), Gordon Clapp (General 'Howlin' Mad' Smith), Michael Cumpsty (Secretary Forrestal), V. J. Foster (major on plane), Kirk B. R. Woller (Bill Genaust), Tom Verica (Lieutenant Pennel), Jason Gray-Stanford (Lieutenant Schrier), Matt Huffman (Lieutenant Bell), David Hornsby (Louis Lowery), Brian Kimmet (Sergeant 'Boots' Thomas), David Rasche (senator), Tom Mason (John Tennack), Patrick Dollaghan (businessman), James Newman (local politician), Steven M. Porter (tourist), Dale Waddington Horowitz (tourist's wife), Lennie Loftin (justice of the peace), David Clennon (White House official), Mark Thomason (military censor), Oliver Davis (young James Bradley), Sean Moran (waiter), Lisa Dodson (Iggy's mother), John Nielsen (Senator Boyd), Jon Kellam (Senator Haddigan), Ron Fassler (Senator Robson), Denise Bella Vlasis-Gascon, Jenifer Menedis, Joie Shettler, Vivien Lesiak (luncheon singers).
Filmed at Iwo Jima, in Washington DC, Chicago, the Los Angeles region and Iceland.
Dedicated to Phyllis (Huffman) and Bummy (Henry Bumstead).
Dist.: Dreamworks-Paramount (USA), Warner Bros. (international). 131 mins.
On February 23, 1945, the fifth day of the battle of Iwo Jima, six Marines raise the American flag on top of Mount Suribachi. Fortuitously, photographer Joe Rosenthal snaps the shot that will immortalize the event. The military staff realizes the impact that such an image could have on public opinion, and it ends up on the front page of every major newspaper. At the request of the White House, three survivors of the flag-raising are enrolled to promote the war effort back home, notably the sale of Treasury bonds. They are greeted as 'heroes' everywhere, but soon find the media circus intolerable.

Letters from Iwo Jima
Dir.: Clint Eastwood. *Prod.*: Clint Eastwood, Robert Lorenz, Steven Spielberg, for Malpaso and Amblin Entertainment. *Exec. Prod.*: Paul Haggis. *Sc.*: Iris Yamashita, from a story by Iris Yamashita and Paul Haggis, and from the book of Tadamichi Kuribayashi's letters and drawings ed. by Tsuyuko Yoshida, *Picture Letters from the Commander in Chief*. *Ph.*: Tom Stern (Technicolor). *Steadicam*: Stephen Campanelli. *Prod. Des.*: Henry Bumstead, James J. Murakami. *Cost.*: Deborah Hopper. *Edit.*: Joel Cox, Gary D. Roach. *Stunts*: Buddy Van Horn. *Sp. effects*: Michael Owens, Matthew Butler, Bryan Grill, Steven Riley, Digital Domain. *Mus.*: Kyle Eastwood, Michael Stevens, orch. by Lennie Niehaus.
With: Ken Watanabe (General Tadamichi Kuribayashi), Kazunari Ninomiya (Saigo), Tsuyoshi Ihara (Baron Nishi), Ryo Kase (Shimizu), Shido Nakamura (Lieutenant Ito), Hiroshi Watanabe (Lieutenant Fujita), Takumi Bando (Captain Tanida), Yuki Matsuzaki (Nozaki), Takashi Yamaguchi (Kashiwara), Eijiro Ozaki (Lieutenant Obuko), Nae Yuuki (Hanako), Nobumasa Sakagami (Admiral Oshugi), Lucas Elliott (Sam), Sonny Seiichi Saito (medic Endo), Steve Santa Sekiyoshi (Kanda), Hiro Abe (Lieutenant Colonel Ciso), Toshiya Agata (Captain Iwasaki), Yoshi Ishii (Private Yamazaki), Ken Kensei (Major General Hayashi), Ikuma Ando (Ozawa). Akiko Shima (lead woman), Masashi Nagadoi (Admiral Ichimaru), Mark Moses (American officer), Roxanne Hart (officer's wife), Yoshio Iizuka (tired soldier), Mitsu Kurokawa (suicide soldier), Takuji Kuramoto (Ono), Koji Wada (Hashimoto).
Filmed in Barstow, on the island of Iwo Jima, and at the Warner Bros. studios, Burbank.
Production title: *Red Sun, Black Sand*
Dist.: Warner Bros./Dreamworks. 141 mins.
Entrusted with the last bastion capable of protecting Tokyo from American bombers, General Kuribayashi sets up his unorthodox defence system on the flanks and inside Mount Suribachi rather than on the beach. Aware that he can only forestall the inevitable, he prepares his troops for the ultimate sacrifice. Ordered to fight to the last man, the 22,000 defenders dig underground tunnels. For most, it will be their grave. Among them are two young soldiers: Shimizu, a hard-liner who was trained in the military police, and Saigo, a baker torn from his family and determined not to die in vain.

2008
Changeling
Dir.: Clint Eastwood. *Prod.*: Clint Eastwood, Brian Grazer, Ron Howard, Robert Lorenz, for Malpaso/Relativity Media/Imagine Entertainment. *Exec. Prod.*: Tim Moore, Jim Whitaker. *Sc.*: J. Michael Straczynski. *Ph.*: Tom Stern (Technicolor, 2.35 scope). *Steadicam*: Stephen Campanelli. *Prod. Des.*: James J. Murakami. *Art Dir.*: Patrick M. Sullivan, Jr. *Cost.*: Deborah Hopper. *Edit.*: Joel Cox, Gary D. Roach. *Stunts*: Buddy Van Horn. *Sp. effects*: Michael Owens, Steven Riley, CIS Vancouver, Pacific Title and Art Studio. *Mus.*: Clint Eastwood, orch. by Lennie Niehaus. Mus. arrang.: Kyle Eastwood, Michael Stevens.
With: Angelina Jolie (Christine Collins), John Malkovich (Reverend Gustav Briegleb), Jeffrey Donovan (Captain J. J. Jones), Michael Kelly (Detective Lester Ybarra), Colm Feore (Chief of police James E. Davis), Jason Butler Harner (Gordon Northcott), Amy Ryan (Carol Dexter), Geoff Pierson (S. S. Hahn), Denis O'Hare (Dr. Jonathan Steele), Frank Wood (Ben Harris), Peter Gerety (Dr. Earl W. Tarr), Reed Birney (Mayor Cryer), Gattlin Griffith (Walter Collins), Devon Conti (Arthur Hutchins), Eddie Alderson (Sanford Clark), Michelle Gunn (Sandy), Jan Devereaux, Erica Grant, Antonia Bennett, Kerri Randles (operators), Morgan Eastwood (girl on tricycle), Madison Hodges (neighborhood girl), Ric Sarabia (man at diner), J. P. Bumstead (cook), Debra Christofferson (police matron at train), Russell Edge, Stephen W. Alvarez (reporters at train), Pete Rockwell (reporter at precinct), John Harrington Bland (Dr. John Montgomery), Pamela Dunlap (Mrs. Fox), Roger Hewlett (Officer Morelli), Jim Cantafio (desk sergeant), Maria Rockwell (police matron at precinct), Wendy Worthington (reception nurse), Riki Lindhome (examination nurse), Dawn Flood (morning nurse), Dale Dickey (patient), Sterling Wolfe (Briegleb's aide), Mike McCafferty (ticket vendor), David Goldman (administrator), Anthony DeMarco, Joshua Moore, Joe Kaprielian (abducted kids), Muriel Minot (secretary), Kevin Glikmann (male orderly), Drew Richards (holding officer), Hope Shapiro (medication nurse), Caleb Campbell, Jeff Cockey (back-up detectives), Zach Mills (news vendor), Kelly Lynn Warren (Rachel Clark), Scott Leva, Rich King, Clint Ward (Mounties), Michael Dempsey (man on street), Peter Breitmayer (Chairman Thorpe), Phil Van Tee (councilman), Jim Nieb (reporter at hearing), Lily Knight (Mrs. Leanne Clay), Jeffrey Hutchinson (Mr. Clay), Brian Prescott (courtroom bailiff), Ryan Cutrona (judge), Mary Stein (Janet Hutchins), Gregg Binkley (jury foreman), William Charlton, Cooper Thorton (prison guards), E. J. Callahan (warden), Asher Axe (David Clay), Devon Gearhart (Winslow boy), Austin Mensch (boy in coop).
Filmed in Los Angeles.
Dist.: Universal Pictures. 141 mins.
The year is 1928. One March evening in Los Angeles, as she comes back from her work as a telephone supervisor, Christine Collins discovers that her nine-year-old son Walter has disappeared. Five months later, the LAPD inform her that the child has been found in Illinois. When the boy gets off the train, Christine faces an impostor, but the police insist otherwise. She endeavours to prove that he is not her son. Her unrelenting resistance gets her committed to a mental hospital. In the meantime, a young Canadian confesses to having helped his cousin, a Riverside County farmer, to kidnap and murder some twenty children.

Gran Torino
Dir.: Clint Eastwood. *Prod.*: Clint Eastwood, Robert Lorenz, Bill Gerber for Malpaso/Double Nickel Entertainment. *Exec. Prod.*: Jenette Kahn, Adam Richman, Tim Moore, Bruce Berman. *Sc.*: Nick Schenk. *Ph.*: Tom Stern (Technicolor, widescreen). *Steadicam*: Stephen Campanelli. *Prod. Des.*: James J. Murakami. *Art Dir.*: John Warnke. *Cost.*: Deborah Hopper. *Edit.*: Joel Cox, Gary D. Roach. *Sp. effects*: Steven Riley, Pacific Title and Art Studio.
Mus.: Kyle Eastwood, Michael Stevens. 'Gran Torino' by Clint Eastwood, Jamie Cullum, Kyle Eastwood, Michael Stevens, int. by Jamie Cullum, Don Runner. 'Psalm XVIII' by

Benedetto Marcello, arr. by E. Power Biggs. 'Esto Es Guerra' by Neiver A. Alvarez, Jesus A. Perez-Alvarez, int. by Convoy Qbanito. 'We Don't F*Around' by and int. by Budd-D, L.B. & Buddah. 'The Bartender' and 'Maybe So' by Renzo Mantovani, int. by Renzo Mantovani, Doug Webb. 'Appreciation' by and int. by L. P., Buddah, Cuzz & L. B. 'Hmoob Tuag Nthi' by Elvis Thao, Cheng Yang, Joseph Yang, int. by Rare. 'All My Hmong Mutha F*Kaz' by and int. by Buddah.

With: Clint Eastwood (Walt Kowalski), Christopher Carley (Father Janovich), Bee Vang (Thao), Ahney Her (Sue), Brian Haley (Mitch Kowalski), Geraldine Hughes (Karen Kowalski), Dreama Walker (Ashley Kowalski), Brian Howe (Steve Kowalski), John Carroll Lynch (Barber Martin), William Hill (Tim Kennedy), Brooke Chia Thao (Vu), Chee Thao (Grandma), Choua Kue (Youa), Scott Reeves (Trey), Xia Soua Chang (Kor Khue), Sonny Vue (Smokie), Doua Moua (Spider), Greg Trzaskoma (bartender), John Johns (Al), Davis Gloff (Darrell), Tom Mahard (Mel), Cory Hardrict (Duke), Nana Gbewonyo (Monk), Arthur Cartwright (Prez), Austin Douglas Smith (Daniel Kowalski), Conor Liam Callaghan (David Kowalski), Michael Kurowski (Josh Kowalski), Julia Ho (Dr. Chang), Maykao K. Lytongpao (Gee), Carlos Guadarrama (head latino), Andrew Tamez-Hull, Ramon Camacho, Antonio Mireles (latino gangbangers), Ia Vue Yang, Zoua Kue (Hmong flower women), Elvis Thao, Jerry Lee, Lee Mong Vang (Hmong gangbangers), Tru Hang (Hmong grandfather), Alice Lor (Hmong granddaughter), Tong Pao Kue (Hmong husband), Douacha Ly (Hmong man), Parng D. Yarng (Hmong neighbor), Nelly Yang Sao Yia (Hmong wife), Marty Bufalini (lawyer), My-Ishia Cason-Brown (Muslim receptionist), Clint Ward (officer), Stephen Kue (Officer Chang), Rochelle Winter (waitress), Claudia Rodgers (white woman neighbor), Vincent Bonasso (tailor).

Filmed in Detroit, Michigan.

Dist.: Warner Bros. 116 mins.

Retired autoworker Walt Kowalski has just lost his wife. Estranged from his grown sons who have joined the middle class, he lives alone with his old dog. A veteran of the Korean War, he resents his neighbors, a family from the Hmong community that has overtaken the area, but comes to the rescue when young Thao and his sister Sue are attacked by local gangbangers. The grateful neighbors introduce him to their way of life and culture. To his surprise, Walt finds he has more in common with these foreigners that with his own family, but as he grows closer to Thao and Sue, he becomes ensnared in a conflict that is bound to rekindle his old traumas.

2009
Invictus

Dir.: Clint Eastwood. *Prod.*: Clint Eastwood, Lori McCreary, Robert Lorenz, Mace Neufield for Revelations Entertainment/Man Company and Malpaso. *Exec. Prod.*: Morgan Freeman, Tim Moore, Gary Barber, Roger Birnbaum. *Sc.*: Anthony Peckham, from the book *Playing the Enemy* by John Carlin. *Ph.*: Tom Stern (Technicolor, widescreen). *Steadicam*: Stephen Campanelli. *Prod. Des.*: James J. Murakami. *Art Dir.*: Tom Hannam, Jonathan Hely-Hutchinson. *Cost.*: Deborah Hopper. *Edit.*: Joel Cox, Gary D. Roach. *Line Prod.*: Genevieve Hofmeyr. *Rugby adviser*: Chester Williams. *Sp. effects*: Michael Owens, CIS Visual Effects Group.

Mus.: Kyle Eastwood, Michael Stevens. 'Invictus 9,000 Days' by Diana Ruiz Eastwood, Emile Welman, mus. by Clint Eastwood, Michael Stevens, int. by Overtone and Yollandi Nortjie. 'Shosholoza' arr. by Gobingca George Mxadana, int. by Overtone. 'The Crossing (Osiyeza)' by Johnny Clegg, int. by Overtone and Yollandi Nortjie. 'Victory' by Reuben Khemese, int. by Soweto String Quartet. 'Anderlecht Champion' aka Ole´ Ole´ Ole´ – We Are The Champions' by Armath and Deja, int. by Overtone. 'Hamba Nathi', int. by Overtone and Yollandi Nortjie. 'God Defend New Zealand' by Thomas Bracken and J. J. Woods, arr. by Guy Jansen. 'Nkosi Sikelel´iAfrika' by Enoch Sontonga. 'Die Stem van Suid-Afrika' by Cornelis J. Langenhoven and Reverend Marthinus L. De Villiers. 'Colorblind' by Daniel Po, int. by Overtone. 'World in Union '95' by Charlie Skarbek and Joseph Shabalala, based on music originally comp. by Gustav Holst int. by Ladysmith Black Mambazo and PJ Powers; also int. by Overtone.

With: Morgan Freeman (Nelson Mandela), Matt Damon (François Pienaar), Tony Kgoroge (Jason Tshabalala), Julian Lewis Jones (Etienne Feyder), Adjoa Andoh (Brenda Mazibuko), Patrick Mofokeng (Linga Moonsamy), Matt Stern (Hendrick Booyens), Leleti Khumalo (Mary), Marguerite Wheatley (Nerine), Patrick Lyster (Mr. Pienaar), Penny Downie (Mrs. Pienaar), Sibongile Nojila (Eunice), Bonnie Henna (Zindzi), Shakes Myeko (Minister of Sport), Louis Minnaar (Springbok coach), Danny Keogh (Rugby President), Dan Robbertse (Boer), Robin Smith (Johan De Villiers), David Dukas (Captain of 747), Grant Swanby (Co-Captain of 747), Josias Moleele (face painter), Langley Kirkwood, Robert Hobbs, Melusi Yeni, Vuyo Dabula, Daniel Hadebe (presidential guards), Jodi Botha (high-school boy), Hennie Bosman (high-school coach), Refiloe Mpakanyane (Jessie), Jakkie Groenewald, Murray Todd (Johannesburg cops), Japan Mthembu (local cop), Albert Maritz (Springbok manager), Sello Motloung (Mandela's doctor), Meren Reddy (Minister of the Environment), Lida Botha (Mrs. Brits), Susan Danford (Mrs. Cole), Sylvia Mngxekeza (Mrs. Dlamini), James Lithgow (New Zealand PM), Malusi Skenjana (NSC firebrand), Bart Fouche (prison guard), Johnny Cicco, Wayne Harrison (staff members), Ashley Taylor, Gift Loetlela (team crew), Kgosi Mongake (Sipho), Given Stuurman, Vuyolwethu Stevens, Ayabulela Steven (township kids), Nambitha Mpumlwana (trophy wife), Andre Jacobs (TV announcer), McNeil Hendricks (Chester Williams), Zak Feaunati (Jonah Lomu), Scott Eastwood (Joel Stransky).

Filmed in Cape Town, Johannesburg and Pretoria.

Dist.: Warner Bros. (in association with Spyglass Entertainment). 134 mins.

South Africa is about to host the 1995 Rugby World Cup. After years of banishment from international competitions, the standing of the Springboks is at its lowest. Nelson Mandela,

in the first year of his presidency, has to confront his own party, the ANC, which is determined to eliminate a hated symbol of the apartheid regime. In keeping with his policy of dialogue and reconciliation with the white minority, the great leader supports and galvanizes the players, particularly their captain, François Pienaar. Giving Pienaar a copy of his favorite poem ('Invictus' by William Ernest Henley), he reveals what he expects from the team and the tournament: 'We need inspiration. In order to build our nation, we all need to exceed our own expectations …' Miraculously, they did.

Miscellaneous

Eastwood was the executive producer of a documentary by Charlotte Zwerin, **Thelonious Monk: Straight No Chaser** (1988). *Dist.*: Warner Bros. 89 mins.

His intervention also led Warner Bros. to handle the international distribution of **The Last of the Blue Devils** (1980), a documentary by Bruce Ricker on the Kansas City jazz scene during the 1930s.

He has since 'presented' **Tony Bennett: The Music Never Ends** (2007), a documentary he co-produced with director Bruce Ricker for Rhapsody Films Inc. Production in association with RPM Music Productions and Thirteen/WNET New York. *Exec. Prod.*: Ted Sarandos. *Co-Prod.*: Amy Schewel. *Edit.*: Joel Cox. *Narrat.*: Anthony Hopkins. *Dist.*: Red Envelope Entertainment. 87 mins.

Other Malpaso productions include:

Ratboy (1986)

Dir.: Sondra Locke. *Prod.*: Fritz Manes. *Ass. Prod. and Ass. Dir.*: David Valdes. *Sc. and Ass. Prod.*: Rob Thompson. *Ph.*: Bruce Surtees (Technicolor). *Prod. Des.*: Edward Carfagno. *Make-up*: Rick Baker, Greg Nelson. *Edit.*: Joel Cox. *Mus.*: Lennie Niehaus.

With: Sondra Locke (Nikki Morrison), Robert Townsend (Manny), Christopher Hewett (tutor), Larry Hankin (Jewell), Sydney Lassick (Dial-a-Prayer), Gerrit Graham (Billy Morrison), Louie Anderson (Omer Morrison), S. L. Baird (Ratboy), Billie Bird (medium), Gordon Anderson (Ratboy's voice).

Filmed in Los Angeles and Northern California.

Dist.: Warner Bros. 104 mins.

The Stars Fell on Henrietta (1995)

Dir.: James Keach. *Prod.*: Clint Eastwood, David Valdes. *Sc.*: Philip Railsback. *Ph.*: Bruce Surtees (Technicolor). *Prod. Des.*: Henry Bumstead. *Edit.*: Joel Cox. *Mus.*: David Benoit.

With: Robert Duvall (Mr. Cox), Aidan Quinn (Don Day), Frances Fisher (Cora Day), Brian Dennehy (Big Dave), Francesca Ruth Eastwood (Mary Day), Billy Bob Thornton (Roy).

Filmed in Texas.

Dist.: Warner Bros. 110 mins.

Though it is not a Malpaso production, the following film features many Malpaso veterans:

Rails & Ties (2007)

Dir.: Alison Eastwood. *Prod.*: Paul Federbush, Robert Lorenz, Peer J. Oppenheimer, Barrett Stuart. *Sc.*: Mickey Levy. *Ph.*: Tom Stern (Technicolor). *Art Dir.*: James J. Murakami. *Cost.*: Deborah Hopper. *Edit.*: Gary D. Roach. *Mus.*: Kyle Eastwood, Michael Stevens.

With: Marcia Gay Harden (Megan Stark), Kevin Bacon (Tom Stark), Miles Heizer (Davey Danner), Marin Hinkle (Renee), Eugene Byrd (Otis), Bonnie Root (Laura Danner).

Dist.: Warner Bros. 101 mins.

Eastwood composed the score for:

Grace is Gone (2007)

Dir. and Sc.: James C. Strouse. *Prod.*: John Cusack. *Song*: 'Grace is Gone' by Clint Eastwood (mus.) and Carole Bayer Sager (lyrics).

Cast: John Cusack, Emily Churchill, Rebecca Spence, Jennifer Tyler.

Dist.: The Weinstein Company. 85 mins.

Eastwood executive-produced and narrated Richard Schickel's documentary series, **You Must Remember This: The Warner Bros. Story** (2008), a Lorac production of a Warner Home Video release, in partnership with American Masters (PBS).

Eastwood is credited as executive producer on **The Dream's On Me** (2009), Bruce Ricker's documentary about songwriter Johnny Mercer (an original Turner Classic Movies production).

Index of Titles

Author's Acknowledgements

This book owes its existence to the subject himself. Over a period of some twenty-five years one of the most private of our great American filmmakers agreed to sit down with me and endure the ritual of the interview. We stuck to matters close to his heart: film and jazz, Carmel and Hollywood, the history of America and, occasionally, his own personal journey. He always comported himself with the simplicity and humility that are his trademark.

The idea of a book emerged in the course of these numerous exchanges. It kept growing as I visited him on the sets of his films, from *Heartbreak Ridge* to *Invictus*, and also during the shoot of *A Personal Journey with Martin Scorsese Through American Movies*, for which I interviewed him on the western and his position within the history of that genre. (As a matter of fact, *Unforgiven*, a milestone film, was the only picture made after the 1970s to be included in the marathon documentary.)

Among his collaborators past and present, I would particularly like to thank Lenny Hirshan, his agent and long-time friend; Joel Cox, the editor of his films since *The Outlaw Josey Wales*; Robert Lorenz, his producer since *Blood Work*; Judie Hoyt, the linchpin of Malpaso for years; Jenniphur Ryan, Deana Lou and Jessica Meier, who have succeeded her; and Joe Hyams, the master publicist who was Eastwood's man at Warner Bros. Very helpful as well were Richard Fox, who runs Warner Bros. International in Los Angeles, and Marquita Doassans, Eastwood's long-standing press attaché in France.

One man to whom we are all indebted is Pierre Rissient. He is the one largely responsible for the discovery of Clint Eastwood in Europe as he helped spark a critical recognition that has kept expanding on both sides of the Atlantic. As Eastwood's friend and advisor, he was able to persuade him, in particular, to take control of *Letters from Iwo Jima* as a director as well as a producer. Thanks to Pierre, I had the privilege of meeting and interviewing Mr Eastwood at a critical juncture: when he was shedding his 'heroic' image to tackle riskier character parts such as Bronco Billy, the Honkytonk Man or the sex-addicted cop of *Tightrope*.

It was Pierre, again, who facilitated many of the following encounters. I was happy to dedicate to him my documentary, *Clint Eastwood: A Life in Film*. While on the subject, I also have to thank my co-producers Laura Briand, Serge Lalou and the team at Films d'ici. The Iwo Jima chapter of this book is a compendium of the eight hours of conversations with Eastwood that I filmed in Burbank and Carmel.

I am grateful to my old friend Michel Ciment and the magazine *Positif*, who have covered Eastwood's career with remarkable consistency. Most of the following interviews appeared originally in the magazine (nos. 287, 295, 380, 397, 400, 445, 459, 512, 530, 552, 573, 587). I also recommend the one Ciment published on White Hunter, Black Heart in issue no. 351 (May 1990). Among my favorite references were the in-depth interview conducted by Nicolas Saada and Serge Toubiana at the time of *Space Cowboys* for *Cahiers du cinéma* (no. 549, September 2000) and the well-researched tome by Fuensanta Plaza on the director's collaborators, *Clint Eastwood/Malpaso* (Ex Libris, Carmel Valley, 1991).

Great support also came from those who enabled me to screen Eastwood's films time and again over the years: Kent Jones and Justin Bateman, the archivists of Martin Scorsese's video collections; Mary Lea Bandy, Laurence Kardish and Joel Siegel of the Museum of Modern Art, New York; Jean-Max Causse and Jean-Marie Rodon, who never stopped programming and reissuing Eastwood's films in their Action cinemas in Paris; Hervé Dumont, who celebrated Eastwood as an 'ambiguous marginal' at the Cinémathèque Suisse in Lausanne; Bertrand Tavernier and Thierry Frémaux, who kept the gates wide open for him at their Institut Lumière in Lyon.

Allow me to salute, as well, the friends, cinephiles, critics and connoisseurs who have encouraged me either in Paris or Los Angeles: Yves Alion, Olivier Barrot, N. T. Binh, Sylvestre Clancier, Lorenzo Codelli, Marie Demart, Fabien Gaffez, François Forestier, Jean-Pierre Garcia, Hopi Lebel, Bruce Ricker, Nicolas Saada, Laurence Schifano, Joel Siegel, Mohamed Tahiani, Christian Viviani.

The book you are holding could not have seen the light of day without the passion and loyalty of Claudine Paquot, François Maillot, Alexia Renard and their team.

I would like, finally, to dedicate it to my wife Carole Wilson, who shared with me every step of its creation.

Opposite page: An artist who is a free agent: Clint Eastwood on the set of *Mystic River* (2003) in Boston.

Photographic credits

Sources:

Bifi: pp.33, 118–9; Clint Eastwood Collection: pp.2, 13, 16–7, 18, 19 tr, 20, 21, 25, 27 b, 28–9, 39, 62, 67, 68, 69, 70 t, 71, 88, 89, 93 b, 94 b, 98b, 104, 107, 110–1, 112, 118, 122 tl and bl, 123, 124 c and b, 137 b, 177, 183, 238; Collection Cahiers du cinéma: pp.4, 6, 19 tl and cl, 21 br, 22–3, 27 t, 30, 31, 38, 40–1, 44–5, 46, 48 tl and cl, 52, 53, 54–5, 57, 58 t and bl, 59, 60–1, 64–5, 70 b, 73, 74, 75, 76–7, 79, 81 t, cl, br and cr, 83, 84, 85, 86–7, 88 b, 89 b, 91, 92, 93, 94, 95, 96–7, 98, 99, 101, 102, 103 b, 104–5, 108 t and c, 109, 113 tr, 114 t and c, 118–9, 122, 123 tr, cr and br, 124 c and b, 125, 126, 127, 128, 129, 131, 132, 133, 134, 135, 136, 137 c and b, 138–9, 140–1, 142, 143, 144–5, 147, 148, 149, 150, 151, 152, 153, 154–5, 157, 158, 159, 160, 161, 162–3, 164, 165, 167, 168, 169, 170–1, 172, 173, 178, 179, 180–1, 182 c, 185, 186–7, 189, 190, 191, 192–3, 194, 195, 196, 197, 199, 200, 201, 202, 203, 205, 207, 208, 209, 210, 211, 213, 214, 215, 216, 217, 218, 219, 221; Collection Cahiers du cinéma/D. Rabourdin: pp.36–7, 48 bl, 116–7, 120 l, 121 b, 182 t; Collection CAT's: pp.48–9, 63, 112 b and tl, 113 tl and b, 114 b, 115, 204; Collection Cinémathèque Française: pp.26, 32, 34, 35, 42, 43, 81 bl, 108 bl and br, 121 t and c, 124 t, 182 b; Collection Noël Simsolo: p.103 t; Screen grabs: pp.19 br, 50, 51, 58 cl, 68 b, 118 t and c, 137 t, 174, 175, 184.

Credits:

© Arturo González Producciones Cinematográficas/Constantin Film Produktion/Produzioni Europee Associati: pp.22–3, 108 t and cl, 109 tl and tr; © CBS Entertainment: pp.18, 19; © CLM: pp.30, 32, 33, 34, 35, 81 bl, 116–7, 118 t; © Columbia: pp.58 cl and bl, 142 b, 143, 144–5, 151; © Constantin Film Produktion/Ocean Film: p.31 b; © Deputy Corporation/Kit Parker Films: p.182; © Lewis Milestone Productions Inc.: p.81 cr; © Little Bear/PELF: p.85 t; © Malpaso: pp.118, 118–9, 121 t and c; © Paramount Pictures: pp.113 tl, 122 cl and tr; © Toho Company: p.31 t; © Twentieth Century Fox: pp.81 br, 94 b, 99 c and b, 122 cr, 137 c; © United Artists: pp.81 t, 108 c, bl and br, 109 b, 123 tl; © Universal Studios Inc.: pp.25, 26, 27, 28–9, 70 b, 98 t, 99 t, 112, 113 b, 122 br, 182 t, 201, 202, 203, 204, 205; © Vulcan Productions/Reverse Angle International: p.165; © Warner Bros. Inc.: pp.2, 4, 6, 13, 21 tr, tl and br, 36–7, 38, 39, 40–1, 42, 43, 44–5, 46, 48, 48–9, 50, 51, 52, 53, 54–5, 57, 58 t, 59, 60–1, 62, 63, 64–5, 73, 74, 75, 76–7, 79, 83, 84, 85 b, 86–7, 88, 89, 91, 92, 93, 94 t, 95, 96–7, 98 b, 101, 102, 103, 104–5, 110–1, 113 tr, 114, 115, 120–1, 121 b, 124 t, 125, 126, 127, 128, 129, 131 (photograph by Ken-Regan Camera), 132, 133 (photograph by Sam Emerson), 134 (photograph by Sam Emerson), 135 (photograph by Sam Emerson), 136 (photograph by Ken-Regan Camera), 137 t, 138–9 (photograph by Ken-Regan Camera), 140–1 (photograph by Ken-Regan Camera), 142 t, 147, 148, 149, 150, 152, 153, 154–5, 157, 158, 159, 160, 161, 162–3, 164, 167, 168, 169, 170–1, 172, 173, 174, 175, 188, 201, 202, 203, 204, 205, 207, 208, 209, 210, 211, 213, 214, 215, 216, 217, 218, 219, 221, 222; © Warner/Malpaso/Paramount Pictures & Dreamworks: pp.177, 178, 179, 180–1, 183, 184, 185, 186–7, 189, 190, 191, 192–3, 194, 195, 196, 197, 199.

Cover illustrations
Front cover: Clint Eastwood on the set of *Flags of Our Fathers* (2006) in Iceland.
Back cover: Clint Eastwood and Marianne Koch in *A Fistful of Dollars* (1964).

Cahiers du cinéma Sarl
65, rue Montmartre
75002 Paris

www.cahiersducinema.com

Revised English edition © 2010 Cahiers du cinéma Sarl
First published in French as *Clint Eastwood. Entretiens avec Michael Henry Wilson*
© 2007 Cahiers du cinéma Sarl

ISBN 978 2 8664 2576 0

First edition designed by Paul Raymond Cohen
Graphic adaptation, cover design and typographic design of this edition
by Hans Dieter Reichert
Printed in China